HITTING THE MAT

The Making of a State Champ or
At Least a Good Man!

*I know you're going to be inspired by this book. It's a
rare look inside the sport of wrestling.*

Dan Gable

DAN BLANCHARD & BRIAN PREECE

Editor: Scott Schulte

FOREWORD

I first met Dan Blanchard several years ago through my autobiographer, Scott Schulte. Dan was one of the proofreaders of my New York Times Bestselling book, *A Wrestling Life: The Inspiring Stories of Dan Gable*. Dan had also come out to the U.S. Olympic Wrestling Trials with Scott in Iowa that year while he was still writing his book, *A Sprint to the Top*.

Also, many years ago, I was interviewed by Brian Preece. He came out to cover the NCAA wrestling tournament when Cael Sanderson won his fourth title. Brian mentioned that, like Cael, he too is the son of a famous wrestling coach from Utah. Brian's father is the legendary coach, Dennis Preece.

When Dan had finished his book, *A Sprint to the Top* I read it and was really impressed with the young wrestler in it. I particularly liked the message it sent out to our young men and women out there about doing something hard, being a self-starter, and building character. I was happy to endorse it.

With that said, I was even happier to write the foreword for this book, *Hitting the Mat: The Making of a State Champion or at Least a Good Man* by Dan and Brian. These two gentlemen, former wrestlers, coaches, educators, and fathers, are great ambassadors for the sport of wrestling. They genuinely understand how wrestling helps young men become good men.

I know you're going to be inspired by this book. Here you will get a rare look inside the sport of wrestling. You'll appreciate how fathers

INTRODUCTION

This is a good book written by Brian Preece and Dan Blanchard. I look forward to getting a copy after this book, *Hitting the Mat: The Making of a State Champ or at least a Good Man* comes out.

It's odd how, after all these years, I keep getting drawn into wrestling. For years I tried to hide from my notoriety. Then one night after I had retired, I was asleep in bed, and suddenly I was wide awake. And this vision flashed in my mind. "Stand in sunlight if you expect to be heard." For years I had hidden from the talent that God had given me. Now he was telling me that I needed to use my ability in wrestling for the benefit of others. I offer my help here.

Oddly after this vision, I no longer felt self-conscious about my win over Gable. Embracing the success and using it to help others was the key. I hadn't realized it until up to that point. Since then, I have enjoyed being around wrestling a lot more. And I am using every opportunity to help others learn wrestling skills and develop the character that wrestling creates mentioned in this book.

I think this book exhibits these traits of becoming a good man through hard work. It's one thing to be a state champion, and another to be a great person that everyone loves and respects. This is a difficult thing to do because one doesn't get it by commanding respect, but by earning it through helping others grow to their greatest ability. And then to continue to contribute to our great wrestling family.

Larry Owings

and sons make this demanding journey into the battled-tested realm of wrestling to come out at the other end as better men.

Hey, it's not that Dan and Brian's journey is perfect and without failure, but it is real. Both speak powerfully of important mentors. They acknowledge the broader community of support that every coach, father, and competitor will need along the way in this great sport of wrestling, and in the real world after wrestling.

Dan Gable

ENDORSEMENTS

As I read through the book, it occurred to me that working to create self-esteem is among the values wrestling teaches - or certainly can teach. There are a lot of great wrestlers speaking in the book. And it's very interesting to have the duel perspectives of Dan Blanchard and Brian Preece. You'll enjoy Dan, the former champion wrestler rooting for his son. And you'll equally enjoy Brian Preece's perspective who wrestled for his father, one of Utah's greatest coaches but wasn't in love with the sport. Now, all these years later, Brian is glad he wrestled and understands what wrestling did for him. Non-wrestlers and wrestlers who aren't having the time of their lives, will truly appreciate Brian's perspective on wrestling.

In addition, during today's times, we need good men and good leadership more than ever. Character and values are slipping away. It's worrying me. And it should be worrying you too. This book and the values it's trying to teach are timely, extremely valuable, and is something everyone should be exposed to.

I think the book is wonderful. Chances are you will too.

Terry Davis

Author of Vision Quest Book/Movie

I think "Hitting the Mat" is an extraordinary story that shares the details and experiences of wrestlers growing through the sport of wrestling. It's amazing to see the growth and maturity through wrestling not just in a wrestling season, but through the experiences of families on and off the mat. The sport of wrestling, it's truly one small family. This great book will help show the growth in wrestling and also in life

Rulon Gardner
Olympic Champion

Dan and Brian have a very unique story about the father-son journey through the sport of wrestling and how it creates that special bond that positively impacts both of their lives forever. This is a must read for wrestling families and a valuable and enjoyable read for everyone else as well.

Ken Chertow
Olympian

Hitting the mat helps you see things from different perspectives. If you are an athlete or if you are a coach you can learn from the back and forth dialogue of Brian Preece and Dan Blanchard. Dan helps you see things from the dad/coach perspective and Brian more from the son of a coach perspective. Coaching your son can sometimes be one of the hardest things someone can do. And learning from both Brian and Dan can help you navigate that difficult process better. I would highly recommend this book to all!

Jeff Newby
USA Wrestling Utah
Executive Director

Dan and Brian literally bring it home. We lose our inhabitants and win in our hearts. The proverbial question is answered. Wrestling is not always about winning. Incredibly impactful. But yet. Its subtlety *draws you into the deeper waters of this epic journey between a father and son. Due diligence and the commanding knowledge of our craft has won the day. Outstanding!*

Rodney Smith
Olympian
Bronze Medalist

A rare look into cause and effect of an athlete's journey. Brian and Daniel guide you through the very real lessons learned as a young wrestler, and juxtapose these to their own understanding of how those lessons have played out a positive role in their own lives.

Katherine Shai-
Six-Time U.S. National Team member

Brian Preece is the son of one of the greatest wrestling coaches in America. Coach Dennis Preece who won more state team titles, and coached more individual state champions than just about anyone. No small task in a state that produced the likes of Cael Sanderson. Coach Preece had an uncanny knack of getting more out of an athlete than anyone I've ever seen. Brian Preece tells an unbelievable story of his father, a basketball player turned wrestling coach, whose teams were virtually unbeatable. It's a fascinating story by Brian and Dan for anyone in any sport.

Ben Ohai
2-Time NCAA All-American (BYU)
Inductee into the California and Utah Wrestling Hall of Fames
Inductee into the Brigham Young University Athletic Hall of Fame

It was an honor to be one of the first readers of this exciting new book. It has been a long journey towards an excellent life for both Dan and Brian. They are great sons, great wrestlers, great dads, and great coaches. So glad to be endorsing this book and their journey towards a better life for all using a great sport of wrestling! Good luck and hope many young kids benefit from reading this book.

Shirzad Ahmadi
22X World Champion

It has been my pleasure to witness Dan Blanchard's development as a wrestler, coach, author, parent, and then a parent/coach. In his latest endeavor with this book he shares an amazing inside look at his son's individual journey towards personal excellence through wrestling with some help from Brian Preece.

John Bennett
World Champ

I know this book and the good it will do for our youth well. I also know Dan Blanchard and his son Dakota represent. Furthermore, I know what wrestling has done and the kind of good men it has built across this country of ours, especially in Utah were Cael Sanderson, Rulon Gardner, and Brian Preece's father, the legendary Dennis Preece reside. This book and the sport of wrestling are the perfect combination to building better men and women.

John Knapp
KT KIDZ Coach

I'm really excited about this book and what Dan Blanchard and Brian Preece are doing for wrestling. Their book gives an inside peek at the father-son dynamic in this demanding sport. Through doing something extremely hard, like wrestling, our young men (wrestlers), and our older men (fathers), develop together as they grow closer together and become stronger and better men. All wrestlers and wrestling families should pick up a copy of this book.

Jack Clark

Executive Director

U.S. Wrestling Foundation

Award winning author Dan Blanchard and Brian Preece have another winner in their book "Hitting the Mat." Their insight following Dakota's journey in the sport of wrestling is honest, refreshing and enlightened. This includes their reflection on the daily grind of our sport, the physical and mental demands, and the small achievements and failures, The wrestling background of both authors makes this is a must read for wrestlers, parents and coaches.

Ken Destefanis

National Wrestling Hall of Fame-CT

AUTHORS

DAN BLANCHARD- Father and Coach of Dakota, the boy we're trying to make a state champ or at least a good man in Connecticut. Dan is a bestselling and award-winning author, speaker, educator, and TV Host.

BRIAN PREECE- The son of the famous coach Dennis Preece in Utah. Brian is a Board Member of Utah Sports Hall of Fame Foundation, Championship Wrestler, Sports Writer, and Utah Teacher Fellow.

EDITOR

SCOTT SCHULTE- New York Times Bestselling Author of, "A Wrestling Life: The Inspirational Stories of Dan Gable." Speaker, Sports Writer, Championship Wrestler.

CONTRIBUTOR

TERRY DAVIS: Author of the book, *Vision Quest*, which was made into the Hollywood blockbuster movie, Vision Quest. Terry is writing a sequel to Vision Quest and has contributed an essay in the back of this book on what wrestling did for him.

CONTENTS

CHAPTER ONE

FATHERS AND SONS

Dan Blanchard: A little over 14 years ago, I gave up wrestling because of him. Now, 14 years later, he is entering high school as a freshman, and I'm back in wrestling ironically because of him.

When my wife had told me all those years ago that she was pregnant again, I was, like always, in the middle of another hectic wrestling season. As a matter of fact, back then, it seemed like I was always in the middle of another busy wrestling season because I was coaching wrestling year-round. I used to coach football, too, but a few years earlier, I gave up football when my first daughter was born, so I would have some time to be a father to her.

Now I had a son on the way, and my wife was in my ear about being there for him too so I could be a real father. I agree with my wife that being a father was the most important job I could have. And being a father was something that I needed to do well. I didn't want to be that father that was always off coaching other people's children rather than being with my own. I didn't want to be that coach that might find himself someday in the position of his team competing against his son's team. I didn't want to be that coach that trained the guy who would try to beat my son. I didn't want to be that coach that was supporting and encouraging the guy battling my son on that mat someday.

After 14 years of coaching wrestling at all levels, I walked away from the sport just like I had done earlier with football for my daughter. I walked away from wrestling after coaching for 14 years and didn't look back so I could be fully present for my son and help him in everything he does to the best of my abilities.

However, life has a way though of throwing curve balls and change-ups at us. So, here I am now 14 years later with a son about to enter high school. And without any encouragement from me, because I wanted him to live his own life, he decided out of the blue that he wants to try wrestling in high school. He has never wrestled a single day leading up to this decision of his to begin this journey. I'm a bit surprised, but happy as all heck because I know wrestling will make a better man out of him. But, as his father, and protector, I'm also worried because I don't want him to get beat up or hurt.

Let me take a moment to give you some backstory. I had a great career as an athlete. I was a two-time state champion wrestler and twice a Junior Olympian. I also had a great run as a coach, where I coached a plethora of State Champs, some All-Americans, and even one National Champion. During those 14 years of coaching, I coached at all levels and was twice the Junior Olympian Coach as well.

Now, as a 48 year-old man, who has been living a post-wrestling life, I have put on some middle-age weight. I can no longer wrestle like I used to. I can't run or lift weights as I did before. I've had a total hip replacement, shoulder surgery, and a torn bicep. Also, I still need surgery on my other shoulder, too. Sometimes I feel like wrestling broke a few parts on me, and I can't help but wonder if my son should wrestle or not…

Upon further reflection, though, I realize that I have no regrets and would do it all over again if I had the chance. The hardships of wrestling build character. It helped mold me into a good man who was surrounded by other good men who didn't allow me to take the easy way out or make excuses.

Now, as a father who is raising a son of his own, shouldn't raising my son to be a good man, be one of my most important jobs? If I can pull that off, then my son will have a better chance of someday raising his own son to be a good man who will be a man of character, and someone who understands sacrifice and hard work. And who knows how far down the line this chain reaction can go from one good man raising another good man… who raises another…. And another… And another…

And when considering all of this wrestling and raising good men, I thank God that perhaps I can start this chain reaction of good men with some help from the world's oldest and toughest sport… wrestling!

Brian Preece: My journey in wrestling really started shortly after birth as I'm a son of a (famous) wrestling coach. I was born in Vernal, Utah in September of 1965, while my father (Dad) was in his second year of teaching. As a young teacher who loved athletics, he was eager to do whatever his administration asked him to do. He was asked to be an assistant wrestling coach. My Dad had no real experience in wrestling. He played basketball in high school and dabbled for a week in the sport as a junior in high school because he really liked the wrestling coach. But doing basketball and wrestling at the same time proved too difficult.

My Dad growing up was known to be a bit of a trouble maker, and he loved to fight. There were reported stories that he and his two best friends would look for trouble around town on weekends, and if they couldn't find a fight, they would fight each other. My Dad was the son of a rancher. But he sought a different life and went off to college, first at BYU and then later at Colorado State College (now known as the University of Northern Colorado). Colorado State College in Greely, Colorado, was known as a teacher college, meaning everyone that graduated there earned a degree in teaching. That is where he met my Mom. His involvement in a fraternity gave him a new interest in wrestling. One of their favorite activities was to attend the wrestling matches.

The head wrestling coach was dismissed, and all of a sudden, my Dad was promoted to be the head coach. My Dad was simply a coach in every sense of the word. Whatever he coached, he had success. He had the magic to relate with kids, understand the nuances of that sport's strategy, and teach the requisite skills in an understandable way for teenagers. And he was the master of the old fashioned pep talk. He also knew how to be a student of the game. My Dad was also an innovator. He started one of the first youth wrestling clubs in the state of Utah, and of course, I would be a participant.

However, there was immense pressure to be good, and it was very hard. It wasn't always enjoyable. I remember my first competitive tournament at around nine years old. I won, but I felt the pressure like everyone's eyes were on me. I felt like a lot of people wanted me to lose just because I was Coach Preece's kid.

I couldn't agree more with Dan's assessment above of wrestling's demands, as he makes this journey with his son. It's tough to be a son of a coach and/or father who was a state champion. These circumstances add a lot of extra pressure to a sport that already has plenty of it. To me, wrestling is the hardest sport a youngster can do. And it's not just the physical demands of the sport. It's the nature of the competition itself. I've seen over the years a lot of big-time football athletes admit they just can't deal with the pressure that comes from the one-on-one nature of the sport. In that dual meet, everyone there sees who won and who lost. You can't hide amongst other teammates and blame the loss on "the line that didn't block" or "the wide receiver that dropped the ball." And unlike other individual sports, you can't hide among the sea of competitors. If a cross-country runner takes tenth place at a meet, one has to ask, "Is that good or bad"? When it's just two competitors, "second place" really stings.

Of course, being a parent (or even an interested party) of a wrestler can be excruciatingly painful. But probably hardest for fathers. There is definitely ego involved. It's your blood out there competing, your genes are on the line. And since fathers (but increasingly more mothers) are the first coaches for their sons (and daughters), their ability (or inability) to teach technique is also on display. And what they have instilled in regards to character and how their child handles victory and defeat will be seen by all.

Though my Dad is in the National Wrestling Hall of Fame and won nine state titles and had lots of state champions and state placers, our father-son (wrestling) journey was far from perfect. There were times when I "quit" the sport, and a couple of times where my Dad "kicked me off the team". Generally, my Dad was a better coach for other people's kids than maybe for me. But, regardless, he was still the best coach I ever had in any sport. My younger brother who took state (I managed fourth) might have a different take. But reading about Dan's experience and his journey with his own son from above brings back a flood of my own memories, which were mostly good, but not always. Hey, that's wrestling…

CHAPTER TWO

THE ADVENTURE BEGINS

Dan Blanchard: "Dad, can you bring me to your old friend John Knapp's to wrestle before the regular season begins?" asked my boy Dakota.

"Wow! You want to go big time here with KT KIDZ Wrestling! I guess you're really serious about this wrestling thing." I responded to my son Dakota as I was a bit caught off guard with his sudden and sincere interest in wrestling.

To tell you the truth, I thought I would have a few more months before any of this wrestling stuff happened if it happened even at all. And I knew that my wife, Dakota's mom, wasn't going to be happy with Dakota's sudden interest in wrestling. And she certainly wasn't going to be pleased with him replacing his fall sport of cross-country running so he could do pre-season wrestling training.

This new change in our family schedule wasn't going to be easy on any of us. We have five children who are all involved in extracurricular activities. So, one can imagine the juggling we already do to get our family to where they need to be.

Now, throw into the mix me also driving Dakota 45-minutes away every Monday, Wednesday, and Friday night this fall so he can wrestle with Coach John Knapp. Then throw in a mother's natural tendency to worry about her kids, and you all can already see how this was going to complicate things. This new arrangement Dakota was promoting wasn't going to be an easy sell to my wife.

Well, thankfully, my wife, Jennifer, Dakota's mom, finally relented. However, she did let us know repeatedly loud and clear how she wasn't a big fan of Dakota wrestling, and me being 45-minutes away three nights a week.

Now, Dakota and I were off in the car to his first pre-season wrestling practice at Coach John Knapp's place. John is my old East Hartford High School wrestling teammate from the old days. He is also my former Junior Olympian teammate. We both spent some time together in Iowa, the home of Dan Gable, the best wrestler, and wrestling coach who ever lived. Now, all these years later, John Knapp is one the top wrestling coaches in Connecticut, and perhaps even the whole country.

So, I knew with confidence that my boy would be in good hands at KT KIDZ Wrestling in Rocky Hill, Connecticut. And to tell you the truth. I did think it was a good idea to get my boy some pre-season wrestling with me, and my old buddy John Knapp before Dakota's regular high school season began. It just makes sense to prep him, so he doesn't get beat up on day 1 in his high school season. And to see if he likes the sport before he jumps all the way in. Once the official season starts, he won't be allowed to quit. He'll have to finish what he started.

And once Dakota officially begins his high school wrestling season, he is going to be competing against kids who have been wrestling for years. This is usually a formula for getting beat up a lot. And getting beat up a lot in front of your classmates isn't much fun. And makes some kids want to quit.

I don't want Dakota's wrestling career to be over as soon as it starts. I want him to have a fighting chance at this. So I'm thrilled he asked me about my old buddy John Knapp. My boy Dakota surprised me here. Maybe he already knew somehow what I had been thinking. Or he somehow knew what I would be thinking about pre-season wrestling before I even realized I had been thinking it.

As we pulled up in the car at John Knapp's first pre-season practice, I might have been more nervous than my boy Dakota. Hey, John and I came up together, and I knew John's practices were going to be hard. And I also knew that kids there would be well-trained. Furthermore, Dakota isn't in wrestling shape and was still a novice.

Surprisingly Dakota held his own pretty well in his first practice at KT KIDZ Wrestling with just the moves I had been showing him in our unfinished basement. However, I could see him getting more and more tired as practice went on. At one point, he tried to come off the mat, telling me that his vision was blurry. I told him to get back out there that wrestling isn't over until the coach says it's over. He bravely went back out there. However, he was out of gas, and the next few wrestlers put some pretty good moves on him. Dakota was now in some uncharted territory. And I wondered how he would respond to it.

When practice was finally over, Dakota practically stumbled off the mat and out to my car. Then he got a calf-cramp trying to get in my vehicle that was painful as all heck. While cringing in pain, he said that he liked wrestling and that this sport isn't for wimps right before he passed out and slept all the way home.

"Wow!" I thought. My boy got a taste of wrestling tonight and felt first-hand what it was like to be more tired than he had ever been before in his entire life. And furthermore, he said he liked it and that this sport wasn't for wimps before he passed out. Dang! That's cool as hell! Maybe he won't be one of those kids who quits once they get to feel what wrestling is all about. Perhaps he'll stick it out and will wrestle with his school team in the winter, too. And maybe the sport of wrestling will help me make him a good man someday... Let's not get ahead of ourselves, though. Let's wait and see what next week brings...

Brian Preece: Unlike Dakota, I didn't enter my high school days full of excitement for the sport. Our school district didn't allow ninth graders to compete in high school. That has now changed. But, back then, in ninth grade, I competed in junior high in our school district that consisted of about 12-14 junior highs in the center part Salt Lake Valley. The junior highs were divided into two divisions, and I placed second in both division and district. I lost to the same wrestler twice. Ironically, he was trained in my Dad's Little League program and attended the junior high that fed into the high school where he was coaching.

However, there were no inclinations that I would attend the high school where my Dad was teaching and coaching. It was actually clear across the valley from where I lived. I would go to the local, more affluent high school where educational outcomes were significantly better. However, something interesting happened. My Dad, at age 41, decided after four years at his new high school to quit teaching altogether and sell insurance. I wasn't sure exactly what this might mean for our Dad-Coach-Son relationship. But to be honest, it was somewhat of a relief that I wouldn't be competing against the school where he coached. There were also a couple of wrestlers in my weight class at his school that were tough (okay, pretty much impossible) to beat. But I wasn't sure if he would be around at my practices a lot or just what my wrestling life would be like.

As my first high school season approached, I didn't have Dakota's sense of excitement nor his dedication to improving. In fact, I made it emphatic with my father that I was done with off-season wrestling, whether it be spring, summer or fall. I genuinely liked "team wrestling," meaning wrestling for my school and the comradery that it brought. But I just wasn't that interested in Saturday freestyle tournaments in the spring or wrestling Tuesday and Thursday nights with other wrestlers from other schools during the fall. I think my Dad was uneasy with my interest level and dedication at this point in my career. However, he accepted it because at least I was still wrestling.

My actual first high school coach was young as coaches go, in his late 20's. He wrestled at Oklahoma State where he was an All-American and at BYU. I really liked him. We had a strange team in the sense that we were small in numbers but high on quality. There were 12 weight classes at this time, and we couldn't even fill a team. But we would do better in tournaments because we had three or four wrestlers that would always make the championship finals. We had about 10-12 wrestlers on the team and there was only one weight, my weight, where we had multiple wrestlers. I lost my first wrestle-off, and now Coach Preece's kid was the only jayvee wrestler on the team.

Between my ninth and tenth grade year, I had grown about two inches and went from weighing 95-100 pounds to around 115-120 pounds. I wasn't the most natural athlete, and now I was struggling with a growth spurt, which would continue over the next two years. In the four years from grades 9-12, I nearly grew a foot and put on about 65 pounds in natural weight. I was gangly thin and tall for my weight class. And as a sophomore, I was finally going through puberty. But I had no natural strength. It wasn't that the guy that beat me in the wrestle-off was all that much better, he was just too strong for me. So I decided to suck down from 112 pounds to 105 pounds. I naturally weighed close to 120 pounds, so it was tough at first, even though I had some experience cutting weight as a youth wrestler. More concerning to me was that I had to beat out my closest friend on the team for varsity, and I felt terrible about it. But then the guy who had originally beat me out for 112 pounds spot quit the team. So my 105-pound teammate moved up to his spot and I remember feeling happy because I wouldn't be taking something away from my friend.

CHAPTER THREE

DOING MORE

Dan Blanchard: Well, another week and two more wrestling practices are under our belts. In the last chapter, I shared with you that my son Dakota's first preseason wrestling practice had caused him to become so tired and worn out that his vision became blurry. Also, his calf painfully cramped up while trying to get in the car, and then he quickly passed out on the car ride home.

The next day, when Dakota was rested, and feeling normal again, I spoke to him about how he had felt the night before. I told him that ironically if he wanted to get beyond that feeling of being wiped out beyond belief that he was going to have to do more.

Now, common sense would say that if you are already physically wiped out, then how the heck would anyone expect you to do more? Well, I suppose, being a wrestling champion, or even just a good man that can battle through the pain and fear isn't very common. So, sometimes you have to do the uncommon thing. Sometimes you have to do the thing that you may believe doesn't make sense, such as doing more when you think you can't do anymore. But, doing more is what will make your future easier.

Hey, either way, you're going to pay. So, you might as well pay now by doing more. This will help you be in a better position later to play rather than pay in front of all of your family and friends when you wrestle your next opponent. If you don't pay now, you'll surely pay later in a place where you'll be much more embarrassed when your opponent plays with you in front of your home crowd. I know I wouldn't want that to happen. What about you? Are you willing to pay the price now?

Well, I don't know if this all sunk into my son Dakota's head or not. Or if the fact that we did more drilling and less live wrestling in practice caused the workouts to be easier this week at John Knapp's KT KIDZ Wrestling program. But, surprisingly, both nights this week, my boy Dakota stayed awake during the car ride home and physically appeared to be fine both on the mat and in the car going home.

Tuesday night's car ride home was a bit humorous. Well, let me frame this by saying that many times the humor doesn't come during the moment, but rather later when we think back on it. Let me explain what I mean. During Tuesday's practice Coach Knapp and Coach West had shown the wrestlers a slide by wrestling move and then sent them off to their little special places on the mat to practice it. The slide by move is not the easiest move to master. So, my son was struggling with it, of course. And as any good father would do, I kept trying to instruct him from the side of the mat without stepping onto the mat. After all, I am a parent, not a coach. And I'm wearing work shoes, instead of wrestling shoes. You can picture this, right?

Well, no matter what I said to my boy from the side of the mat, it just didn't seem to help him do the move correctly. So, I finally resorted to being less technical and tried to put it in the simplest form of communication as possible that I could think of at the moment. Every time he did the move, he then turned and looked at me, and I kept just simply saying, "Get your head out of the way when you're trying to slide by him." Simple, right?

Well, now here comes the funny thing that I alluded to above about the car ride home on Tuesday night. As I was driving and talking to Dakota about practice, he said, "Hey Dad, I was trying to get that slide by move right, but every time I looked up at you, all you said was to get my head out of the way. And I had no idea what you were talking about. But, you just kept repeating to get my head out of the way, anyway."

Wow! Parenting and being a parent trying to coach your son from the side of the mat is humbling. I was a bit stunned and at a loss of words at that moment when Dakota basically said I wasn't helping him. Dang! He kept looking to me to tell him what he was doing wrong, and all I could eventually say was to get his head out of the way. I might as well have been speaking Greek to him because he had no idea what the heck I was talking about. And I didn't seem to know what other words to use to communicate with him in a way that he could understand. And furthermore, here we are in the car driving home, and I still couldn't seem to figure out what to say to him either. But those imperfect or maybe even screwed up exchanges that took place between us in wrestling practice tonight burned in my head. Hmm…

Well, forty-five minutes later our car pulled into our driveway, and we got out and went into our house. Inside I decided to leave that whole slide by thing alone for now and just instruct, or better yet, show my son Dakota a couple of minor things on defending himself better. For example, he didn't know what to do that night when his opponent was on top and grabbed his ankle. In addition, I also taught him how to better defend himself against the double leg attacks by staying on his feet more and not allowing his knee or hip to drop to the mat.

Furthermore, I also let Dakota know that he only had to improve just a little bit every week. And now if he knows how to free his ankle when he is on the bottom, and better defend the double leg attack, even if it's just a little bit, then he's already improved some for the week. And if he keeps making these tiny improvements every week, then he's going to be just fine for this upcoming season.

During Thursday's practice, I noticed Dakota is scrambling a little bit better and not always giving up the easy points when he seems to be in some trouble. I've been drilling into his head never to take the easy road, and never to give up the easy points even when he's in trouble. Dakota needs to make his competitor earn every point against him. He needs to make his opponent know every single second that he's in a fight so Dakota can physically and mentally wear him down. After all, didn't the great Coach Lombardi from the Green Bay Packers' fame say something about fatigue makes cowards of all of us? I say let's use that sound advice to make cowards out of our opponents.

While finishing up the practice that night, Coach John Knapp came over and stood next to me, and we both watched Dakota wrestle. My old buddy John said, "Dan, Dakota is pretty good for a kid that has never wrestled before." I whole-heartedly agree. Then Johnny also said, "Heck, he might even be more athletic than you were at that age, Dan." I was happy with this comment, too; however, I must admit that I wasn't entirely sure what to make of that one. I was thinking. "Hey, what do you mean more athletic than me!"

Well, when I got home that night and told my wife, she said that Johnny is probably right and that now I'm supposed to be proud of my boy's athletic abilities. And you what? I then agreed with her, too. And I am indeed proud of Dakota's athletic ability. And it in no way diminishes what I did on the wrestling mat when I was his age.

Now that I've pushed my ego aside, let's wait and see what roller-coaster wrestling ride this preseason at KT KIDS wrestling is going to take us on next week…

Brian Preece: As I read Daniel's reflections on Dakota this week, I reflected a bit myself on whether I was more athletic than my father. I actually didn't feel that athletic until my college days where I finally stopped growing. Then for some reason I got more athletic. I gained speed, strength, and improved my coordination. I could hit a golf ball about 300 yards even without very good equipment. By the time I left college, I could bench press close to 300 pounds. My friends in college actually thought I was athletic. Then when I was playing intramural football, two friends from my high school days asked if they could join our team. In regards to our days from high school, they were much more athletic. But they were shocked by just how athletic I got in college and told me so. I was now their size and faster. And what was cool was that they noticed. For the first time in my life, I actually felt athletic.

I remember after losing my semifinal match at state my senior year, my Dad came over to me to console me. He knew I was devastated, and I told him, "I was going to take this like a man." His words to me were a bit shocking. "Brian, I never thought you would get here. I'm very proud of you."

So evidently, my own impression of my general lack of athleticism in high school seemed to be generally shared by my father. And at the saddest point of my life, his words were actually comforting. I took them to mean that "I did pretty well for what I was given."

However, in reality, compared to most humans my age walking around at that time, I was probably reasonably athletic. It's not like I'm a Niles Crane from the TV series *Frasier*. I might have made our school's basketball team if I focused my efforts there. And I did make our school's golf team for a couple of years. I could play tennis decently, too. I actually possessed pretty good eye-hand coordination, but that's not something that is all that valuable in wrestling. There are no balls to catch or to hit.

My younger sister and brother were "the athletes of the family." My sister did four sports in high school and my brother did three. My brother ended up being a state champion wrestler and my sister was a key player on a state championship volleyball team. But by college-age, I was probably the most athletic of the Preece siblings, at least I can make a better argument at Thanksgiving dinners. That's the tricky thing about athletics and life. Some people peek out earlier or later than others.

In regards to wrestling, my Dad never wrestled with his wrestlers. Like ever. At least I never saw it, even when he was younger. In his later years, he often coached in street clothes. I actually played basketball and golfed against my Dad more than we ever actually wrestled. Growing up, the weight difference between my Dad and me was pretty enormous. I was small, he was a big guy. And when I was growing up, he smoked and drank socially. But since he was actually a basketball player in high school and not a wrestler, maybe this wasn't all that shocking. And he could play a decent game of golf. He even played a little freshman football in college. Unlike Daniel and Dakota, we weren't both wrestlers. I was a wrestler, and he really wasn't. And that's what was unusual about my father as a coach. He outcoached coaches who were college All-Americans and state champion wrestlers. One of his best friends, Ben Ohai, who coached at another school was an NCAA finalist. He brought my Dad in all the time to talk to his team and be a clinician. But my Dad also picked his brain for technique all the time. Coaching is not actually doing, it's actually showing someone how to do something. And also all the tangibles of making a kid believe in himself. That's what made my Dad one of the greatest coaches ever.

Perhaps being a bit opposite from Daniel, I actually like to brag about my wrestling success despite being a "bad athlete." I thought it was cool to learn years later from a coaching colleague that wrestled in high school the same time I did, that their team had a nickname for me. It wasn't flattering, but it is still pretty darn cool that I had a nickname. They called me "The Leech" by the way.

I stressed to my athletes that they don't have to be the best athlete in the world to be successful. I told them that my biggest asset I had as an athlete and wrestler was my brain. I shared with them how in all my matches that I ever wrestled in youth high school, and college that I always knew the score. Well, all except for one wild match that I had in high school, which makes for an amusing story that I'll share with you later. I stressed for my wrestlers to find their own style and make their opponents wrestle their style. And surely, I had a lot of wrestlers that were much better natural athletes than myself and ultimately better wrestlers than I ever was. And that was more than okay. I was coaching my wrestlers to be state champions, and yes the reality was that only a small handful would ever make it there. But I wanted state championships for all of them. But more importantly, I wanted them to be good men, good women, and good people regardless of where they placed in the states.

CHAPTER FOUR

THE LEARNING CURVE

Dan Blanchard: I feel like my 14 year-old boy Dakota is already changing for the better, thanks to wrestling. When I showed him moves at home this week, he actually said, "Thanks." Wow… is all I can think. I guess wrestling really is putting him on the path to be a good man someday.

Early Tuesday evening, on our way to practice, I had a talk with Dakota about the importance of sucking it up. I stressed how crucial it is to suck it up, especially when you're tired and really don't want to. I had plenty of time to get my message across during our 45-minute car ride to John Knapp's KT KIDZ Wrestling practice in Rocky Hill, Connecticut.

I shared with Dakota that during the 3rd period when we're all the most tired we've ever been in our lives, is when the real men come out to play. I let him know that most guys are just trying to get through the third period. Some others, however, seem to flip that 'seize the day' switch in their heads instead. These kinds of guys go into the carpe diem mode that third period. They're not even thinking about just surviving that 3rd period. Instead, all gears are firing, and they're now thriving in their own element of toughness. This is where these champs and good men really pick up the pace to a point where it becomes punishing for their opponent to try to keep up.

I have actually seen this all-out pace done in the All-American rounds, where a wrestler cried because his opponent set such a punishing tempo in the last period. It's a killer instinct to win by making the other quit. And if you're already winning, then it's a killer instinct to pin your opponent, rather than just settling for winning the match on points.

Soon we arrived at practice where Coach Knapp and Coach West showed some defensive strategies to the double leg takedown. I was pretty happy about it because Dakota was having some trouble stopping the double leg attacks of some of his better opponents the week before. The coaches explained that our first line of defense is our head position and hand position. They showed how to hip-in and bury your opponent's head, push his hips back to extend and weaken him, and then showed a great way to grab your opponent's ankle and slowly circle around to the back of him while driving him down to the mat with your own hipping-in pressure. I feel like this could be a good move for my son Dakota to help him defend the double leg attack because he has long legs and arms. Unlike me... I'm assuming he must have gotten that longness from his mother's side of the family.

After practicing the moves for a while, we went into the live wrestling part of the night. I couldn't wait to see what Dakota can do tonight now that he knows a little tiny bit more than he knew last week.

The first six-minute match, he wrestled against a really good kid who schooled my son in the combat sport of wrestling. I'm slightly frustrated, and my heart breaks some for my boy. Now he looks a bit worn out after this rough match. Hopefully, the next match will be better…

Unfortunately, the next match wasn't any better, though. It might have been even more painful than the first one. I can feel the pain in my own shoulders as the 2nd boy is also schooling Dakota in the combat sport of wrestling. This boy has a half-nelson so deep that it looks like my boy's shoulder is about to pop out. Dakota showed a lot of guts out there fighting it off, but this boy, just like the first one, was just too much for him at this point.

Tonight there were a few times I saw the frustration on Dakota's face. He couldn't do much to defend himself against his opponents. Then add in the pure exhaustion from fighting off his back. Hmm... There was a part of me that felt bad for my boy. But then there was another part of me that thought that the wrestling practice mat is a way better place than the real world for him to get a few early lessons in getting beat up. Here, in a safe environment, he can learn how to deal with feelings of frustration and not being able to accomplish what he wants to.

On the way home, I told him that I was proud of how well he hung in there and didn't quit when he felt overmatched, and everything seemed to be going wrong. I also told him that I would teach him how to build a base from the bottom and defend that half-nelson before next practice. Then I asked him if he wanted to sleep on the way home, but he said, "No." Hmm… that's an improvement compared to how worn out he was last week.

Oh, yeah, I almost forgot to tell you this. Another positive is that Dakota was able to hit an arm-drag on both of his opponents tonight.

And both were a lot better than him. But, regardless, he successfully took them both down to the mat anyway. Pretty cool, huh?

Thursday night got off to a great start as I noticed Dakota's slide-by move was looking a little bit better. The kid he was drilling with was doing a great job of helping Dakota better understand, and execute it. And occasionally Coach John Knapp intervened and re-coached some of the finer points of the move so Dakota could do it more effectively. At one point, Dakota even said to me, "I think I finally know what getting your head out of the way means now, dad."

I'm beaming as we all move into the live wrestling part of the practice. I'm thinking that after doing a little homework or wrestling work at home, Dakota should do a bit better tonight than he did on Tuesday night. Boy, was I wrong. The first six-minute match Dakota wrestled a very good kid who had his way with my boy. Dakota was clearly over-matched and fighting for his life out there again. However, a bright spot was that Dakota once again hit his arm-drag and successfully took this older and more experienced boy down to the mat.

The next boy and six-minute match was a repeat of the first one. Another great older and more experienced wrestler who also schooled Dakota and bent the heck out of him. I didn't like to see my boy being manhandled and bent all up like that. I wanted to help him. But, I also knew he had to take his lumps out there all by his lonesome self. No one could take those lumps for him if he were going to improve. Dakota could get bent like crazy, and that would be okay as long as he didn't break too much. And this would help him learn how to be a better wrestler and a better man.

Another bright spot of the night was that Dakota successfully hit another arm-drag for a takedown on this kid, too. Dakota didn't think much of this minor success, but I certainly did as I did a fist-pump off on the side of the mat.

At the end of this match, I figured Dakota's gas tank was empty. And maybe I was being a bit too protective, but I was happy for him that practice was over. However, I was wrong, and practice wasn't over. Coach West yelled to find another opponent. Dakota wrestled a third six-minute match and then two rounds of round-robin. I wondered where Dakota was finding the energy and will to fight on, but somehow he did. And I'm so proud of him.

During this trying period of time of watching my exhausted boy trying to hang in there, I felt a tap on my shoulder and turned around to see who it was. It was Vinny Knapp, the father of Coach John Knapp. Mr. Knapp is the guy who always seemed to look out for me when I was just a kid. He used to pick me up and drive me to some wrestling practice or tournament somewhere so I could practice my fighting on the mat, instead of on the streets.

I am extremely grateful for all that Mr. Knapp did for me when I was growing up in the rough and tough East Hartford. I was delighted to see him again and chat with him for a bit. Our conversation of catching up undoubtedly made it easier for me to deal with the hardships that my boy was going through on the mat at that same exact moment.

Finally, the practice was over. It was a very frustrating week. However, every coach in that wrestling room stopped Dakota before we left and told him he did well and that his tiny improvements are visible. Coach John Knapp instructed him to keep his head up because he's getting nailed with half-nelsons left and right. I guess we'll have to work on those half-nelsons again at home.

When we got in the car for the long ride home, I asked Dakota again if he wanted to sleep. And again he said, "No." Again, I thought, "Wow." Then he blew my mind with what he said next, which was, "Dad, they're better than me because they have put in more time and work than me."

"Dang" was all I could say. He's really starting to get it. Effort applied over time… That's the game-changer… And that's the developer of champs and good men… Now we're both eagerly looking forward to next week.

Brian Preece: As I read about Dakota's experience, I think it's really cool that he is learning and willing to try new moves. In ninth grade I had done organized wrestling for six years. And I was pretty set in my ways and I invented my own style of wrestling based on the fact that I was tall and gangly and very slow-footed. My Dad actually didn't try to change me much. He was one that tailored techniques around the individual wrestler. He wasn't a cookie-cutter style of coach, where all his wrestlers had to have the same style of wrestling. But as for me, I had a limited number of moves that I would do, especially in takedown wrestling.

My strategy was always to shoot first and take the match to the ground because I had trouble defending myself. In my adult coaching years, I learned a lot of funk defenses that I enjoyed employing, but wrestling wasn't this evolved in the 1970s and 1980s. So I would shoot a bad double leg, and then try to maneuver to my favorite move, which was an outside fireman's carry or "kelly" as my Dad would call it. If my opponent hung his arm, or even better under-hooked me, I would dump him with the carry. I was pretty good about getting back points even against better wrestlers through this dump. My complimentary moves were a short-drag, or under-drag depending on what you want to call it. And a switch off to a high-crotch and then changing back to a double leg finish.

One thing I could generally say is that I wrestled my style of match 99 percent of the time. I still lost plenty of times, about a third of them, but one had to beat me wrestling my style of match. I did, however, change my style against one guy. It was in what I thought would be the last match of my career. I was wrestling for third place in the state tournament my senior year. And I told my Dad that I was going to wrestle on my feet, meaning that I wasn't going to take the match instantly to the ground. I figured I wasn't going to take state anyway. And third place versus fourth didn't matter that much to me. I just wanted to try something new and have some fun. I lost 1-0. But oh well, it was in some ways the most fun I ever had wrestling. It was sort of the feeling maybe Dakota had in his first few matches.

I bring up the fun because I see how Dakota, even though he's getting thrown around a bit, is having fun and learning the sport. And what's cool is that he's trying to apply what he is being taught to competitive situations. Dakota has a much better attitude than I had about the sport at his age. I had more experience, and I was set in my ways by the time I was his age. But as I went into my high school season, which was the tenth grade, instead of Dakota's ninth grade, I went from winning most of the time in junior high to losing more than half of the time in high school. That was really frustrating.

Sometimes I wonder what was going through my Dad's head during this time. Was he thinking that he should have made his son wrestle differently? I know he wondered if I should have wrestled JV, especially in bigger tournaments. But my high school coach my sophomore year insisted that I wrestle varsity. He tried to change my style and couldn't figure out why I couldn't defend myself. I know wrestling on my knees frustrated him. But after a while, he seemed to get why I wrestled that way.

As I read about Dan's and Dakota's week, I also thought of my coaching days. I thought about the excitement of seeing my wrestlers learn new things and then apply them in competition. I didn't have a great youth wrestling program feeding my school. And a lot of my wrestlers started wrestling in their ninth-grade year or even after. I even had a few seniors come out and try the sport.

During this time, I tried hard NOT to coach my wrestlers on how I actually wrestled. However, if some of them found themselves in the positions I was in much of my high school career, I knew exactly what they needed to do. But I built my program on giving my wrestlers the tools to be able to compete decently without a lot of experience. So we really emphasized conditioning, and great defense, or what I would rather call "counter-offense." When Daniel talked about teaching his son how to defend the half-nelson, I was saying, "Right on." We have to give our wrestlers the ability to protect themselves on the mat in the bottom position.

We felt if we could get our wrestlers to actually wrestle longer in matches, their superior conditioning would pay off in wins. In high school wrestling, I'm a firm believer that positioning is more important than moves. It's great to have a lot of moves in your bank account, but bottom line, even the best wrestlers use a small set of techniques. But the best wrestlers have perfect positioning from their stance to how they wrestle on the mat. My wrestlers could always repeat my two rules of wrestling on demand: 1) Head up and back straight. 2) The low-inside man wins!

CHAPTER FIVE

TAKING STEP FORWARD

Dan Blanchard: As the next week of pre-season wrestling rolls around, Dakota tells me in the car on the way to practice that he isn't feeling 100%. I wonder if his interest in wrestling is fading, or if he's still feeling the effects of last week and those really tough kids he had to wrestle against on both nights…

However, once practice starts, Dakota looks fine, so I'm no longer concerned. I kind of drift off a little bit to daydream about how I wish I knew these moves back in high school that now my freshman son is learning before the season even begins. These moves are firing up my imagination on what would have been possible if I knew back then what I know now.

Drilling and instruction go well. Now comes the live wrestling part of the practice. I'm still feeling a little nervous as I remember what my son Dakota went through last week when he wrestled one tough kid after another.

Dakota gets partnered up with a kid that he looks slightly bigger than, but in wrestling, that doesn't mean much. The whistle blows for the six-minute match, and Dakota gets the first takedown. He then rides his opponent for most of the first period. Unfortunately, he doesn't really know what to do to turn his opponent to his back successfully. Eventually, his opponent escapes and then Dakota takes him down again before time runs out. The next two periods went well for Dakota. I'm a bit relieved thinking about how this match was good for Dakota because it will give him a chance to get some of his confidence back after the beatings he took last week.

The second practice match kid also appears slightly smaller than Dakota, but he looks athletic and wiry. I noticed this kid earlier in the night, and he's a pretty good wrestler. Tangling with this kid should be good for Dakota now that he has a little bit of his confidence back.

The whistle blows, and once again, Dakota gets the first takedown. I'm impressed because I know this kid is pretty good. However, once on the mat, it becomes painfully apparent that this kid has a lot more experience than my son Dakota. This kid quickly reverses Dakota and then throws the leg in. Dakota doesn't know what to do. He hasn't been taught leg-wrestling yet. They roll around a lot, and Dakota misses a few opportunities like grabbing his opponent's head when it's hanging. He just doesn't know yet what to do. His opponent ends up pinning Dakota a few times while down there on the mat rolling around.

However, on the positive side, Dakota does seem to be a little bit better fighting off the half-nelsons tonight with at least these two kids. Also, every time Dakota was on his feet tonight, he successfully took his opponents down to the mat. I think Dakota's athleticism is really helping him a lot in neutral. And so is the drilling on our feet in our unfinished basement

On the ride home, Dakota feels pretty good even after doing some extra pull-ups on his own after practice. We talked about his matches, and he felt good about the first one but frustrated that he couldn't do anything with the second kid, especially after he threw a leg in. I remind him that he was only outmaneuvered on the mat, but he had dominated the neutral position. He seems surprised that he had had that much success. I was surprised that he didn't realize that while his opponents were better on the mat tonight, he was better on his feet tonight... I guess that's the way our human psyche works. We rarely see ourselves fully in the positive light that we should. We focus too much on what went wrong.

Before the next practice, I show Dakota on his bedroom floor how to keep his hips lower while riding his opponent so he doesn't get rolled so easily. I also teach him how to ride the ankle so he can slow down his opponent and help keep his hips lower if he gets a guy really tough and wiry on the bottom. We both end up with rug burn knees.

During Thursday's car ride over to Coach John Knapp's KT KIDZ Wrestling place, Dakota surprised me again when he asked, "How do you score? How do you get a takedown?"

Wow, I was shocked! I had apparently forgotten how new he is in the sport of wrestling. He's had some success, especially on his feet, so I guess I just naturally felt like he was a lot further along than he really is. Lesson learned... The humbling way... Boy, do kids have a way of doing that to us adults, don't they?

In practice, that night, Coach John Knapp and Coach West showed an excellent arm-bar series. One of the tilt moves looks to me like a variation of the old freestyle gut-wrench move. Again, I think, I wish I knew that move in high school. Well, to tell you the truth, I knew the high school folk-style arm-bar tilts, and I also knew the international freestyle gut-wrench. However, I had never considered putting the two of them together to score on my opponent. Wow! Wrestling sure has advanced here in Connecticut since I had coached wrestling fourteen long years ago.

During the live wrestling portion of practice, Dakota gets paired up with a pretty good kid who he wrestled a few weeks ago. This kid had his way with Dakota back then. Tonight the whistle blows, and Dakota gets the first takedown. Wow! He really is getting better on his feet! Later in the match, Dakota gets a beautiful double leg where he lifts his opponent and throws him down for another takedown. I was very impressed, and so was Coach John Knapp as he walked by and yelled, "Way to go, Dakota! You're already 100 times better than your father was!" Johnny grins ear to ear and gives me a little head nod and wink.

My son Dakota certainly has improved, especially on his feet. Unfortunately, though, this second kid, too, had his way with Dakota on the mat pinning him several times in the down position. Dang… I wish I had a small mat at home so I could work with Dakota more in the down position. Almost all of our work so far has been up on our feet. Thankfully he's getting better in neutral. But unfortunately, he's still getting torn up down on the mat.

Overall, Dakota and I are both happy with his performance tonight, both physically and mentally. But again, he got hammered with those half-nelsons. Guess I have some more work to do with him. We also need to watch some wrestling videos soon so he can see how the scoring in wrestling works. And lastly, we better keep going to these

KT KIDZ Wrestling practices. These practices are helping a lot in our quest for Dakota to have a fighting chance on his first official day of high school wrestling on the Monday after Thanksgiving. Hopefully, the regular season, too, will be another successful leg of our journey in building a state champion, or at least a good man someday out of my boy Dakota.

Brian Preece: As I read about Daniel and Dakota's journey this week, I too wished that I knew then what I know now. And this applied both to my competitive experiences as both a wrestler and a coach.

I do remember the exact move or maneuver that derailed my dreams of being a state champion. It became so ingrained that as a coach, it became a staple in our top offense. The move I speak of is the Churella. It's named after Michigan great Mark Churella. He coached at the University of Nevada Las Vegas, or UNLV, at the time when I was wrestling in high school. In fact, coaches and wrestlers at this time period in Utah didn't yet call this move the Churella. They called it "The Brighton" because Brighton High School used this new move on top with a lot of success back then.

I can remember my semifinal match at state vividly. I was winning 4-3 and on bottom to begin the last round. I was in a great position to score and win the match. But then my opponent, Mark Romine of Brighton, hit me with the Churella twice to turn me to my back and beat me 9-4. As Daniel described his son Dakota's match where he didn't know how to counter the top leg wrestling techniques of his foe, it brought back this memory for me. Like Dakota, I had shown superiority on my takedown wrestling, scoring two of them against my opponent only to get completely outwrestled on the mat.

However, when I turned more to coaching, I made this move, and the series of moves that went with it was part of our top offense. I even taught this series to my younger brother Scott. He made it part of his repertoire on top offense on his way to taking state some seven years later.

Over the next few years in Utah wrestling, the Brighton would be called the Churella. Yet, I wonder if Mark Churella actually invented the move or if it was just named for him because he used the technique a lot and won a NCAA title. But all credit to him. I won't say that I invented any moves. But the way I instructed the step-thru Turk series, and incorporating the Churella into the series, was cutting edge in Utah wrestling. It is really a boost to your coach ego when other programs are calling techniques your wrestlers use by the name of the school where you coach.

Of course, wrestling is an evolutionary sport, and that's why I love it. There are moves to counter moves to counter moves to counter moves. And nothing in wrestling has seen more incredible developments than counter wrestling on takedowns, or what people might call funk or scramble defenses. I fully embraced it as a coach. And I think I was outside the norm as I encouraged creativity from my own wrestlers to even "invent" their own techniques. Of course, I wasn't wholly laissez-faire with all of this. I still had my two guiding principles to position (head-up, back straight, and low-inside man wins). When I was an assistant coach at West High School, Coach Dan Potts and I had what we would call "Slime Practice" after the regular practice was over. This time after the official practice is where we would explore the creative aspects of the sport and work with wrestlers individually.

We called it "Slime Practice" because we were teaching those "slime" techniques that would help our wrestlers become competitive quicker, while also enhancing the methods of our more advanced grapplers. And the techniques were individualized to each wrestler's weight, body type, and strengths as a wrestler. Slime Practice was entirely optional. And the format was usually us, as coaches, answering questions put forth by the wrestlers. We again let our wrestlers guide the instruction. But we had a lot of wrestlers like Dakota, who were new to the sport, and curious about learning. And in any regular practice, you always have to stretch, condition, and wrestle, along with those team announcements, so sometimes there isn't enough time to teach technique and refine skills. And of course, in the typical high school wrestling practice, the same methods tend to be coached to every wrestler regardless of body type, weight class, and experience.

So much of mastering wrestling is just experience and exposure. Dakota was learning how to defend against the half nelson but then found himself being overwhelmed by top leg wrestling techniques. But over time, Dakota will learn how to fight legs. I lost my semifinal match my senior year from a move neither my Dad nor myself had seen before. Here it was too late to apply those nontraditional things to my own high school wrestling career. However, I was able to add these slime techniques in coaching my wrestlers and even help my younger brother win state. So I am glad time is on Dakota's side to continue learning.

CHAPTER SIX

WHEN MORE IS MORE AND WHEN
LESS IS MORE

Dan Blanchard: It's Monday night, and once again, Dakota and I are back in the car heading to another preseason wrestling practice. And we're doing this after consuming another dinner in seven minutes or less. These preseason days are so busy. As a matter of fact, all of these autumn back-to-school days are busy. I feel a little bad today because I didn't do any drilling with Dakota this past weekend. He came to me Friday night about 9:30 after I just had gotten home from work to drill, and I told him, "I have been going non-stop since 4:00 A.M. that morning, and I was just too tired. We'd do it over the weekend."

Well, guess what? I ended up working one of my multiple part-time jobs that supplements the pay of my full-time teaching job. I worked all day on Saturday, and again all day on Sunday. The weekend passed, and I didn't drill any wrestling moves with my boy, Dakota. Hmm… I'm going to have to figure out a way to do better by my son. He deserves at least that much… even if I am just trying to pay the bills, which seems to be a never-ending uphill battle.

During practice tonight, Dakota seemed to be doing well. A funny kind of thing happened at practice. Coach John Knapp quickly referenced defensive moves off of the bottom position that he never wants to see his wrestlers use. The funny thing is that when I used to wrestle, I used those two moves he referred to frequently. I even used to show those moves to my wrestlers when I was a coach.

Coach Johnny Knapp instead showed what the wrestlers should really be doing when on the bottom, instead of those two moves. And after some reflection, I had to give it to Johnny. His way was indeed better than my old way.

Bear with me for a moment, and I'll try to explain the reason his way is better than mine. In the old days, a wrestler would hit one of his moves on me, and then I would counter it with one of my moves. In Coach Knapp's way of wrestling, one counters his opponent's moves at the beginning of the move, instead of at the end of it. Johnny's approach doesn't even allow the opponent to hit the move in the first place. My old way did allow my opponents to execute the move and then I attempted to counter it after it was completed.

When I spoke to Johnny that night about the brilliance of this way of wrestling through not even allowing the opponent's move, he said, "Our goal here is to beat the top five wrestlers in the country, not the bottom five."

Wow! That's Powerful, I thought…

My son, Dakota, is getting some great coaching here. If he continues this, then by the end of next year, his sophomore year, he could be more technically sound than I am in the sport of wrestling.

Not sure how I feel about him being better than me by the end of his sophomore year. However, I guess I feel good and bad. I'm very proud and happy for him if he can indeed pull this off. But, I'm also wondering if I should go buy some wrestling shoes and begin brushing up some, so I don't become obsolete. I really would like to be able to continually add to my son's wrestling education throughout at least his high school years before he is out of my league.

Tonight's live wrestling segment was all down on the mat. At first, I was a little nervous because this is an area of weakness for Dakota. But then I rebounded and was grateful because I know Dakota needs some extra mat time so he can learn what to do down on the mat.

On this night, I found myself continuously yelling out, "Head up! Look away!" At one point, Dakota got one of his opponents in a cradle, but didn't know what to do until I yelled, "Put your knee in his back and pull him over it." He did and successfully pinned the kid.

Cool!

All and all, it was a pretty good night of wrestling for Dakota. It got even better when on the long drive home he said, "Hey, Dad, you want to know why I'm going to be really good at this sport someday? It's because you didn't force me to come here and wrestle. It's because I want to be here. And I want to get better at wrestling."

Wow! He's already beyond his years… And I'm starting to see the good man coming out of him…

I'm kicking myself a bit on Wednesday night's drive after another seven-minute dinner. Once again, I didn't have a chance to work with Dakota, between the last wrestling practice and this one. Again, I got home late last night from work. And tonight I got home just in time to eat, and then dash out the door with Dakota for that 45-minute car ride to John Knapp's KT-KIDZ wrestling practice.

During the ride, Dakota took a short nap. When he woke about halfway there, we talked a little bit about life. Dakota told me that school has been burying him with homework, especially his math class. The math teacher gave him 50 math problems tonight that he had to do before I'd take him to wrestle. Dakota didn't think it was fair. He thought maybe the math teacher should only give him 15-20 problems to solve. Dakota was frustrated that he just hasn't had any time to himself lately since school started back up. Things are different for him now. He is in high school, and there is more expected of him there than there was in middle school.

I told him, "I get it, buddy. I hear you. I have no time either. And I know it's hard." However, as a high school teacher myself, I'm not picking sides because I can see the arguments on both his side and his teachers' side…

Once we got to practice and warmed up, Coach West and Coach Knapp reviewed the bottom moves we had learned on Monday night. And then the wrestlers got busy working on them again.

Next, the coaches showed some top techniques of better positioning oneself and knocking the bottom wrestler off balance so he'd be weak. This was good, I thought. We all like being in strong positions while making our opponents weak.

The time spent in mat wrestling was helpful for my son, Dakota, but as we all already know, these things take time. Dakota still wasn't entirely sure what to do out there tonight during the live wrestling part. He doesn't have any muscle memory for it yet.

At one point, Dakota got so frustrated after another roll left him getting pinned again that he walked over near me and asked me what he's supposed to do. I instructed him to leave the rolls alone, and just work a strong base, wrist-control, and then just stand up.

With the next kid, he tried this, and it actually worked! I was so happy that he decided to listen to me. You all know how teen boys are. Them actually listening to us, doesn't happen every day. Back in neutral, Dakota took his opponent down, and I found myself then yelling, "Cover his hips!"

Soon after, Dakota surprised me again. His opponent was getting away from him, and Dakota attempted to drop down to his opponent's ankles to bring him back down to the mat. It didn't work. The kid still got away. But hey, at least he tried, right? He's listening... at least a little bit...

The car ride home that night was exciting. Dakota mentioned how nice the other boys at wrestling are and that they try to help him learn some of the moves. We talked about how hard and demanding wrestling is, and how it's a badge of honor to have wrestled for even a little bit. I told Dakota that it's good to do hard things. And because wrestling is so hard, it brings out a brotherhood in wrestlers that unites them no matter where they come from or what they look like. Wrestlers will help each other out and show each other moves. They will share what they know with each other.

Wrestling creates a real brotherhood, and that's what we need in this world... more brotherhood. People who are involved in a brotherhood don't go shoot each other like some of the kids are doing out there these days... We wrestlers and coaches are doing our part to further that brotherhood. We are developing good men with the promise of a brighter and stronger future. These future men, who know combat on the mat, don't need to use violence to get what they want in the real world.

Hopefully, this weekend I can find some time to work the front-headlock series with my boy, Dakota. I've noticed a lot of his opponents are leaning too much in the neutral position. They're attempting to protect their legs from being shot upon. But by overcompensating for one problem, they are unknowingly creating another problem that hopefully Dakota can capitalize on. A few snapdowns into front head-locks might help him score a few points next practice if I can find some time to work with him. Well, I guess we'll just have to wait and see what the weekend brings…

Brian Preece: When Dakota said to Daniel, "Hey, Dad, you want to know why I'm going to be really good at this sport someday? It's because you didn't force me to come here and wrestle. It's because I want to be here. And I want to get better at wrestling," it brought back a flood of memories from my youth and my own son's decision not to wrestle.

On the latter, I was more than okay with my son's decision. He was born with Sensory Processing Disorder, and that is a game-changer on many levels. He has done cross-country and track and field, throwing the discus and shot-put, and that is fine with me. He is involved with some clubs at school, very actively involved in his church groups, and he does a great job at school. When he was old enough to maybe wrestle, I had retired from being a head coach at my school. I really never brought it up much again, letting both of my children gravitate to their own interests. I believe wrestling is a wonderful sport and builds character. But it's not the only thing that creates character and can shape positive values in young men and women.

Dakota's words ignited thoughts about when I was young with my father. The word "forced" is a tricky one. I don't think I was ever chained to the car or anything, but there was an incredible amount of coaxing, and even Mom and Dad guilt trips sometimes to get me to wrestle.

I can remember back to those days growing up in Vernal, Utah, and having to drive to the Wasatch Front (Salt Lake or Utah County) for a Saturday freestyle tournament. For the most part, I dreaded those trips. The tournaments were so long back in those days. There were no staggered start times like we use for youth tournaments these days or Track Wrestling. Since the drive was three hours away, it often meant waking up at around 4:00 A.M. to make some early-morning weigh-in.

There were also one or two guys I could rarely beat so I would faithfully come home with that silver, or bronze medal if I had a bad day. And predictably those medals are somewhere in my shed today collecting dust. Most were not engraved. But my Dad went the extra mile and took the time to engrave them himself when we got back home. I guess maybe some 45 years later, I might be able to connect some of those medals with some of those tournament experiences.

But most of these early wrestling experiences weren't that great for me personally. There were some fun times in-between matches, but a lot of these tournaments finished up late at night, sometimes close to midnight. My Mom usually volunteered as a "pair master," and she was great at it. But it also meant that she was there to the bitter end, even if I was done wrestling several hours earlier. I would try and often succeed in sleeping on the car ride to and from our destinations. But getting home in the wee hours of early morning wasn't always my cup of tea.

There is guilt now thinking that maybe I should have been stronger or more eager about wanting to do these youth wrestling events. Now I am fully aware of the sacrifice of time and money my parents put into me wrestling, as well as the other sports I did, too. But I was too young to understand that fully back then. So, as a 9 year-old boy, who wanted to please his parents, especially his father, off to the meets, we went.

And at these wrestling events, I felt pressure to not only partici-pate but also to do well. And I'm sure my Dad felt some pressure that I attend and do well, too. Being a coach's son, and a legendary coach's son on top of that, came with a lot of pressure--for both father and son. I know that every once in a while, you get a coach's son that is not that good. Maybe that might even be a blessing. However, I was good enough for there to be a lot of pressure, again for both father and son. And there was always some coach's son that was doing better than I was doing. And that hurt a little bit for both my Dad and me.

As I said in a previous paragraph, there was always one kid who always beat me. His name was Todd Norton. He wrestled for the Brighton program in Salt Lake Valley. Brighton had a great youth pro-gram and high school program. It was the dominant large-school high school program in Utah from the mid-1970s through the 1980s. Todd was a year ahead of me in school and took state when I was a sopho-more. He would beat me in the quarterfinals that year, which was the last time we ever wrestled against each other. But I liked Todd a lot. He always made sure I didn't feel too bad.

I remember, after a match one time, Todd picked me up in a bear hug and carried me around. He was a stud on and off the mat. And his parents were awesome. I especially liked his Dad. I think after a while, my Dad accepted that Todd was a better wrestler. And he was older, so it seemed that my losses to him were at least somewhat acceptable. Todd's parents were great people.

I bring Todd up because he was one of the guys that made some of my past youth tournaments tolerable. There were others too. When I was in a Little League program in my hometown, some of the guys like Ryan Siddoway, Mike Smith, George Cook, Mike Slaugh, Gary Murray, and Kary McNeill, who I would wrestle against in high school to a 5-5 tie, were fun to hang out with as well. Remember, youth tour-naments were long back in the day, and one had to keep themselves entertained with any adventure they could. We probably wrestled a lot more in between our matches than we actually did in the competition. We found equipment in the gym to play on until we would be inevita-bly told by some adults to get off of it. That's usually when our Dads came over and told us to get ready for our next match.

But by my sophomore year in high school, I had had enough with all the extra wrestling. Even though we had moved to the Salt Lake Valley by then, and the traveling wasn't that bad anymore, I was burnt out from all the preseason/postseason wrestling practices and compe-titions. Most of my medals were silver and bronze unless Todd took the weekend off. Again, I was just done with all this wrestling. There were still aspects of wrestling that I liked, and that was hanging out with my teammates. Or, more specifically, my school teammates rather than club teammates that I didn't go to school with.

I knew I was pretty decent at wrestling, and it did give me some amount of identity. At my junior high and high school, I was the kid that was "good at wrestling." So I brokered a deal with Dad that I would continue to wrestle in high school, but I was done with the off-season stuff. And when I did anything off-season, like a camp or a clinic, it was entirely my idea now. I showed up every now and then while in high school to a freestyle meet. But that was usually to officiate rather than wrestle. I also remember after my sophomore high school season, I went down to a grocery store and got a job. I knew they would want me to work Saturdays, and that was more than okay with me. But this conscious decision to get away from preseason and postseason wrestling, except for that rare case, made a huge difference in my attitude with the sport. And that's probably why I am still involved with wrestling today.

Sometimes less is more!

I hope that Dakota keeps loving the sport and that Daniel keeps listening to his son on the matter.

CHAPTER SEVEN

DEDICATION

Dan Blanchard: I noticed for the first time tonight that the leaves here are beginning to change colors. It's a brisk Monday night on Columbus Day in early October in the northeast part of Connecticut or the quiet corner, where I live with my family.

Things have been a little rough here since my son, Dakota's, last preseason wrestling practice over at KT KIDZ. I had good intentions and planned on working with him over the weekend on that front-headlock series I've been telling him about. But, unfortunately, I got sick and spent most of the weekend in bed. On Sunday night, I was determined to show Dakota that front-headlock, even if I had to crawl out of bed to do it. However, now there was another obstacle. Since I usually do not sleep much regularly, my back couldn't handle laying most of 48 hours in bed, and now my back has gone out on me.

Now it's Sunday night, I'm still sick, a bit dizzy, and I can't move too well because of my back spasms. However, I'm determined to help my boy. I feel a bit like I'm in a wrestling match of my own while trying to get out of my bed and get down on the floor to show Dakota the front-headlock. My wife soon walks by and yells at both of us. And

I eventually end up back in bed trying to get well again. Hey, regardless of how it looks, though, I'm still calling the front-headlock instruction a victory for the boys.

To compound the complexity of things, my wonderful mother-in-law wants to take our whole family to do a Halloween outing on Monday night up in Rhode Island. Furthermore, my wife strongly encourages Dakota and me to do the family thing instead of going to wrestling on the upcoming Monday night. I left the decision up to Dakota, and he picked wrestling. Miraculously, my back pain and cold let up enough in time for me to get in the car and drive Dakota to wrestling practice on Monday night. Thankfully, I had that day off from teaching school.

On the way to practice, Dakota talked about the upcoming physical education test at his school next Thursday. His goal is to break the six-minute mile. Last year as an 8th grader, he did it at 6:08. We also talked about him doing the necessary work in his Math and Latin classes. And then he took a little nap for the rest of the ride. I guess school talk bored him.

Upon arriving at practice, I noticed the Columbus Day Holiday caused the number of wrestlers at practice to be a little less than usual. Unfortunately, Coach West couldn't make it either. Coach Knapp ran practice alone tonight. The calf injury he had last week seems to be better as he is no longer limping. Aging in this sport is tough…

Tonight Coach Knapp showed some pretty cool breakdowns from the top riding position. Fortunately, Dakota was able to utilize some of these moves almost immediately in the live wrestling part of the practice. My son, Dakota, looks like a new wrestler out there this week on the mat. Against his first few opponents, he kept his hips low and covered his opponent's hips well. He even managed to trap his opponent's arm, just like Coach Knapp showed earlier.

At one point when Dakota was on the bottom, and his opponent was riding him high, Dakota even bucked-up his hips, and his opponent fell off of him. Dakota was then able to gain a two-point reversal. I haven't even shown him that buck-up move yet. "How the heck did he know how to do that?" I wondered. Well, it certainly seems like he is gaining a better understanding of hip-riding and good hip position. Knowing those two things better certainly will help him a lot in wrestling.

Near the end of practice during Dakota's six-minute live wrestling match tonight, Dakota wrestled a tough kid. However, my son got the first takedown and then successfully rode his opponent for the whole first period. Pretty cool. He's getting better. At the end of the first period, Dakota is up 2-0.

The next two periods of this six-minute match didn't go as well for Dakota. His opponent got him into several cradles that exhausted him. His opponent also put him in a couple of can opener moves while leg-riding him. I was scared that this boy was going to injure my boy when he was making a wish with my son's legs. I could see the pain on my boy's face, but I stayed put and let my boy fight through it, which he did. I asked him about it later in the car, and he said there was no way he was going to let another kid injure him, or pin him.

Dakota looked wiped out at the end of practice. And surprisingly, he even asked me to feel his tongue, which, by the way, was as dry as sandpaper. He took a few swigs of water, a few minutes to rest, and then did extra push-ups, pull-ups, and then went back to do more push-ups again. Pretty impressive, I thought, as I silently watched while leaning against one of the wrestling room's padded walls.

Surprisingly, all the way home, one would have never known that Dakota just worked himself to near exhaustion in wrestling practice. He was excited and pumped up as we talked about wrestling. When we pulled into our driveway 45-minutes later, he asked me how we got home so quick. "It felt like we just left wrestling," he said

I'm pretty happy for him. And now if I can only find some time to work on those cradles and can openers before his next wrestling practice, so I don't have to watch him suffer through them again. I know the next day will be another marathon day for me, and I won't be home until late… but I'm going to try my best. And if I fail, well, at least I still have Coach Knapp and Coach West to teach Dakota what he needs to know next at KT KIDZ Wrestling. After all, making a young boy into a good young man is a team effort, right?

And speaking of that team effort, or a village raising a boy into a good man, my wife called me on my way home on Tuesday after a long day at work teaching followed by me taking and passing my real estate exam. Unfortunately, it's tough to raise a family on just a teacher's income, regardless of how good you are or how hard you work. However, that's a topic for another article on another day.

So, getting back to the village, and my wife. She is on the phone, and she is upset with Dakota. He's acting immature again by dragging his feet when she asks him to do something. And then he is trying to turn her request into a debate. She's mad, and she wants to take away wrestling from him on Wednesday night.

I want her to take away electronics instead. Now we don't always see eye-to-eye on everything, though. I tell her that Dakota likes electronics, but he doesn't need them. But, he does need wrestling because wrestling is hard. And hard things build character and help him mature. I promise to talk to him when I get home.

When I do finally get home, I go to Dakota's room and speak to him. I let him know how he is supposed to be maturing and doing his duty as a good son by listening to his parents without debating. After a little more talk, I work with him on the cradle and can opener move. Hopefully, he'll be better prepared come Wednesday night. And hopefully, he's maturing.

Wow! Wednesday night is here. And I didn't see this coming. But I should have. I rushed home Wednesday night from a long day at work and found Dakota sick. I guess he has what I had. Dakota won't be going to practice tonight. Nor will he break that six-minute mile in school on Thursday. He might have to wait until next year's school physical education test to break the six-minute mile. But hopefully, a dream deferred isn't a dream denied, right? And hopefully, I'll find some extra time around my side jobs this weekend, and if Dakota is well enough, we'll do some drilling. It will be nice for Dakota to have more exposure to some wrestling moves before he goes back for Coach John Knapp's next Monday night wrestling practice.

Wish us luck... nothing ever comes easy... especially when you're trying to build a good man!

Brian Preece: Daniel's story reminded me of quite a few things.

Dakota's desire to break six minutes in the mile also brought up memories of how bad I am at running and one memory in particular.

It was when I was wrestling at BYU. One of the assistant coaches was Olympian Mark Fuller. During preseason conditioning, we would do a lot of running I guess. And he wanted to take BYU to the "next level" and have us actually do three workouts a day. The one around lunch hour was optional, and I took the option not to do it.

It was a beautiful autumn afternoon with temperatures maybe in the high 60's when we took off on a long run. And I was really bad at running. I was recruited to wrestle 150/158, which I guess in Coach Fuller's eyes meant I should have been a bit more athletic. Our final destination was to end up at one of the grass fields after practice after running maybe three miles or so with lots of hills. When I came in second to the last place barely finishing ahead of our third-string heavyweight, Coach Fuller lit into me. I was doing the best I could, and he wasn't settling for it.

My Dad was the only coach I ever talked back to in my entire life until I snapped at Coach Fuller with, "I'm a wrestler, not a cross-country runner." I remember him getting a bit mad. I think I might have been the reason the team did some extra sprints on the field. We did 100-yard buddy carries and threshold carries where we had to run 100 yards while carrying our partner like one would carry our bride over the threshold.

Now, years later, Coach Fuller and I have developed a healthy respect for each other. And I have come to realize that he really just wanted to take our program to the next level and help me become a better wrestler. That's all. It was nothing personal.

I also remember my junior year in high school, after I didn't make the golf team, going out for cross-country thinking it would help me get ready for wrestling. I think my father was actually pleased. One workout later up a canyon, where we were running at 7,000 feet plus altitude, ended my foray into distance running.

I did eventually, however, ended up helping manage our football team by keeping stats. I think this ended up being a good thing because I became close with our football coach Ray Groth. He was our weight lifting coach, and he worked with me a lot on weight lifting. I probably couldn't even bench 100 pounds when I came into high school, but I remember benching 230 pounds by the time I was a senior. I made the "1000 Pound Club," which was recognition we got for bench pressing, squatting, and deadlifting more than 1000 pounds. I know I competed against a lot of wrestlers stronger than I was, but since I was on the taller side, my leverage with decent strength went a long way.

I was really good at riding and turning. I still own the school record for near-falls earned in a season. I think my length, and being left-handed helped. So as a coach, I always coached my wrestlers to ride both sides, and with brand new wrestlers, I always had them start the referee's position left-handed. I figured they didn't know the difference anyway.

I remember as a head coach only missing one practice when I went to a business conference with a young lady I was dating. A fight broke out between two of our wrestlers, so I guess after that I went to practice rain or shine. Or even when I had a 103 degree fever and strep throat (and when I got strep throat again a few days later). It's not that I didn't take sick days off teaching, but if I was coaching, I made it. I should say I missed one meet when my son was born. I think I can be excused for that.

I can certainly relate to Daniel's struggle to teach and coach when you're sick and so forth. I remember when I broke my neck (not sure exactly how) during the 1999-2000 season. I remember over Christmas break my neck started hurting and my back and then my left arm started tingling a lot and then sometimes it would go completely numb. The initial x-ray didn't show a break, so I did a lot of physical therapy. I went over during my preparation (or free) period so I could always make practice. I got through the season in a lot of pain, but our team finished in the top ten, and we had two grapplers that finished second in the state. Then a couple of months after the season, I remember walking through the gym, and I asked a basketball player for the ball to shoot a free throw. I thought it was strange when it traveled about 10 feet instead of 15 and was at least three feet to the left. I shot another one with a similar result. My therapy sessions were over, but I felt I needed to go in to see the doctor again. They did an MRI, and it showed a fracture. Under the knife, I went.

But teachers and coaches are a dedicated and crazy lot. I took a week off after my neck fusion surgery. But since I was the Assistant Athletic Director, I went to a softball game anyway just a few days after my surgery. I just figured this is what you do. I remember my Dad got an award for never taking a sick day in his 12 years of teaching at Uintah High School.

My own assistant coach (Darren Hirsche) took just one sick day in about 22 years of teaching. And that day was when I injured his shoulder, demonstrating a move, and he had to go to the doctor. He was mad as heck that he couldn't get an appointment after school, instead of during school hours. Well, now that I think about it. He did take a week off with flu-like symptoms in his last year of teaching. He came back a week later, worked for a couple of more weeks, and then was diagnosed with Huntington's disease and had to leave the profession. My best friend would pass away less than three years later.

I look back in awe at his dedication and that of my Dad. I truly respect Daniel for getting through things and his desire to help Dakota learn wrestling. But I think that's what wrestlers do. When we're on our backs, we do everything we can to get up off and get back on our feet. Just like in wrestling...

CHAPTER EIGHT

ATTITUDE OF GRATITUDE

Dan Blanchard: Wow! This week is off to another crazy start. Dakota and I snuck in a quick drilling session with some instruction that quickly wore me out late Sunday night. After about 15 minutes, my shirt was soaked, and I felt exhausted. I was a bit concerned because I shouldn't have been so tired. I guess I had a tough week. And to think that I still had a few more hours of work ahead of me tonight with my weekly columns that I have to finish writing and submit before I can go to sleep, or maybe even just pass out.

Monday night comes around quickly. And I find myself driving Dakota to KT KIDZ Wrestling in Rocky Hill, Connecticut, while chewing the last few bites of my dinner once again. The drive is a pleasant one as Dakota talks to me about fitness. I eventually jumped in with a stroll of my own down memory lane sharing the good old days when I was a kid who had a bike, but not video games. We were always riding bikes, and playing a game or two, or maybe even three, of pick-up ball with the kids in the neighborhood.

We never had adult supervision during these games or bike rides. The only rule was that we had to be home in time for dinner, or we might not get dinner. Dakota said he wishes it was still like that now.

And I wholeheartedly agreed with him. There was something special about those days…

Tonight's wrestling practice is a little bit different. My old buddy and wrestling comrade, Coach Johnny Knapp, isn't there. So Coach West is running the show. Also, since Marc Guberti, one of the world's top ten podcasters has just asked me to speak at his virtual summit this upcoming Thursday night. So, I am going to spend the first 30-minutes of wrestling practice doing some homework for the show I will be doing.

Homework or not, though, I keep looking up at Dakota and take brief breaks to watch Coach West demonstrate a great high-crotch (High-C), and a single leg series. I'm still a little concerned, though with how Dakota will do considering he was just recently in bed sick.

However, he walks by me and tells me that he feels good. So, here we are. Showtime! Live wrestling begins, and Dakota gets paired up with a very good, older kid who beat him up pretty good several weeks ago. The whistle blows, and Dakota gets the first takedown. Cool! His opponent escapes though, and takes Dakota down. He throws in both legs to leg ride. Dakota bucks up, grabs his opponent's head, and pulls it down under him to put the kid on his back for a near pin.

"Wow!" I just showed Dakota that move last night when I was huffing and puffing feeling old and out of shape. But, regardless, here he is tonight using it. Eventually, the other kid scrambles and gets away. But I don't care. I'm thinking, "Way to go, Dakota! That's progress!"

Dakota's opponent looks a little angry, and he becomes more physical. He takes Dakota down again and turns him to his back. Dakota surprises the heck out of his opponent and me by hitting an explosive high back bridge. This move causes his opponent to roll over and ends with Dakota landing on top of him and pinning him.

"Dang! That was amazing!" I'm silently screaming inside. Well... I must admit that someone there might have heard something coming out of me.

His opponent becomes even more physical and rough, but Dakota doesn't back down, and he gives it right back to him. I'm wondering, "Where the heck did all this toughness in Dakota, my little boy who ain't so little anymore, come from?"

What an improvement Dakota has made! The other boy might have outscored him, but it was a close match. And even more important... Dakota showed a lot of guts out there...

Leading into his second match, Dakota was exhausted from fighting so hard in his first one, but he still seemed to be in his tough physical mode from the last match. He immediately hits a vicious double leg lift takedown that forcefully drives his opponent into the mat and stuns him. This kid is another good wrestler. He eventually recovers and reverses Dakota.

For the next almost six minutes, the two boys brawl out there on the mat. At one point, Dakota's opponent slaps a very deep half-nelson on him and also manages to catch Dakota's wrist and yank it down his back. The boy is punishing my boy now. It looks like Dakota's arm is about to pop out of his socket. His head and neck are being violently twisted at the same time. Dakota is exhausted, I'm wincing, and I don't know how he is going to survive this one… but he somehow does…

Dakota shows tremendous guts and courage as he refuses to be put flat on his back, no matter how tired or how painful it is. I practically have a tear in my eye for my young boy, who is beating the odds. At this very moment when life is beyond difficult, he acted like a man by refusing to give in… I wish I could still wrestle like that… I miss those days… But, for me, it was easier to go through it when I was young than to watch my son go through it now while I'm older.

Eventually, the whistle blew, ending the match. I don't know how Dakota gets to his feet, but he does as Coach West yells out, "Find another partner!" By process of default, because Dakota took too long to move, he ends up staggering over to a much bigger, very athletic, and very experienced boy.

"Oh, no. Not him" is all I can think.

The older boy was one of the better ones in a room of a bunch of good wrestlers that I've seen so far. He tooled on my exhausted and dazed boy. And even though the other boy was putting on his own wrestling clinic out there, he was decent to Dakota and didn't pound him or punish him. I was grateful to the young, fine man for conducting himself in such a manner. He was a real stand-up guy. And a great wrestler.

Coach West finally blew the whistle and yelled, "Do 90 push-ups and practice is over." Dakota looked over at me and showed me his tongue again like he had done last week. And like last week it looked like sandpaper again. My poor boy. "Okay, only 90 push-ups, and he's done. And he can then rest and get some water," I said to myself.

Dakota ended up being one of the last boys to leave the wrestling room that night. He slowly and arduously powered through 115 push-ups and then did 10 pull-ups on top of that.

I don't know how he did it. Pure determination I guess. I was so proud of him. And so was Coach West as he mentioned on our way out the door that if Dakota keeps it up, he might have a chance of making his varsity wrestling team this winter as just a freshman. That was pretty cool because I know that is one of Dakota's goals. He wants to wrestle varsity as a freshman, just like his dad did.

On our way home, even though Dakota had reclined the front passenger seat again so much that it looked like a recliner, he looked like he was recovering nicely. We had a great conversation about how important the old Greek values of mind and body are. And everything seemed to be going well when he dropped a bomb on me that he had injured himself.

"What?" I thought. "When?"

Right before live wrestling, he had grabbed his water bottle and sat down at the very end of the bench. The bench fell over, and he landed right on his tailbone on the hard cement floor. And now it was painful for him even just to sit in my car. My heart jumped up into my throat because I've had a tailbone injury before, and it caused me excruciating pain for about a week. And it made it very hard for me to move around well and fight back in practice.

Let's hope Dakota is a quick healer. And if he does heal quickly, let's hope I have time to work with him before his next practice. I have to teach him how to defend and break out of that 2 on 1 arm hold his opponent had on him a few times tonight that he didn't quite know what to do about… And that switch, too. He got burned a few times tonight on that move.

The next night, which is Tuesday night, I get home a little late from work and immediately ask my wife how Dakota is doing with his tailbone. She thinks he's okay. He hasn't said anything all day about it. After a quick dinner, I go upstairs to my boy's room to work with him on how to defend the 2-on-1 arm tie and the switch. He tells me he is fine, but I only want to work with him for a few minutes this time, just in case he isn't okay. He mentions to me near the end of our short session that his knees hurt. I look confused, but then regain my senses and look down at my own knees. I notice that we both had a little case of rug burn on our knees from this short session of mat, or maybe I should say rug wrestling instruction.

Before we know it, it's the next day and Dakota and I are back in the car driving to wrestling. I'm really starting to appreciate the 45-minute of father-son time rides. It's bringing me closer to being the kind of father I want to be in developing my boy into a real man.

After some small talk, we landed on the subject of girls. I explain to Dakota that real men always respect women. And that some immature boys may think it's funny or cool, or even manly to disrespect women. But it's not. They're just showing their lack of maturity and that they're really not real men yet.

Later in the car ride, Dakota asked me what he should be doing on the bottom position because he's having some difficulty there. I don't mean to simplify it too much here, but I basically say, "Just stand up. Use your athletic abilities, and just stand up. And if you can't, then get wrist control, strong base, and then stand up. Learn to do that first, and then you'll have a chance on the bottom. Then you can slowly learn the other bottom stuff."

Tonight's practice was a little different again. I wasn't studying, but this time I had to be on a conference call for one of my side jobs with the American Federation of Teachers. From a distance, I watched Coach Knapp, and Coach West show the wrestlers a pretty cool hammerlock and arm-bar series that they practiced over most of the next hour.

My conference call ended just in time for me to be back mat-side for the live mat wrestling to yell to Dakota to either look away or to stand up. To his credit, he tried his best to do both.

At the end of mat wrestling, I saw that Dakota had that sandpaper tongue again while heading into his six-minute match against another really good kid. I'm going to have to remember to tell Dakota to drink more water during the daytime when he has wrestling that same night.

Dakota's opponent was good. He nailed Dakota with a couple of ankle picks. At one point, Dakota catches him in a front headlock, but the boy just drags out of it and takes him down anyway. I'm also going to have to remember to show Dakota a better front headlock. One that doesn't allow his opponent to so easily drag out of it, which I do in the car on the ride home.

We only did one six-minute match tonight, but combined with everything else, the boys were all exhausted. Coach West yelled for all of them to go home after a few minutes of intermittent jogging and sprinting up and down the wrestling mat.

Dakota walked off the mat with all the other boys to get some much-needed water. Then he headed back out onto the mat to pop out

70 pushups. Dakota was the only person on that great big wrestling mat area at that time. I was proud of him for being able to stand all alone to work hard at something he apparently now believes in. After the pushups, he headed over to the pullup room and popped out a bunch of those, too. I didn't say a word. Just watched in admiration...

We were once again the last ones to leave. Coach West yelled over to Dakota asking him how school was going. I smiled because the village raising the child was busy at work again. On the way out that night, Dakota looked Coach West in the eye, shook his hand, and said, "Thanks, Coach."

Dakota wouldn't have even thought to do this sort of thing a few months ago. Also, the 45-minute car ride each way is a pleasure now. It is something I am really looking forward to doing tonight. It's a blessing in disguise where I'm seeing with my own eyes, and hearing with my own ears the transformation of my boy slowly developing into a good man... One that can even now at 14- years old look you in the eye, shake your hand, and say, "Thanks."

Brian Preece: Daniel's story brings back memories of my coaching days. Sometimes it isn't the victories or championships won that is most important but the lessons of the practice room. And sometimes, what means more to you as a coach is when an athlete tells you, "Thanks." Maybe it was just 'thanks' for showing them a technique. Perhaps it was taking the time to talk with them about wrestling or life. Or maybe it was after they won a big wrestling match. I really was impressed with Dakota telling his coach, "Thanks."

I always tried to show gratitude as a coach to my athletes and I thanked them every day for their time and efforts. I genuinely respect anyone that comes into that wrestling room and sticks with it, whether they take state or hardly win a match. Again, I see wrestling as the most demanding sport. Not only does it have physically challenging practices and competitions, but the one-on-one aspect of it is truly mentally and emotionally demanding. Again, in a dual meet, everyone there knows who won and who took second place. You can't hide among a sea of competitors or among other members of your own team.

And let's face it, the wrestling practice is grueling. A typical workout involves some long-distance endurance running. Hard drilling. And conditioning, which usually for me, meant short bursts of rigorous activity. And then, of course, combat (or wrestling). In my technique sessions, I often incorporated quick sprint work, or what I called shorties for short walls. If we were doing longer running, we would run the length of the wrestling room. But a "shortie" as I called it was after the technique session, I would yell "10 shorties". And that meant the wrestlers would sprint all-out the width of the wrestling room, which basically was the width of the wrestling mat. And I expected a full-effort sprint. The idea with shorties was not to let the wrestlers get too cold during the technique sessions. However, in addition, it also built up stamina. And I believe it helped wrestlers regain their attention span for further instruction. After shorties, we usually had a one to two minute water break. Yes, I was a "new school" coach that let my wrestlers drink water in practice, about every 15-20 minutes. I believe hydrated wrestlers work harder and learn better. But early on in my coaching career, I had to learn to go from old school to new school. My father was definitely an old school coach. I learned that part of this new school coaching was actually showing appreciation to my wrestlers every day for their work.

I do think my attitude of gratitude worked. There wasn't a practice where a wrestler or two didn't thank me. And like any human being, I liked feeling appreciated. The same goes for the classroom. It feels nice when a student thanks you for teaching them something, or for a lesson well crafted.

But of course, the most meaningful appreciation usually comes years after. When maybe you bump into a former wrestler at the grocery store, or when they introduce you to their own children at a wrestling tournament. At my retirement open house, I had an opportunity to thank my wrestlers, and parents of my wrestlers. They, of course, reciprocated their appreciation for my efforts. But perhaps the most important thank you I got was from a former athlete after my best friend, and longtime assistant coach, passed away.

The former wrestler in question wasn't even really a wrestler. He dabbled shortly but then decided to become our team manager. And he was one of the best managers we ever had. He also was a manager in our baseball and football programs. Now he teaches high school Spanish in the Midwest. I will always cherish his letter because he reached out to me at a painful time in my life. It was like he knew exactly what I needed to hear. And his expression of appreciation for his coaches made me feel pretty good quite frankly. So when Dakota tells his coach thanks at the end of a tough workout, trust me as a coach, this makes us feel good inside like we are making a difference. Coaches, like athletes, need affirmation too.

CHAPTER NINE

BALANCE IN ALL THINGS

Dan Blanchard: My wife and I are a little frustrated right now. When I feel like this, I try to remind myself that Dakota is still only 14 years old. And... It took me 48 long years to become the man that I have become today. It was not a perfect journey. And I am still not perfect.

You see, progress is like a twister circling around and around. We're trying to move forward in developing my son into a good man through doing something very difficult. And that difficult thing is wrestling and shooting for a state championship. However, his progress is going to be circular like a twister. Sometimes the winds of change will blow him forward into new successes, and other times it will circle him right back to where he was before. But, as long as we keep Dakota moving in the right direction, things should be okay. However... On the flip side, there will be moments of frustration when he seems to be stepping backward.

Last Wednesday night, I was so proud of Dakota for looking his wrestling coach in the eye, shaking his hand, and saying, "Thank you" like a real man at the end of his practice. And then this weekend he play-punches his sister in the gut harder than he should have done. I snapped at him not to do that again. His mother jumped in, too. My wife, Dakota's Mom, complained that she has already told him not to do that.

Dakota looks at us, confused, and says he was just playing. He doesn't seem to know why we're giving him a hard time. I tell him that he is never to hit a girl or anyone in his family, playing or not. He's frustrated and voicing his own opinion as he goes to his room to get away from us.

The back-talk or arguing that he didn't do anything wrong is what really gets under our skin. Back in the day, our parents would have rained all hell down upon us if we back-talked or argued with them. I would have never voiced my opinion when I knew that my parents thought I was wrong.

I was afraid of my Dad when I was a boy. However, in contrast, though, I must admit that I am happy that my boy isn't afraid of me. I don't think people should live in fear of their family members. However, there is still a struggle there between kids and parents, and our past parenting practices and present. Check out the poem I wrote that was published on this push-pull dynamic between my son and me, and almost all fathers and sons: http://granddaddyssecrets.com/the-cyclical-father-son-storm/.

Welcome back. Hey, it's a terrible thing to live in fear. And that's why I go the extra mile to make sure that my kids know I love them, will play with them, show patience with them, and will joke around with them while still offering the parental guidance that they need.

So, over the weekend, even though Dakota and I didn't see eye to eye, I still spent some time with him working on his wrestling. However, he did have to wait until after my younger daughters' soccer games, my oldest daughter's driving practice, and a few hours on one of my side jobs.

It was a busy weekend. But Dakota and I did manage to sneak in a little time together. We worked on some foot sweeps, a defense to the cradle, and a quick cheap tilt that is usually good for a quick two points. This tilt usually leaves one's opponent flat on his stomach where one is weak and can be better controlled, and attacked further. Also, I show Dakota a limp arm out for when his opponent has a whizzer/overhook on him.

Our Monday night 45-minute car ride is starting to become kind of typical now. We talked about life, being a real man, and school, of course. Dakota's grades are pretty good, but I did receive an email this morning that his algebra grade dropped to a C-. Dakota says he knows where he messed up, and he will fix it. I'm good with that answer for now...

At practice, Coach John Knapp and Coach West show some pretty cool defensive moves to the switch, as well as some great go-behinds off of short hooks, and then a front headlock. This former 2X State Champion, 2X Junior Olympian, and 2X Junior Olympic wrestling coach, loves watching and learning the finer details or nuances and subtleties of Coach Knapp's techniques. After Coach Knapp explains them, they seem so simple to do while also making a move so much more effective.

My attention to practice is snatched away when I find my phone ringing. It's Scott Schulte. Scott lives almost all the way across the country in Utah and is a New York Times Bestselling Author of a Dan Gable book. Scott tells me that he has been following my blog. He has been studying the pictures I have put up there of my son Dakota. And he believes that I should work cradles and leg-riding with Dakota due the way he is built.

I say goodbye to Scott Schulte as live wrestling begins. And believe it or not, Dakota gets the first takedown again and then puts his opponent into a cradle. During this match, Dakota gets a few more takedowns and captures his opponent in a few more cradles. He pins his opponent several times in the cradle. I can't help but wonder how the heck Scott Schulte knew that he'd probably be pretty good at cradles. In the end, Dakota does very well in his first six-minute match. He even uses the move I showed him the night before of the limp arm out to get out of a whizzer/overhook, and secure a takedown. And he even finally hits a zook that worked! And worked well, indeed!

For his second match, Dakota faces a tougher opponent. However, he once again gets the first takedown. But eventually gets reversed. His competitor then sinks a painfully deep half-nelson, but Dakota somehow fights it off. Next, the kid throws in legs on Dakota. Man! I have to teach Dakota some leg wrestling. I guess Scott Schulte was right there, too. Finally, the other wrestler catches Dakota in a cradle. Ah… I've got to find some time to work with him on both the offensive and defensive moves around cradles.

For the third match, my 130-pound boy approaches a 160- pound boy. I'm a little nervous here because I know that sometimes injuries happen during moments like this one. I'm a bit relieved, though, when the boy says he's too heavy for Dakota and begins to walk away. However, Dakota insists, and they end up wrestling anyway.

I watch anxiously and witness Dakota once again getting the first takedown and then actually pins the kid. Back on their feet, the bigger boy gets Dakota in a bear hug and muscles Dakota down on to his back. But Dakota refuses to be pinned and fights off his back. Dakota even reverses the boy and pins him instead.

Dakota finishes up practice with 110 push-ups and 40 pull-ups. We shake Coach Knapp's hand and say goodbye as he asks me if I can get Dakota down to practice in November more than just two nights a week. I think this sounds awesome, but I don't know how I'd do it with my hectic schedule. And to his credit, Coach Knapp knew this and was thinking out loud of possible ways for Dakota to get to practice on the nights I have other commitments. I'm grateful to have such a good old buddy, and now a great coach for my son.

On the way home, both Dakota and I spoke excitedly about this night's practice and how much Dakota has improved in such a short time. Coming from a tough background myself, I tell Dakota that I must admit that I thought his life was way too easy for him to have this kind of mental toughness in him at such a young age. But somehow he has that mental toughness, and he has a lot of it.

I also mention Coach Knapp's offer to train him more nights a week. But Dakota surprises me a bit when he says that he is taking some pretty tough classes in school, and Dakota doesn't know how he'll be able to keep up with his schoolwork if we get home after 10:00 at night more than twice a week. I'm a bit caught off guard by Dakota's statement and ability to compartmentalize his life at such a young age. I'm really impressed with his ability to quickly assess the new situation. All the while, not forgetting about how important school is. I think I sense that the good man inside of him is growing again.

Well, time flies, as it will, and we're once again back in the car on another Wednesday night heading to KT KIDZ in Rocky Hill to meet up with Coach Knapp and Coach West. In the car ride over, Dakota mentions how he doesn't like the fact that they only get gym class twice a week in high school. I wholeheartedly agree with him and feel that kids should have gym class five days a week. I feel strongly about the old Greek values of mind and body. And studies in Texas have proven that when kids exercise, they learn better.

While at practice, I have to participate in another phone conference for one of my side jobs. I watch from a distance as Coach West is teaching some defensive moves to a single leg where he wraps the guy up like a pretzel in a move called a spladle. Next, Coach West shows some offensive moves off of the single leg. And then he finishes up the instruction part of the evening with a fireman's series.

Live wrestling starts, and the wrestlers are put into groups of three. Dakota gets the first takedown against both the first guy and then the second guy. However, the second guy is pretty good. And he recovers, gets back to his feet, and hits Dakota with a nice fireman's carry that puts Dakota on his back. Dakota successfully fights his way off of his back, though.

At this time, I learned something very interesting from one of the assistant volunteer coaches named Coach Joe. He informs me that the numbers of wrestlers have gone down across the World. And that the rise of the female wrestlers is what saved wrestling from being eliminated from the Olympics. As a history teacher, I can't help but make the comparison or how our U.S. women played a vital role in WWII and might have saved us in that fight, too.

I'm grateful for what our women did way back then in WWII. However, I didn't know about the whole female Olympic wrestling thing. But thanks to Coach Joe, now I do. And I'm extremely thankful again for the role our women played, and their ability to fight that good fight that saved our Olympic Wrestling. Now we need even more females to wrestle in the oldest and greatest sport mankind, and womankind has ever known.

Practice ends quickly. There wasn't a lot of live wrestling tonight. Dakota and I stay a little extra to work a bit on some cradles and leg wrestling. I feel bad I didn't get to this sooner. But, regardless, it was kind of neat for me to have that individual time with Dakota on an actual wrestling mat instead of on the carpet floor in my upstairs bedroom.

The ride home was awesome! After Dakota and I stopped for gas again like we do every Monday and Wednesday night, we talked all the way home about wrestling. Come to think of it, even when I was standing outside the car pumping gas, I opened Dakota's door and talked to him more about wrestling. I shared some strategy on how to drop his hip level and split his opponent's legs when he knocks his guy to his butt. I can't help but sometimes feel excited. Sometimes I feel like I'm a kid in a candy store when Dakota and I are driving home talking about wrestling. We go back and forth the entire way home. We even continue to speak about wrestling as we're walking back into our home…

We're now another week closer to Dakota's first high school wrestling season. I'm impressed with how far Dakota has come. And I feel grateful that on Day 1 of his regular high school wrestling season he is going to have a real fighting chance of defending himself. Now he is going to be able to take his abilities to the next level. His great attitude, myself finding a way to get him to his preseason wrestling practices, and the amazing and very effective coaching he is getting from Coach Knapp and Coach West has really helped him develop.

It really does take a village and a team to raise a child. And for many, many years, I have been part of that village helping other peoples' kids. And now I'm really enjoying and truly appreciate watching a village at work with my son, Dakota. Way to go World! Way to go Team! Way to go KT KIDZ Wrestling! And way to go Village!

Brian Preece: Dan's writing has me really buzzing on many fronts.

It was cool when Daniel mentioned his friend Scott Schulte. It's through Scott that I was introduced to Daniel and his incredible blogs (and this project we are working on together). However, I first became acquainted with Scott as a coach. He was an assistant coach at one of the most successful large-school wrestling programs in Utah. And Scott and I also have another thing in common as we were also sportswriters for newspapers of about the same size in circulation. However, my main vocation was teaching, where Scott's was journalism. I was a typical teacher-coach (who wrote for the newspaper as a side job) where he coached as a side job to his main gig of being a sportswriter. I never knew of Scott's true writing excellence until I read his book on Dan Gable. Scott recently moved closer to where we live, and we communicate almost daily.

Also, as I read Daniel's story and how he spoke of Dakota's ability to compartmentalize his life. I applaud Dakota for recognizing that academics are important and recognizing limits and maintaining balance in life. And sometimes we, as adults, need to realize that young people these days have a lot on their plates. School to them is like our full-time jobs are to us, and like many of our jobs, school requires more work outside of normal hours. I think Dakota is telling his Dad, and his coach, that I enjoy wrestling, but I also need to take care of what is most important for me right now, and that's school.

Speaking of academics. It is something that we truly valued in our program, not just something we gave lip service. We have banners in our wrestling program to recognize our state placers. And we also have a banner recognizing our Academic All-State wrestlers. I named my best friend, "Assistant Head Coach," and he was also our Academic Coach. He had a Juris Doctorate. But instead of going into law, he chose to go into teaching and coaching. And we both saw the importance of academics in athletics. We had two grade checks within the grading term. We weren't afraid to hold out wrestlers that weren't performing in the classroom or were missing class.

I know it cost us a lot of points in tournaments and maybe some dual meets here or there. But we hoped that we got the message across, the books come first. We would also hold study halls before practices or when we had meets. We fit in a study hall before weigh-in. And about every day, in our post-practice comments, we talked about being good students and good citizens. We also welcomed open communication between our coaching staff and the teachers. We not only wanted to know how our athletes were doing in the classroom, but we wanted our colleagues to know we would take action if there were shortcomings. And at our team banquet, we took significant time to honor our academic wrestlers. We had a Scholastic Wrestler of the Year Award, too.

One season, one of our best wrestlers wasn't doing his best according to his parents. His Mom wanted him to have A or A- grades in all of his classes. When Mom said he wasn't going to wrestle until his grades improved, we supported her decision. I remember telling him after he missed placing in state by a match his junior year, which maybe missing a lot of meets and practices for academics might have made a difference in him getting on the podium. I didn't say this to be cruel, but my point was that he knew his Mom's expectations. And that for his senior year, I didn't want him to miss any more practices or meets. But I would always support his Mom.

Now, my father would think I was crazy. And in a similar situation, he actually told a parent, "No way is your son missing the meet. Eleven other guys are depending on him. Find another way to punish him versus punishing our team". And I see the argument.

But this young man I was coaching learned from this experience, he kept his grades up to his Mom's standards. He didn't miss a meet or practice his senior year and placed second in state. Instead of missing most of our overnight trips and tournaments, he was now able to take part. One of them, he was unseeded and then beat a returning state champion from a different classification in the first round of the tournament on his way to a gold medal. This boy was also our school's first-ever wrestler to compete in the NHSCA Senior Nationals held in Pittsburgh (now Virginia Beach).

On girls wrestling. It is becoming big in Utah, and in 2020-21, our state high school athletic association will officially sanction it. How it will exactly work is still in the works. We have six classifications in athletics in Utah (I know, way too many). But we don't have enough girls yet to make six classifications viable for them.

I am a pioneer of sorts in girls wrestling. It all first started in 1984 when I was freestyle official my senior year in high school. There was a girl from the hometown I grew up that was wrestling. She was beating a lot of the boys. It was causing quite the stir and Dads were putting pressure on the officials and the tournament directors about allowing her to wrestle.

At the state freestyle meet, she had reached the championship match. And by that time, the outrage had reached such a point no one would officiate her match. My Dad looked at me and said, "Son, you are going to officiate her match," that really ticked off a lot of people. I had never felt so much pressure in athletics, even as a competitor, in officiating that match.

But when my father said this match was going to happen, and him at that time being the winningest coach in Utah history, people backed off and let the match happen. She actually got beat by a point, but her Dad thanked my Dad and me for having the courage to stand up to everyone else.

She would have become a good high school wrestler, but the forces were so against her at that time, she decided not to wrestle in junior high and high school. I don't blame her because she, and her family, went through a lot of garbage they shouldn't have had to. However, many years later, her daughter would place in state as a wrestler.

Later, when I was an assistant coach at West High School in Salt Lake, we had the first girl that actually wrestled in high school in our state. It was incredibly hard on her at times. And we as coaches didn't navigate things perfectly. Her harshest critics were her own "teammates" for the most part. The whole thing became a media circus as well. And some of our best wrestlers didn't care for it. Our team, her senior year, finished second in state. We had two state champions, one of which ended up wrestling in the Dapper Dan, and winning it. I think over time, she did win the support of most of her teammates. She never won a match but came to practice every day. It was nice that in her second year, another girl came out for the team. We felt uneasy, as coaches, forcing anyone to work out with her, and many refused and were supported vehemently by their parents. So it was nice she had a workout partner.

When I relocated to Provo High School to become a head coach, I coached the first three female wrestlers in our county and the third and fourth girl, high school wrestlers, in our state's history. This was just over 20 years ago. One of our girls was the first-ever wrestler to compete in a varsity region meet. But at that point, many boys refused to wrestle her. And that actually helped us win the J.V. region tournament one year by a single point when she made the semifinals because of a forfeit. Her opponent would have easily defeated her. And lucky for us, he was from the school that was our main competition. But so it goes, and we took home the trophy with no regrets!

But things have really changed in Utah. Just over 10 years ago, we had a girl place second in state. Candace Workman was from the school where my Dad won all his state titles. She nearly made the Olympic Team. She has coached women at the Olympic Training Center. And coached our Utah's Girl's National Team.

Following in her footsteps are two other girls Hailey Cox and Sage Mortimer. They have made world teams and have had huge successes nationally, and even internationally. Mortimer placed at state her freshman year and became the third girl wrestler ever to place in our high school state tournament. But even more impressive, she became the first female wrestler ever to place competing against all boys at the USA Cadet Nationals in Fargo, North Dakota.

So girls wrestling has caught on, and in the unofficial state meet in 2020, 141 girls competed. Wow, how things have changed. I'm also so glad I was an early proponent of the concept as both a coach and through my sports journalism efforts. And I think female wrestling did save Olympic wrestling and will be crucial in maintaining, and perhaps even adding more college programs.

CHAPTER TEN

PLAY-WRESTLING TIME

Dan Blanchard: We're coming up on Halloween, and I don't know where the time has gone. It's dark and cold in the mornings now when I leave for work. And it's dark and cold at night when I get home.

My son Dakota has improved in wrestling during this preseason beyond my expectations. And another jam-packed weekend consisting of early mornings and late nights just ended. Unfortunately, I didn't really get a chance to work with my son, Dakota, on his wrestling moves.

However, at least once a day, as we passed each other, Dakota gave me a hug that usually resulted in him bear hugging me, followed by a little play wrestling for a few seconds. I hit him with a nice lift during one of these moments. And then I showed him how to do it.

Also, I have noticed recently that some of my wrestling moves don't work so easily anymore on Dakota. But, I guess this is good because it means he's getting better, and not that I'm necessarily getting worse. In addition, it also means that I now get a chance to show my son Dakota sequential or chain-wrestling.

For example, Sunday night Dakota underhooked me while we were passing each other in the kitchen. I hipped in to load him up on my hip for a simulated throw. However, he backed out, not allowing me to load him up. But then I came right back with an opposite direction underarm spin where I did load him up for a throw. But, I then stopped halfway through the move with his feet just off the ground to explain to him how I did it. And because he is athletic, he might actually be able to surprise a few people by hitting this second-move underarm spin on them. My wife gets some credit here too, though for not yelling at us this time to not break anything in the kitchen.

In addition, there is another benefit here, as well. Going through this sequence with Dakota made me feel a little athletic again. It even made me feel wise, well, at least in the ways of the wrestling world anyway. And to top it off, I must admit, I felt valuable again in the wrestling world because I'm still able to hit and then teach this more advanced move, and of course others like it. Furthermore, I think I felt this way because I still have some experience and knowledge that my son Dakota doesn't have yet. Even though he is being taught by one of the best out there, Coach John Knapp of KT KIDZ Wrestling in Rocky Hill, CT. His old man can still teach him a thing or two, hopefully, for a long time to come...

Well, once again, Monday night arrives quickly. I get home as fast as I can from work only to find Dakota in bed sick, however. And Wednesday night, there won't be any wrestling practice because of Halloween. So, I guess Dakota will not have any wrestling practices this week. I'm slightly disappointed because he is sick, and he won't be able to prepare himself this week for the upcoming season.

However, I've also been around long enough to know that this is all part of life. It's just how things go sometimes. Furthermore, I was up late last night with my daughter, Dakota's sister, because she had a 104-degree temperature. So, I guess it only makes sense that Dakota would be sick, too, eventually.

Although, something good does come out of this, though... As soon as I leave Dakota's bedroom, I bump into my two youngest daughters waiting for me in the hallway wearing their soccer practice uniforms. And you can probably guess what happened next. Yup! You got it! They asked me to go with them and their mom to soccer practice since I wasn't bringing Dakota to wrestling. I guess there really is a silver lining in every cloud, huh?

Watching my two youngest daughters was fun. It was a little cold sitting outside under the lights, though. At least wrestling is inside where it's usually warm. But, regardless, watching my daughters play soccer was worth it. And when I finally got back home, Dakota was awake and in the kitchen. He asked me if I'd drill wrestling moves with him. But, I declined. And then I told him to go back to bed, and we'll see how he feels tomorrow night.

He gave me a very disappointed look that broke my heart a little. But, I'm not in this fathering business to take the easy way out. Instead, I'm doing what's right. And I'm doing what's right even when I don't feel like doing it. And it's especially important to do what's right when it's hard to do because that's usually when it's most important to do what's right. And the right thing here was for Dakota to go back to be and get well, regardless of how his young machismo and love for the sport of wrestling was protesting.

Over the next few days, Dakota and I play-wrestle a few more times. He grabs me in the kitchen again and attempts to load me up on his hip. I hop over and load him up on my hip instead. However, when I was jumping over, my heel accidentally banged the pantry door. So, as I'm loading Dakota up on my hip telling him how I got him this time, my wife is yelling at me not to break anything in the kitchen. A few more similar play wrestling situations occur over the next couple of days. And we're back to having some fun as only two wrestlers can, even if one of them is a bit old and a bit broken.

Dakota looks like he is feeling better. We're both anxiously waiting for Monday night's practice. Time is ticking. We only have a few more practices before Thanksgiving. And everyone knows what happens on the Monday after Thanksgiving here in New England. Wrestling season starts!

What? Wait! Hold the presses! I said, "Hold the presses!" Wow! There really is a silver lining in every cloud, isn't there? We just had an unexpected development over here. My gym suddenly closed, and it forced me to go to a gym in the next town over in Willimantic. Once there, they told me I could bring a free guest with me as long as the guest was at least 14- years old.

Dakota is 14 years old. So, this weekend I found some time to bring Dakota to the gym. I have wondered for 20 years what the first day of my son and I in the gym together would look like. Now I know. Maybe we didn't have any wrestling this week. But we did get in our first father-son weight lifting workout. Now we're even more ready for Monday night's wrestling practice! And even more prepared to continue our journey together of building a good man.

Brian Preece: Play-wrestling. Yes, I did it a few times with my father, but we never had an all-out wrestling match. I did it with my younger brother, but we also didn't have a real wrestling match either. In both cases, a weight difference, and age difference, was the major issue. And again, the fact that though my father was a great wrestling coach but never really a wrestler. I guess we could play-wrestle a bit rough, enough to move the furniture in the living room for some space. My Mom, much like Daniel's wife and Dakota's mother, wasn't much into us breaking furniture and putting holes in the wall. And much like what Daniel did with Dakota, when I did play-wrestle with my father, it was to show me a move or a position.

In Utah, we start our wrestling season a bit before they do in Connecticut. We actually begin official practice the first Monday in November, and we can compete competitively the Tuesday before Thanksgiving. Many coaches don't want to compete until after the Thanksgiving holiday. But I preferred to get on the mat as soon as we could. We competed every Tuesday. Later it changed to Wednesday right before Thanksgiving at the Turkey Dart Invitational hosted by Davis High School. Their mascot was the Dart.

At any rate, the end of October does bring a sense of excitement to us wrestling coaches and for wrestlers. I also coached football, but our school rarely made a deep playoff run. Although, in my fifth year as head coach, we made the semifinals, which meant the start of wrestling, and our football season would overlap a week. Since my main assistant coach and I were varsity football coaches, we had to leave the wrestling team in the hands of our two other assistant wrestling coaches that year. November is a fun and exciting time. But it is also very demanding because it's the first part of the wrestling season.

There is a lot of paperwork, equipment inventory, etc. for the head coach to get done. During that year, our football team made it to the playoffs since I coached special teams, I usually could get out early and make it over for the last half of wrestling practice. I always wonder how I made it through that time because my wife and I had our first child that September. I guess you have more energy at 34 than at 54, right?

CHAPTER ELEVEN

A SYSTEM FOR SUCCESS

Dan Blanchard: Monday's 45-minute car ride to KT-KIDZ Wrestling was good. During it, I spent some time sharing some of my high school underclassmen war stories on the varsity wrestling mat with Dakota. I'm trying to work on Dakota's self-confidence and mental toughness. I know he'll have a much better chance of doing well when these two components are intact. He's going to especially need them against the older and more experienced kids who I know he'll be wrestling, just like I had to when I was his age.

Driving up Route 99, the Silas Dean Highway, in Rocky Hill, I asked Dakota if he and his guy buddies play that ranking on each other game that so many young men do. He seemed like he didn't know what I was talking about. Good, I thought. I was kind of happy to see a confused look on his face this time.

I explained how wrestling, football, and the Army taught me a real brotherhood. I never felt like I needed to rank on or bust on my fellow guy friends to make myself feel better. I never felt like I had to establish some kind of silly pecking order among the guys. Unfortunately, though, too many men know sarcasm and putting each other down.

And they all lie to themselves saying it's all done in the name of fun. They say they're just playing.

I explained to Dakota that someday he will most likely encounter these putting down behaviors among his guy buddies. And how regrettable it is that many of us men don't truly understand what real brotherhood is. Unfortunately, too often, we men don't know how to accept and enjoy each other's company without the over-zealous competition and cut downs. Sadly, men do this to each other. Life is hard enough without that kind of garbage in it, I explain.

Busting on my friends is something I never did. And I hope my son, Dakota, never does it either. Hopefully, with the confidence wrestling is building in him, he'll never feel the need to build himself up by putting another down. He'll know in his heart who he is and what he can do if push comes to shove... Like President Roosevelt, he'll speak softly but carry a big stick. Hopefully, he'll speak softly and kindly, and will always have skills big enough to protect himself and his loved ones.

Pulling into the parking lot at wrestling, I mention to Dakota that it feels like we haven't been here in a while. And I can't believe this pre-season wrestling is almost over. As I stop the car in our parking spot, I notice my gas gauge is on empty again. And my stomach is rumbling again because I didn't have enough time to eat enough before we left. Regardless, I ask Dakota if there are any big lessons he has learned so far. A smile creeps across my face when he replies, "Sustained effort over time beats talent." And, "You have to work hard all the time." It's all been worth it, I'm thinking as we head into practice together. I'll get some more gas and food later...

Wow! Where did all these kids come from? My buddy Johnny's wrestling room is full of wrestlers from corner to corner. It looks like his travel team has joined us tonight.

Cool! Dakota should have some great kids to wrestle tonight. My old buddy, Coach Knapp, started practice with a warmup and then a long period of drilling before we went into instruction and then live wrestling.

While the boys were drilling, John's younger brother, Jude Knapp, magically appeared somehow, as if out of thin air. I couldn't believe my eyes. I feel like I haven't seen him since he was still a young boy or at least a young man in college. Now, Jude is taller, thicker, and has a few whiskers. And some of that facial hair might even be grey.

I find out he has been a schoolteacher for 21 years already. And he has been coaching wrestling for almost just as long. It felt awesome to catch up with one of my old wrestling teammates. During my senior year in high school, Johnny was a junior, and Jude was a sophomore. We really do let too much time go by sometimes…

Finally, Johnny called in all the wrestlers to show them a sweet cross-face cradle series that I thought would be good for Dakota because he has long arms… unlike me. And of course, Coach Knapp showed some strategies to make this move more painful, so one's opponent will want to put his knee to his face, be cradled, and then pinned, so the pain will stop.

Live wrestling started next. The wrestlers had to take turns wrestling in two waves because there were just too many of them for the mat space. Dakota was in the second wave with the bigger kids. When he finally got his turn, he wrestled two-minute periods against three different kids. The first kid Dakota wrestled, I hadn't seen before. This stranger got the first takedown on Dakota. I wondered if Dakota was a bit rusty or if this kid was really good. Dakota eventually got back to his feet and got the next takedown. Then time expired.

The next kid Dakota wrestled against, Dakota gets the first takedown and puts him right to his back. I'm wondering if the rust is gone, but then his opponent escapes and gets the second takedown. At this point, I'm still not sure about the rust factor.

Dakota seems to hit his stride against the third kid. He gets both takedowns of the two-minute round. And both times, Dakota puts in a half-nelson, turns him, and pins his kid. "Wow!" I'm thinking. That's pretty cool.

Next, Dakota leaves the mat so the little kids can get another turn. He soon returns for mat wrestling and does okay, but not as well as he did in neutral. I've got to teach him to stay on his opponent's hips better. And when he feels like his opponent is getting away, he needs to get back to the hips, or at least on a leg. Dakota also found himself a couple of times in a position where he could have used a dump move, and a few other times a Peterson roll. But, he doesn't really know those moves that well yet.

Finally, Coach Knapp blows his whistle and yells, One hundred pushups and thirty, and you're done!"

Dakota pops out 150 push-ups and 30 pull-ups. Then we work together on the Peterson roll. However, while teaching him this, I do let him know that I'd rather have him attacking or at least working his way up and out when he's on the bottom. I'd rather not have him carrying his opponent's weight and taking a pounding while hanging out and looking for a roll.

He needs to make things happen. Wear his guy out. Make him carry his weight instead because he's on top rather than the bottom looking for a roll. Then, every once in a while, when it's appropriate, surprise his opponent by hitting him with some kind of roll like a Peterson.

After getting gas, Dakota and I talked wrestling once again all the way home. At one point during the ride, Dakota asked me to turn up the radio. There was an 80's song playing. Wow! This is great, I thought. Now my son and I have another thing to add to the list of wrestling and weightlifting. We both like 8o's music. And you know what? The 80's music seems to be getting better and better as I'm getting older and older!

As we pulled into our driveway at home, I realized that I had forgotten to show Dakota the dump wrestling move after practice... Oh well... I suppose there's always tomorrow... However, I already know it's highly unlikely I'll show him that move since I have another crazy busy day ahead of me. I won't get home until late... Well... at least he has the village in KT KIDZ Wrestling Program on this upcoming Wednesday night. They will help him learn what he needs to know for this upcoming season, which will be here before we know it!

Wednesday night gets here quick. The car ride was a bit frustrating for multiple reasons. But in the end, it was productive. It's never easy explaining to today's kids that they are still kids and that there is a difference between kids and adults, regardless of how tall some kids grow.

In addition, I asked Dakota what he had for dinner.

He says, "Nachos."

Hmm… Not what I would have had if I was wrestling that night…

Well, regardless of the initial stressors of the journey over, the car ride was a good one. It was another opportunity to have a really good conversation. I got to dive deeper into the concepts of respect, values, and how important it is for all of us to control our anger and remain emotionally intelligent. Emotional intelligence is crucial, but sometimes is sadly lacking.

At practice, tonight, Coach Knapp and Coach West introduced a wrestling concept called FLOW. It is basically sparring through wrestling. The boys did this FLOW thing for a while. And I chatted with some of the other fathers there who are also trying to help make their young boys into good men, too.

The other fathers complimented Dakota. They told me he is a fast learner. They also said that in some ways, I was really lucky that Dakota waited so long to begin wrestling. I know this is counter-intuitive, but they said that by waiting and then going straight to Coach Knapp, Coach didn't have to break Dakota of his bad habits. One father shared with me that it took two-years for Coach Knapp to break his son's bad wrestling habits. Now his son is doing awesome!

Tonight's instruction after the FLOW activity was simple but powerful! Coach Knapp showed how most kids tend to sprawl wrong when their opponent shoots on their legs. Johnny showed a way to sprawl and stuff our opponents when they attack our legs. In addition, he didn't just show one way, he showed a whole series on the correct way to defend our legs no matter how our opponents shoot on us. Coach West is a good sport for enduring much of this pain that Coach Knapp dishes out. And again, I wish I knew this stuff when I was still in high school back in the 1980s.

Next comes live wrestling… Dakota gets paired up with a pretty good kid for one six-minute period. Dakota gets the first takedown, but his opponent quickly hits a granby move and is right out of it and back up on his feet. Dakota then looks like he is getting the second takedown, but then at the very last second, the other wrestler wiggles out of it and ends up on top of Dakota.

The kid is pretty good in the top position. He occasionally throws in legs, but can't seem to turn Dakota. Dakota attempts a few switches but is unsuccessful. I yell for him to stand up a few times, but Dakota doesn't do it. I wonder if this is a consequence of his nachos dinner.

Because there are so many wrestlers there again tonight, once again, the live wrestling takes place over two waves. There is a 130 pounds and over wave, which includes Dakota because he is in at 131 pounds. And then there is also the under 130 pounds wave consisting of the little kids.

When Dakota gets his chance to wrestle again, it's through a shark bait round in a group of four wrestlers. They do takedowns. The one who gets the takedown gets to stay in until someone takes him down. All four of the kids in Dakota's group are good. The first kid takes

Dakota down right to his back. Then this kid also takes down the second and third kid. I'm very impressed with this kid whom I've never seen before.

Now Dakota is back up again against this really good wrestler. Somehow, though, this time Dakota takes him down right to his back. Wow! Now I'm really impressed with Dakota, too! Over the next ten minutes, these four young wrestlers battle very hard. Dakota shows a lot of guts out there. Maybe the nachos weren't a problem, after all. Dakota even somehow pops out extra push-ups tonight at the end of practice once again.

The drive home tonight was excellent! Dakota and I discussed at length how critical the eye of the tiger is, and that we mustn't ever lose it. I also explain to him how so many of us humans are really just crabs in a bucket. Sadly, when one of us works really hard to try to climb up and out of our circumstances to the freedom of a better and more successful life, others will grab us and try to pull us back down. Some of this yanking down is obvious, and some of it is more subtle, like when someone calls you a try-hard or a good little schoolboy.

We can't succumb to these obvious attacks. Or even listen to these subtle attacks on our dreams of a better life, which, by the way, will also put us in a better position to help others. Hey, after all, Rudy, from the famous Rudy movie who wanted to play football for Notre Dame, didn't succumb to these overt or subtle attacks on him and his efforts on his dreams, and neither should we.

I'm very pleased and satisfied with our ride home tonight. I think Dakota understood a lot of what I was talking about in becoming a good successful young man. In our driveway, Dakota gets out of the car first. He's quick. It's good to be young, isn't it? I reach over to grab my water bottle, and my eyes land on his declined passenger seat. Once again, the chair looks like he was practically lying down. That seat, at that angle, is beginning to become his signature symbol of our psychological sessions in the car. I'm the quasi- psychologist fielding questions and trying to use some psychology and some experience to help Dakota. I'm trying to help him become a good man on our rides to and from John Knapp's KT KIDZ Wrestling Program.

Dang... I just remembered that I forgot to teach Dakota the dump again...

VILLAGE! I NEED YOUR HELP AGAIN!

Brian Preece: A lot is going through my head as I read about Daniel and Dakota in this chapter.

My first thoughts went to my system of coaching. In both the programs I was at as an assistant, and then later a head coach, many of our wrestlers were beginning wrestlers. As coaches, we are more excited when they are Dakota's age, that being a freshman in high school versus when they are juniors or even seniors. We have more time to make a difference as a coach. A lot of wrestling is learned from experience, and yes, by and large, the kids that wrestled in their youth, if they are coached well and are somewhat athletic, will have the advantage. Certainly, the 3X and 4X state champs that are produced have to come in with some experience to compete to that level right as they enter high school wrestling. But I don't think one has to begin wrestling at age three or four. I've had plenty of wrestlers that have had minimal experience or even no experience until high school do well. Some have even won region titles, placed at state, and even won state.

Some people noticed my successes as a coach with less experienced wrestlers. I just said we had a "system." But it wasn't really that mysterious or anything. As coaches, we just have to emphasize certain things more. The first thing we emphasized was counter offense, which many call defense. I prefer the term counter offense here. The counter offense was something we drilled every single day of practice. I have to say that I was more of a front head into a whizzer guy than just a front-headlock guy. I thought it was easier to teach novice wrestlers to keep their opponents' heads down and away with the front headlock into a whizzer. But, in contrast, I did also show front headlock stuff, especially to my more advanced wrestlers.

We emphasized what I called the five lines of defense, which were 1) head position and getting in the pocket. 2) Hands, always emphasizing that the thumbs be "inside." 3) Forearms. 4) Hips. 5) Funk or scramble defenses. I think #5 is essential because good wrestlers will penetrate defenses 1-4. But teaching these things to novice wrestlers is a bit tricky. So, that's why I invented a lot of different combat games where I put my wrestlers into funky positions and had them wrestle through them. Here, I let them discover what was effective and how height and appropriate pressure helped them win these situations. But bottom line, we have to teach our wrestlers how to defend themselves.

I guess you could say, we also drilled being in a good stance a lot and level change drills. I remember one time when I was at the NHSCA Senior Nationals in Pittsburgh (now Virginia Beach) I attended a clinic for the coaches and wrestlers. The clinician was one of the University of Minnesota assistant coaches. So here we are, some of the more successful high school coaches in the United States with some of the most elite wrestlers in the country waiting to see what stuff this guy was going to share with us. And he spent the entire time talking about stance and mat position. Let's say I took him at his word, though I was doing that even before then. It just helped me reinforce our tact of emphasizing every single day stance and defending yourself and turning that into scoring opportunities.

As for takedowns, we kept it relatively simple. I mean we did duck-unders and elbow passes, we did straight doubles, single-legs, high-crotches and the fireman's carry. I was careful about introducing throws, especially the head-and-arm (or head throw) because, to me, this is a high-risk-low reward move, in my opinion. But at the same time, in certain situations, it's a good move. But you have to give the wrestlers the basics, basics, basics. Towards the end of my coaching career, I actually did more group teaching.

I had two young coaches, Chad and Travis Blevins, who wrestled in California that were really technical. So I had them work with the most elite wrestlers many times. Sometimes, I would split two coaches, Chad and Travis, who were twin brothers, and have them work with what I called the middle group, the wrestlers with some experience. I had another coach that was great at teaching beginning wrestlers. Sometimes we would create a big-man group and work with the heavier wrestlers doing techniques. For the most part, teaching the bigger wrestlers the single leg or advanced funk defenses isn't the best approach. They need specific techniques and strategies that are effective for their size and body types. This smaller group stuff was something I wish I would have done sooner in my career because my more advanced wrestlers really liked it. By the way, my general role was to go between groups, and I really enjoyed that. It gave my assistant coaches some important things as well, the chance to teach and develop more credibility with the wrestlers.

In regards to mat wrestling, I think for more beginning wrestlers, you need to definitely stress the things where they can just defend themselves. How do you counter the half nelson, arm-bars, being tilted and leg attacks. You need to help them identify what is their inside and what is their outside. I always want them to know which is which and work for what I call "outside hand control." I never wanted them to reach to get hand control with their inside arm/hand, as this often leads to them giving up their wrist. I think taller wrestlers can struggle with bottom wrestling, so I teach them a bit differently. They will have a harder time standing up or doing explosive maneuvers to escape. But they can use their length to widen their hips, pressure back and so forth. Here I taught them to get outside hand-control and to pivot on their outside leg to stand-up. I also teach them some side rolls and stuff, maybe not directly to score with the roll but to maneuver the top man off of their hips so they can execute second or third moves. The big thing is to try to teach novice wrestlers to be sticky, if nothing else. If they just don't get turned, they often can wear out their opponents.

On top, I taught the Step-through Turk series as our primary go-to stuff. But I did crossbody and double-grapevine techniques as well. But with my most novice wrestlers, I showed them to start and ride on the left side. This will throw off even better wrestlers.

But probably the best thing you can do for a novice wrestler is to get them in shape. Superb conditioning can win a lot of matches. And when novice wrestlers see this working out for them, they work harder.

Also, I always think it is imperative that at least one coach NOT be wrestling or drilling with the wrestlers. I've visited wrestling rooms where every coach is either drilling or wrestling with their wrestlers. I think it is critically important to have one coach who is free to roam. As I got older, it was usually me who was observing the entire forest. I learned this through my father. When our wrestlers are wrestling, I actively coached and taught. Coaches that work out with their wrestlers often can't see the mistakes that their other wrestlers are making over and over and over. And I'd rather correct them right there in practice when they happen versus a film session or after they lose a match in competition.

But I think I was lucky to have better athletes than a lot of programs, even programs with superb wrestling traditions. But I don't believe that came by accident. My primary assistant and I coached football just about every year. One of us was always coaching sophomore football, and this is where we recruited athletes. We were also popular teachers, which helped us recruit kids. Another thing that helped was that I often asked to teach freshman Geography. A lot of our wrestlers came from our classrooms and the football field. Then when they got in there, we encouraged them to bring a buddy, and sometimes the buddy became the real wrestling star.

One year, one of my future team captains got in a scrap of sorts with a kid in his biology class. The kid was a really good skater who also did some part-time acting in films and television series. After their skirmish that was quickly broken up, the kid on our wrestling team said, "You're pretty tough, you should come out for wrestling." It's funny how two boys that nearly come to blows can become friends, sometimes in a matter of minutes.

In December of his sophomore year, this young man came out for wrestling following his new friend's challenge. He didn't go to state his sophomore year, but I rarely had a kid improve this fast. He took third in the state his junior year. And second in the state his senior year. He won the biggest invitational in Utah called The Rumble, which brought in over 60 teams from several different states. His senior year, he lost three matches, twice to the kid that beat him for the region and state titles. And the third to a wrestler that won the Reno Tournament of Champions and was a 3X state champ in another classification. I usually only saw him do one offensive takedown, a high-crotch. But his counter offense was impeccable. And he couldn't be held down. He was probably the most creative wrestler I ever coached. I wish he would have done some freestyle so he could have wrestled more. He didn't even wrestle 100 competitive matches in his career. That probably hurt him and kept from winning it all. The bottom line, the ways athletes get into the wrestling room, varies quite a bit.

As I was reading about FLOW wrestling, I wasn't sure what Daniel meant. I was wondering if it was what I call "rolling." In our program, rolling meant for the wrestlers to not wrestle all-out but, instead, to just roll around. The idea is to try to connect moves together and chain wrestle. Of course, just rolling around itself had to be taught. Some wrestlers go right to all-out competitive wrestling. If what I call rolling has nothing to do with FLOW, I'd really like to learn about this system Daniel is experiencing. I really love being a student of wrestling like most coaches.

CHAPTER TWELVE

IT TAKES A VILLAGE

Dan Blanchard: Dang! It's Monday night again, and Dakota and I haven't done any drilling for wrestling at all since his last practice. We did manage to get to the gym to lift some weights over the weekend. But, even though lifting is better than nothing, it's still not the same as drilling.

The drive over to KT KIDZ Wrestling in Rocky Hill felt a little bit different tonight. Our conversation continuously jumped from one thing to another, to another. One moment we were talking about wrestling, the next school, then music, then family, then friends, and then back to wrestling.

I don't think either of us came upon any earth-moving insights on the way to practice tonight. I'm not even sure if I gave any good fatherly advice, either. However, besides narrowly avoiding a deer not too far from our house, the one thing I do remember though, is Dakota laughing loudly in disbelief. I told him that back in the old days when Coach John Knapp and I were teammates, sometimes our opponents would refuse to come out to the mat to wrestle us. Instead, they took the forfeit and gave our team the six points so the wrestling meet could just move on to the next weight class. Dakota's disbelief in our opponents forfeiting to us is what stuck out the most in my mind during the car ride to wrestling that night. It was more memorable for me than the near-miss with the deer.

Johnny's wrestling room was full again. This might have been the most kids I've ever seen here. I tried to show Dakota the dump wrestling move right before practice started, but Dakota had to use the bathroom, so we weren't able to sneak it in. The practice began promptly with Coach West running the kids through a quick warm-up. Then, Coach Knapp, had them do some drilling followed by that FLOW-sparring through wrestling activity again.

Next, Coach Knapp showed an excellent series for defending the single leg takedown attacks. He really emphasized for the kids to stop worrying so much about their opponent's head. Instead, he wanted them to crank down on the whizzer, lower their level and leg while attacking the hands. Johnny showed several different strategies to accomplish this technique, depending on what one's opponent was doing.

The wrestlers were all working really hard and sweating a bunch tonight. Dakota and several others looked a bit tired before live wrestling even began. Once live wrestling did finally start, it started with mat wrestling.

Dakota began on top and rode his kid for the entire one-minute period. Although it didn't seem like he did much, at least he didn't let the kid reverse him or get away. Next, Dakota was on the bottom, and again not much happened. I wondered why he wasn't trying to be more athletic and just stand up. Later in the car on the way home, he told me how he felt too tired and that his leg was hurting; so, that's why he didn't stand up.

During the next round of mat wrestling, both of his opponents got the best of him. At one point, Dakota even got cradled and pinned by one of the boys. Both were pretty good.

Neutral was next. Dakota is stronger in neutral. So I was anxious to see what he could do against these two good wrestlers on his feet. On the car ride home later that night Dakota told me that one of them had already been wrestling for ten years.

The boys did takedowns. And the winner got to stay in the winner's circle. Surprisingly, Dakota got the first takedown. And I'm impressed. Dakota looked like he was getting the next takedown on the second kid, too. But at the last moment, that boy turned the table on Dakota and ended up with the takedown instead. Thus, Dakota had to leave the victor's circle.

For what seemed like the next ten minutes or so, these two good wrestlers kept taking Dakota down. There were some close ones, but their experience was just too much for him. Coach West noticed Dakota, who is still green, battling with those tough and experienced kids out there, and he yelled some encouragement. Dakota then hit his old trusty arm drag and got a takedown. This time he stayed in the winner's circle to face the next kid. With the next kid, Dakota hit a beautiful double leg and was driving through his opponent. It looked like Dakota had some newfound life and was going to get the takedown here too, but somehow he came up short and landed on the bottom after a scramble.

Coach West asked Dakota where his head was looking. Dakota's eyes were looking down at the mat during his double leg attack attempt, and thus he ended up down on the mat with the other kid on top of him. Coach West instructed Dakota that if he had been looking up, he most likely would have scored the takedown and been able to stay in the winner's circle. I reinforced this on the way home in the car with Dakota later that night.

Practice ended, and all the wrestlers gathered around Coach John Knapp like he was some wise old warrior that they'd follow to the ends of the earth. It felt like they were all getting ready to go into battle with Johnny. It was a pretty cool sight. And it made me miss those days of yesteryear when that was me who was surrounded by a bunch of young warriors. I now realize I miss the way my young titans looked up to me and were ready to go through a brick wall for me. All I had to do was give the order…

As the room thinned out, I pulled Dakota aside to finally show him the dump wrestling move. Then Dakota popped off some extra push-ups, we said goodbye to the coaches, and then we got out of there.

The 45 minute car ride home consisted mostly of the talk centered on wrestling. And once again, we pulled into the driveway before we knew it. And once again, Dakota's passenger seat was left in the reclined position so far back that I couldn't help but notice it when I got out of the car. This preseason is almost over, and I'm wondering if I'm going to miss adjusting that seat every Tuesday and Thursday morning before I go to work in the early morning?

Wednesday wasn't looking good for practice this week. I had a meeting I had to go to, so I wasn't going to be able to bring Dakota to Rocky Hill. A father of one of the wrestlers graciously offered to pick Dakota up even though he lived about a half-hour away. However, Dakota had been limping a little bit with that sore leg over the last couple of days. You remember that sore leg, right? That's the same painful leg coupled with the exhaustion that kept him from hitting his stand up on Monday night's practice. Wednesday morning, before I left for the gym and then work, Dakota told me his leg was still bothering him. At that point, I thought it would be better for him to rest it.

Sadly, another week with only one practice. And next week will be the same because Wednesday night there won't be any practice due to Thanksgiving being the very next day. Oh, well, regardless, we can't think about what we don't have. Instead, we need to remember to be grateful for what we do have. We have had a fantastic preseason of wrestling with Coach John Knapp and Coach West. I am incredibly thankful for what all these guys have done for Dakota in helping him become a good man. I can easily see the positive changes in my boy in just one short season. And I'm extremely proud of him, the coaching staff, the fathers and mothers that have encouraged Dakota. And I'm thankful for the vast challenges that the sport of wrestling offers that speeds up the process of young boys becoming good young men.

Brian Preece: It does indeed take a village to build a wrestling program as a coach or just to build a wrestler into a state champion, or a great man, as Daniel says.

My father won nine state championships in his 12 years as a head coach at Uintah High School in Vernal, Utah, even though he had very little wrestling experience as a competitor. What were his secrets? I think it's a bit of the village thing Daniel has talked about above and how it does take a village to build a program, or an individual wrestler. And once that village is built, they can make wrestling seem like the coolest thing in the world for a kid to do. That was the secret of my father's success. At his high school, he made wrestling the coolest thing to do in the school. And that made the best athletes want to do it. It was really that simple. It was a simple process but one that took a lot of work, and more importantly, vision.

My Dad was the master of using the media. He worked closely with the newspaper and started his own radio coaches' show. Yes, a high school coach had his own coaches' show. And in the 1970s, I think kids thought it was really cool to be talked about on the coach's show and that the radio would cover their meets.

My Dad always marketed his program. One never went to a dual meet without there being a program. I marvel now at these things because it was back in the day when there weren't home computers or Track Wrestling. But every person coming to the meet got a program on hard-stocked paper. Local businesses advertised on the program. In the final wrestle-off before the season, he actually sold tickets, and it was often a total sell-out. I know my Dad convinced a lot of school staff to help him out with these endeavors.

My Dad might have been the first high school coach in the nation to have a wrestling "half-time" show. Somewhere along the way, he saw some school that had flag twirlers as part of their band or drill team or something. He brought the concept back to his school and talked the drill team coach into starting a group of flag twirlers that would perform at the home meets. Now you had a drill team and cheerleaders at the meets. That's a pretty cool thing for high school boys. And cheerleaders and drill squads also brought their parents to the meets.

He would involve different businesses in his program. A local restaurant always did the pre-match meal after weigh-in. He would even buy his wrestlers matching blazers. He loved it when his wrestlers looked nice. And he thought it gave an intimidating look when they got off the bus in matching blazers, shirts and ties. It sent a message that his wrestlers meant business.

He did a lot of things to recognize his youth wrestlers and their coaches and make them feel a part of the program. He would often have exhibition matches of youth wrestlers before the wrestling meet. I got to wrestle in a couple of them.

And much like the movie "Hoosiers," the whole town would shut down for meets and travel in caravans to the state tournament. I've heard a few people say that it was his program at Uintah that really made the push for the Utah State tournament to be held in college arenas versus high school gyms. The number of people that came to watch from the town was too large, and thus bigger venues were needed. It was estimated that at his last two state meets that he coached, half the town of 8,000 people came to watch the state wrestling tournament. And my Dad had no problem working them into a frenzy. Some say he spent more time doing that in a match than coaching the wrestlers.

But my Dad recognized that the village could really help him build a program and help his wrestlers win matches. From the restaurant owner to the youth coach to the cheerleading and drill team advisors, each had a role. And as a young man, I just thought the whole thing was pretty cool. So while a big part of me didn't always like wrestling, I still wanted to be a Uintah High wrestler. Those guys were treated pretty good, almost like Gods. But there was a lot of pressure to win, though.

However, I never got the chance to be a Uintah wrestler. After winning his ninth state title, we would move to Salt Lake. The issues involved in my Dad suddenly resigning are complicated. But let's say even successful coaches have their detractors or enemies. So by the time I became Dakota's age, my own village was much different than what I expected it to be. But, regardless, I still had my own village. A lot of people contributed to my successes as both a competitor and later a coach. And I believe it is essential to have gratitude and to recognize you aren't doing this alone.

CHAPTER THIRTEEN

DAD'S OFTEN KNOW BEST

Dan Blanchard: Tonight, I took my time eating dinner. It's my son, Dakota's last night of preseason wrestling practice with Coach Knapp and Coach West at the KT KIDZ Wrestling Program in Rocky Hill, CT. It's been one heck of a preseason where Dakota has had a huge uphill battle to face every time we have gone to wrestling because he's still brand new. Everyone there has way more experience than him. However, he has exceeded my expectations and done very well. I'm pleased with the effort and time we have both put into this first leg of our journey to prepare him for his first official high school season of wrestling. Someday, all this extra work might help Dakota to become a state champion or at least a good man.

However… you know how life has a way of making us feel like we're just not living up to the way we envisioned how it would go? Well, once again, Dakota and I didn't do any drilling, nor did we even hit the gym to lift this last week. Dakota was nursing a sore leg in the beginning and middle of the week. Later in the week, I was feeling under the weather. And over the weekend, I was in Boston watching my two youngest daughters play soccer.

As we all can see, there always seems to be a reason for us not getting done what we want to get done. But, in the end, these reasons, or maybe I should say excuses don't really make us feel any better. Nor do they help us move forward towards our life goals. Hmm... Dang... Life...

Okay. Here we go again. One more time. It's Monday night. And we're in the car again. And on this ride over, this father-son dual was having a hard time believing that this was it. The end. This is our last preseason night with my old buddy, and an amazing and innovative coach, John Knapp. And Coach West isn't too shabby either come to think of it. We're going to miss these guys...

On the way over, Dakota talks about how he is pretty excited about his upcoming first high school wrestling season. At least one of his buddies is going out for the team. Dakota hopes his friend makes it and doesn't quit. I remind Dakota that he is going to have to coach his buddy through the hard times, especially in the beginning. We can both still remember Dakota passed out sleeping all the way home after his first few wrestling practices.

We both know Dakota is going to have to help his buddy and teammate understand that the beauty of wrestling is its difficulty. It's so awesome because it's so damn hard. Period! The size of the challenge is what builds the warrior, as well as the good young man. We future good men need to embrace it because, in the end, regardless of how tired we are, it's good for us.

I pulled up to the industrial park building that houses the KT KIDZ Wrestling Program. Dakota and I ran into Johnny's wrestling room. Wrestling practice promptly started, of course. And right away,

Dakota ran out to the front of the pack during the warm-up jog where he stayed the entire time. A smile crept across my face. I remembered myself always giving extra at that age, too, even if it was during just a warm-up.

As far as I'm concerned, being called a "Try-Hard" is a badge of honor. It worked for me when I was young. And those people who knew me best often commented that I would practically WILL MY WAY to a victory sometimes. Now, all these years later, my son seems to be getting closer and closer to understanding what that means. And I'm thankful he doesn't let his classmates calling him a "Try-Hard" bother him either. After all, greatness really is all about effort, isn't it? The growth-mindset stems from EFFORT! Not talent...

Coach Knapp and Coach West put the boys through a lot of drilling again, as well as the sparring once more through a wrestling technique called FLOW. I can see the boys out there on the mat are working really hard, sweating a bunch, and even getting a bit tired.

For live wrestling, Dakota somehow ends up wrestling one really good kid after another. He is forced to fight off one brutal half-nelson after another. I don't know how he does it, but somehow he manages. On the way home, he told me his body went numb on one of them, but he refused to give in.

Wow... I wonder if I would have been able to fight off those, one after another, punishing half-nelsons back in my day like Dakota just did. I know I can't do it today. My shoulder would rip. Heck, I think it might have ripped back then, too. Well, come to think of it, I do recall now that my shoulder did tear one of those times I wrestled a guy that had placed in The Worlds. It still hurts to this day, even after surgery...

Coach Knapp finally calls an end to our last practice that we can attend. There is still one more practice, but my side jobs will keep us from getting to it. Now we had to say goodbye to everyone. We're going to miss all these guys.

Over the last few months, we met and became close to a lot of great wrestlers and great people. I really enjoyed the time I got to spend again with my old buddy, John Knapp. Johnny said that Dakota did a hell of a job and that he wished Dakota could have been there more. He even told Dakota to tell his father to stop working so much because it's screwing up his wrestling.

Getting to know John's protégé Coach West was pretty cool, too. Coach West is a great young man who has undoubtedly developed into a good man. At Johnny's, I also reconnected with several people from East Hartford, where I grew up wrestling and playing football thirty years ago. I became friends with several fathers in that wrestling room, too.

And Beth, one of the mothers there with four adorable young kids was really cool. Her family also did judo on Friday nights in New Britain under Sensei Fox. John Fox is one of my former wrestlers. I coached back in the day, at New Britain High School. Dakota and I are going to miss all of them. I hope we get to see some of the wrestlers and their families again out on the wrestling circuit this upcoming season. But, because we live so far away, I don't know how many of them we'll actually see this winter.

On our last preseason car drive home, I made a special stop to pick up some milkshakes for Dakota and me to enjoy during our 45-minute ride. As we were waiting in the drive-thru line, Dakota and I were talking about the upcoming season. I told him I'm going to try to get down to the last part of some of his practices, and that even though I can't promise him I will be at every single match he has, I'm going to be at most of them.

He said, "Thank You." I was confused. I didn't know what to say. And then as I was about to say something, the intercom went live and asked for my order. I told them two milkshakes, took my foot off the brake, looked at Dakota, and said, "Thank you for what?"

He said, "For being there."

Again I was dumbfounded. That's what fathers are supposed to do. Fathers are supposed to be there. But then again… my father wasn't… and neither was his father… Hmm…

As I pull up next to the window to get the milkshakes, I'm feeling all warm and fuzzy inside because I'm breaking the cycle. And my son is now mature enough to at least say thank you. After I hand him his milkshake, I say, "You're welcome."

On the rest of the way home, we talked a lot about mindset. We also talked a lot about how it's good to be a "Try-Hard" in-between slurping our milkshakes. And when we finally pulled into the driveway and hopped out of the car, I looked back one last time at the passenger seat. Once again, it was reclined a lot. "Ah, we're home," I thought. The next day my wife will say, "What the heck happened to this seat?" while she is getting into the car.

What a great preseason this was. Now it's time to turn the page to the next chapter of Making a State Champion or at least a Good Man out of my son Dakota. But first, we will eat some turkey and stuffing, spend some time with family and friends, and hopefully squeeze in some drilling or at least the gym before next Monday comes… Wish us luck…

Brian Preece: It was great to hear Dakota tell his Dad, "Thanks for being there." My parents were there for me… maybe too much… But at Dakota's age, I never really thought to thank them. At times, I was embarrassed by them. Or at least frustrated by them. But over time, I came to the realization that they were there for me. Dakota has shown great maturity in the recognition of Daniel being there for him and supporting him. I am hopeful that this will always continue.

The time I think my Dad was there for me the most was in my late 20's, and it had nothing to do with wrestling. It was a time when my Dad didn't have the answers I needed. For a man that had a large ego, this realization and his admitting it made us closer.

I was dating this young woman, but it wasn't going well. I wanted more, and she didn't. It was at a time in my life that I wanted to be married and have a family. I was over at my parents, and they could tell that I was frustrated and a bit sad. I was actually breaking down a bit, and I said I wanted to go home. My Dad wouldn't let me leave the kitchen. He physically blocked me from leaving. I remember wanting to deck him. And I was ever so close to throwing that punch. He then yelled, "What do you want, son?" I shouted back, "I want what you have, a wife, a family!" My Dad is emotional, and so am I. We can tear up at any sappy movie, even though I'm a rough, tough wrestling coach. My Dad then asked me to stay at the house and that he would be right back. He made me promise I would stay, and I felt I should honor what he asked. Though I really wanted to leave. He left the house for just a few minutes and retrieved our neighbor, who was a psychologist. I guess he begged him to talk to me. We both humored my father. He was pretty persuasive.

I can't say what was discussed with the psychologist was all that helpful. I mostly whined about my relationship. And I'm sure he gave me some advice. But something more important came out of it. I truly understood the depth of love that my father had for me. My Dad was never afraid to dole out advice to anyone. He had a lot of wisdom about a lot of things. He was a storyteller. It meant a lot to me, maybe not at that specific time, but over time it did. My Dad forsook his own pride and sought out help for me. He loved me that much.

Daniel's story above also made me think about the wrestling community. There is a brotherhood and sisterhood that comes with wrestling. You do grow to sometimes love your opponents, whether they are wrestling against you or coaching against you. I think wrestling people are different that way. I am Facebook friends with three of the wrestlers that I wrestled in the state tournament my senior year. One of them I wrestled five times my senior year (I finished with a 3-2 edge and finished fourth in state and he was fifth). I'm also Facebook friends with other guys I wrestled, as well as a good share of coaches I've coached against. A couple are very dear friends who I would tell my wife to make my pallbearers at my funeral if they should survive me.

Beyond that, I've remained good friends with some of my ex-wrestlers and their parents. Each year, I am the announcer at this big youth tournament called the Beehive Brawl that my friend Andy Unsicker runs. One of my ex-wrestlers, Braeden Woodger, runs the Track Wrestling for it. He also helps me with other tournaments, too. Greg D'Haenens, one of the parents of two former wrestler I coached goes down and makes the brackets for the champions. I coached his oldest son more than 20 years ago. I then helped him get the gig at our state wrestling tournaments, so he makes the brackets there, too. It makes me feel good that I have a bit of my own legacy contributing to the sport in our state in different ways. The bottom line, the connections, and the relationships don't have to end with the wrestling season. Nor do they have to end after one's competitive career. I am glad I've stayed close with a lot of people that I came into contact with through wrestling. And as I get older, I appreciate this aspect of wrestling more and more. I know Daniel understands it, and I think Dakota has an inkling of it as well.

CHAPTER FOURTEEN

THE FIRST "REAL" PRACTICE

Dan Blanchard: Wow! It's finally here. We had a great preseason that ended with the reward of us eating a lot of turkey on Thanksgiving. Dakota and I were lucky enough to hit the gym twice to lift some weights and do a little running on the treadmill over the long holiday weekend.

On Sunday, Dakota and I were supposed to do some drilling, but Dakota woke up feeling sick. He still wanted to drill, but I told him, "No. He needs to rest because the first day of wrestling practice starts the next day."

Hmm… Not sure now how Dakota's very first day of wrestling practice in high school is going to go for him. I imagine it would be very disappointing for him if he has to stay home sick on the first day of the season. Staying home would probably feel like a punch in the gut after preparing so hard for this first day over the last three months.

Well, I guess time will tell how this all will go down…

My Monday workday comes and goes, and I leave work as soon as I can to do my one-hour drive home to see my son, Dakota, at his first high school wrestling practice. I haven't heard yet that he stayed home sick. So I'm assuming that he's in school and at wrestling practice as I'm leaving work.

I get to Dakota's high school in time to see the last few minutes of practice. But first, I have to get by the security guard watching the front door. I learn that Tony, the security guard, is a former state champion wrestler from way back in the day, sometime around when I was born. I share that I was a 1987 and a 1988 wrestling state champion, and that seemed to be enough to seal the deal that Tony and I were now instantly brothers in combat.

On the way out later that night, I introduced my son Dakota to Tony. I share with my boy how I feel pretty good to have a former state champ wrestler watching over our students and athletes.

After signing in, Tony points me in the direction of the back gym. When I arrive there, I meet my son's new high school wrestling coach. Coach Torres looks like the perfect coach for my boy, Dakota. Coach Torres is young, full of energy, and full of passion for the sport of wrestling, and developing young men. It also helps that Coach John Knapp from KT KIDZ Wrestling Program, who we had wrestled during the preseason with, put in a good word with me for Coach Torres.

As I'm talking to Coach Torres, I don't see Dakota anywhere. I'm wondering if he stayed home sick. Finally, my eyes fall upon Dakota in the far corner popping out some extra push-ups. He's with one of his fellow freshman buddies that he recruited to join the wrestling team.

Coach Torres compliments Dakota. Coach says that Dakota is going to do fine and that Dakota was even beating some of the varsity guys today. "Very cool!" I'm thinking. While trying not to smile too big in front of Coach Torres.

On the other side of the mat, I notice the assistant coach. He's a big guy that looks around my age. He sees me and walks over to say, "Hi." As we shake hands, we realize that we actually know each other from our old warrior days.

Thirty-one years ago, and about 1200 miles away in Iowa, my son's assistant wrestling coach Scot Rogers and I were teammates on the same Junior Olympic Wrestling Team. Coach John Knapp was on that team, too. Scott and I haven't seen each other since that time back in Iowa 31-years ago. And now all these years later, this fellow-warrior from my past is helping coach my son, Dakota. Small world, huh? It looks like Dakota has two great coaches now at his high school.

Skipping forward to Tuesday, from what I saw of Dakota's practice, he did well and was able to put a few of his opponents on their backs. However, he wasn't able to hold them there. I'm going to have to work with him though on when to switch off between the half-nelson and reverse half-nelson. I'm going to have to work with him again on fishing for his opponent's head when the other guy has a leg in on him, and they're rolling around the mat. Dakota did, however, get a few cradles on his opponents with those long arms of his.

On our ten-minute car ride home, I shared with Dakota that he should be wrestling with Coach Rogers' son. I noticed during practice that his son was really good. Dakota should wrestle Coach Torres every practice as well, so he can get better.

I also noticed that Dakota was talking funny, kind of nasally, and he was sniffing a lot. Hmm... When we finally pulled into our driveway, Dakota commented that that was a quick ride home. I wholeheartedly agreed with him. We didn't have much time tonight to talk like we had been doing on the 45-minute trips we had been doing from KT KIDZ.

As we get out of the car, I look back at Dakota's seat and think, Wow. The car ride was even too short for him to recline his chair like he had been doing on the way home from Coach Knapp's practices in Rocky Hill. I was kind of sad that we didn't get a whole lot of time to talk. But, I suppose that even a little bit of time for a father and son to talk is still better than no time to speak.

Ah... Dang... I knew it... It's the middle of the week, and Dakota is still sick. It's the first week of wrestling season, and he's staying home sick from school and wrestling... Hmm... Not the perfect start... but building a good man through wrestling is a long road, so I'm not too worried yet...

The end of our first week finishes up with a pleasant surprise. Coach Torres takes our high school wrestling team to wrestle at his alma mater, Windham high school. I'm pumped because I am well aware of the long history of Windham's great wrestling teams and great wrestlers. Dakota will have a lot of very tough kids to work out! And what could be better than that, well, at least for a wrestle, right?

I couldn't stay for the practice because I had other responsibilities to fulfill at home. But when I came back to pick up Dakota, I saw the Windham coach, Coach Risley. We embraced in a big hug like two fellow warriors who hadn't seen each other in many years. And we rapidly spoke to try to quickly catch up on what the other had been doing. It was such a pleasure and such a joy to see Coach Risley again. I was pumped to have my son Dakota receiving some wrestling instruction from another one of Connecticut greats in the sport of wrestling. Check out this amazing YouTube video the Norwich Bulletin did on Coach Risley and Windham High School winning its tenth state championship in wrestling: https://www.youtube.com/watch?v=lvZveN1EWh8.

The ride home was a special one on this day because I had to bring Dakota's friend home, too. So, we all got to spend some time in the car together. Just us men, or emerging men, maybe I should say. We talked about wrestling. I talked about life with the boys, like how they need to learn financial literacy and develop multiple income streams as young men. They need to do this so that when they are adults, they don't become economic slaves like most of us. They can be in charge of their own destinies and become the kind of men they want to become while serving no master.

During our car ride home, another really cool thing happened. My phone rang, and it was an old wrestling buddy of mine, Gus. I put my old warrior buddy Gus on speakerphone. He was also on that Junior Olympic wrestling team with me, and Coach John Knapp, and Coach Rogers. Gus is now a firefighter in San Francisco. He is also the founder of my son's wrestling team. Way back in the mid-80s, Gus was a one-man wrestling team. The things Gus had to do to get my son's team started was way beyond what most of us would have done. You can read a little bit about my old buddy Gus in this New York Times article that was written about him back when we were still young warriors: https://www.nytimes.com/1987/02/24/nyregion/our-towns-one-man-team-a-game-wrestler-gets-off-the-mat.html.

What a treat it was this week for the boys to indirectly meet my old buddy, Gus, the founder of their team. I'm trying to talk him into showing up here on the east coast someday to meet the boys and the coaches of the present-day team.

It really does take a village to raise a child, especially if we're trying to help mold that boy into a good man someday... I can't wait to see what next week brings...

Brian Preece: I have more fond memories of the first day of practice as a coach than an actual wrestler. Because I had been wrestling for such a long time before high school, I can't even think of anything all that memorable about my first high school practice. It was just another practice.

But I sure remember my first day of wrestling practice as a head coach. It was that first Monday in November of 1994. It was actually a morning practice as I did two-a-days. And after several years of being an assistant coach, I was thrilled to lead my own program now.

I was an assistant coach/teacher for five years at West High School in downtown Salt Lake City. My last year there, we placed second in the 4A state tournament. 4A is the classification for the second-largest tiers of school by enrollment. However, the 4A division that year was considered to be the toughest of the five classifications. We had a strong team. We had a wrestler that was first-team All-American and became our state's first wrestler to win his match in the Dapper Dan. The Dapper Dan features the top Pennsylvania wrestlers versus the best wrestlers across the United States. We won all our dual meets that year and won our region tournament. We placed second to state to one of the state's traditional juggernaut programs.

Since I was a son of a famous wrestling coach and our program at West High School was doing great, I guess Provo High had some faith to hire me as their head coach. I had worked at Provo High School as a coaching intern for three years when I was a student at Brigham Young University (BYU). So the school leadership there was familiar with me. It all came together for me to land my first head coaching program at Provo High School.

Of course, it is vital before the wrestling season even begins that you establish some rapport with the returning wrestlers and some credibility as a teacher. With the latter, I was put in a difficult situation. They didn't have a room for me, so I had to move from classroom to classroom for the first semester and teach in these classrooms during the other teachers' prep periods. Getting technology, which at that time was basically a TV/VCR, was sometimes tricky. Most of the social studies teachers were in the same building except for one. This meant I had to leave the building sometimes. I found myself pushing a TV/VCR cart, hoping to get to my next class before the tardy bell rang. Then, of course, trek back before my next class started.

When wrestling season began, and winter set in, teaching became even more difficult. As a newbie teacher, I was asked to teach four different subjects, and Utah class sizes are legendarily large. I had 220 students total to teach. But I had taught over 250 at West High School, so that part didn't really bother me too much. But it was still difficult to balance my teaching load with the responsibility of being a new head coach.

There was an understanding that down the line, I would coach football too, But since I was hired in mid-August, I didn't have to worry about coaching football during my first year. However, I was asked to be the assistant golf coach that year. And to be the "faculty" advisor. Every sport had to have somebody in the faculty on the coaching staff. Now with the dearth of coaches in our schools, that's not a concern and most of our school's head coaches now are paraprofessionals. So I got to work with Vance Law, who was named to be our school's baseball and golf coach. If that name is familiar to you, it's probably because Vance Law played in the major leagues with the Chicago Cubs. Becoming friends with the Law family has been a great blessing to my life. I became an assistant baseball coach, working with the sophomore team. So, you can see my first year as a head wrestling coach at Provo High School was pretty busy. I look back now at age 54, wondering how I did it all. But I wasn't even 30 then, and I still had plenty of energy.

My friend Jess Christen, who was the head wrestling coach before me, would stay on as an assistant. But he was working on getting his Master's Degree and going into administration. Many of the older wrestlers didn't even know I was the head coach at first. However, it became obvious over time that I was the one at practice every day doing more and more of the work. It was nice, though, to have Jess in the room to show me the ropes.

Our school was understaffed, and in December, we hired another social studies teacher. The man we would employ would be Darren Hirsche, who would become my best friend. He was hired to teach social studies and coach football, and we hit it off almost immediately. He also wanted to coach wrestling, and I instantly hired him. Darren was one of the most beloved teachers and coaches in the history of our school. But in his 22nd year of teaching, he was diagnosed with Huntington's disease. He only had missed one day of school for illness in 22 years. But Huntington's disease is one of the cruelest things, and he was forced to take permanent disability. He would pass away in August of 2018 at the age of 52.

I had a good staff when I started at Provo High School. We were also adding a new gymnasium, wrestling room, weight room, and locker areas to our school. I think it ran behind schedule and wasn't finished before the basketball/wrestling seasons began. In mid-January, the facility was completed, which meant we had to move our mats and equipment right in the heart of our wrestling season. So this took a big part of a couple of wrestling practices for sure.

I really didn't know what to expect. My last year at Provo High School as an intern assistant. We took eight wrestlers to state, they lost 16 straight matches, and we didn't even scratch a point. Our sister school (in our two-high school district) closed down its program altogether two years after that. For a year, the school benefitted from that as two of its top wrestlers (the Skousen brothers) came to Provo. One took state, and the other brother took second. And Provo actually cracked the top five as they had another wrestler that took state and a couple of other state placers, too. This was two seasons before I arrived. The success was sort of temporary, however. The program slid back a bit in the standings and finished tenth the year before I arrived. At the same time, West High School was emerging. In my first year, we finished 18th out of 28 schools. Then we surged to about 14th. Then cracked the top ten. Next, we finished sixth. And finally, second in my last year there.

The head coach at West High was Don Holtry, a man I truly love. He wasn't ready to step down as coach, so I felt it was time to make that leap and lead a program of my own. Though I learned a lot from my Dad obviously, and other coaches as well, Don really taught me a lot about the day-to-day operations of a wrestling program. I'm not sure he was always like this as a coach. I think as he got older, he trusted his assistant coaches more and let them do more instruction and have more responsibility. This really helped me develop as a coach. It also showed me that I needed to do that, as well. We had a great coaching staff that also was diverse in approach. That experience also taught me to create a staff like his, not just "clones" of myself but coaches that have different strengths to offset my own weaknesses. It took me a few years, but I made sure I had at least four full-time assistants that I paid who were highly dependable. Some of them were BYU student coaching interns as I had been. I felt it was important to mentor them and make sure they understood all aspects of coaching.

That very first practice as the man in charge was nerve-wracking and exciting. I thought only having 35-40 wrestlers was a bit discouraging as we had nearly 100 athletes in our program at West High. But I was told the numbers were actually up, and I rolled with it. At our peak (at Provo High), we had 70 wrestlers start one season. You never end up with that many, but my idea was that "More lumps of coals in the room meant more possibility of diamonds."

In my first afternoon practice, I just really copied the structure of what we were doing at West High School. Don always had a practice plan. Over the years, I winged it a bit more. "The plan" was more and more in my head. But then, in my last few years, I put the practice plan on the whiteboard for the athletes to see.

The first practice(s) there is always a lot of paperwork for the coach. There is the physical form. The parental-consent form. And if you want to buy a spirit pack (hoodie and shorts) there is a form to fill out too. A lot of our wrestlers were complete novices, so you had to help them find shoes also. I usually waited a few days before I handed out headgears to see who actually stuck with it.

Again, my very, very first practice was actually in the morning. I did two-a-days the first week. Jess thought I was crazy and that I would run off kids. And I probably did. But I felt it was important with an inexperienced team to get them into top physical shape before our first meet so they'd have a chance at a good start.

I did have two returning state placers. I would have had three, but one transferred to another school for football. I had another wrestler that looked very promising. But we had a very uneasy relationship at first, which took some time to improve. Then I had an up-and-coming group of freshmen and sophomores. Some had experience through our youth/junior high program, which wasn't the greatest as compared to other programs in Utah Valley, but they had some experience none-theless.

We had a good junior high coach that knew wrestling. But we had to work within the constraints of the city recreation program, which was frustrating. It was a "non-competitive" model, and they only wanted the wrestlers to practice 90 minutes a day and twice a week with no Saturday competitions. So this meant, as Daniel had to do with Dakota, that some of our wrestlers had to go elsewhere to get more competitive experiences or go it alone. A few did, but most didn't. I would say about half of my wrestlers who stepped into practice that morning had zero wrestling experience. The two state placers were on board; in fact, one had a father who was a head coach in Salt Lake City, and we were friends. He was great. He told his son to trust me implicitly. He called me "the best coach in the state." That was a big boost for my ego and helped me with my own confidence. It also helped me establish credibility with the rest of the athletes.

I knew we had to emphasize conditioning, so I had to sell its importance. And also have fun with it. So we played a lot of games and did a variety of things. I think that's important with a conditioning program. You have to mix it up!

I put in my Step-Thru Turk series, which Jess also did but a bit differently. I let the older wrestlers stick with some of their own techniques that were working for them with just a little tweaking. I also stressed a lot of counter-offense. Jess and I were both stand-up guys, so I didn't have to change things too much there. Another thing I emphasized was telling them they were going to have a life-changing experience with wrestling. I also told them that I appreciated them for taking this leap with me. And I remember saying this over and over. I also kept telling them to just get through the first two weeks, and they would grow to love this sport. And lastly, as Dakota did, I told them to try to bring a friend to practice.

CHAPTER FIFTEEN

REAL FATHERS TELL THEIR SONS THEY LOVE THEM EARLY AND OFTEN

Dan Blanchard: I rushed over to pick up Dakota tonight from wrestling practice. I figured I'd get to see the last ten minutes of this Monday night practice, but unfortunately, I missed it. Dang! I also missed out on finding time this past weekend to get a workout in with Dakota, too. It's so hard to live up to our own visions of the perfect world, isn't it?

As I scanned the wrestling room for my boy, my eyes landed on Coach Torres' big smile. His smile and positive attitude are infectious. He's always a pleasure to talk with. Later in the week, I'd bump into my old friend, Coach Steve Melino in Windham. He is now the top man in Connecticut Wrestling, and he'd tell me that one of his favorite wrestlers of all time is Coach John Torres. I guess Dakota lucked out again with another great coach.

As Coach Torres and I chatted, the wrestling room thinned out. After extra push-ups, Dakota worked his way over to me to say hi and give me a big hug. Dakota and I have that special bond where we hug each other and tell each other we love the other all the time.

Coach worked them hard again tonight. As we continued to chat, Coach Torres informed me of the tough spot Dakota is in because he currently weighs 128 pounds. Dakota is going to have to wrestle-off the team's varsity captain if he tries to compete in the 126-pound weight class. And if he decides to go up to the 132-pound weight class, he'll then have to wrestle-off the team's other varsity captain.

The best spot for my freshman boy to wrestle is the 120-pound weight class. But because Dakota is so lean, he doesn't have the weight to lose. His abs have been looking great lately. However, it also looks like Dakota is going to have his hands full this year with those two varsity team captains. He may not get the recognition for all of the hard work that he deserves this year. But on the positive side, he'll surely get a lot better tangling with the two upperclassmen varsity captains day in and day out.

And besides, there is nothing wrong with wrestling Jayvee, especially if that's the only available place to wrestle. It's better to wrestle in any spot that is possible than not to wrestle at all. And who knows…? I lost my first couple of wrestle-offs as a freshman to a returning varsity starter. And I still ended up on the varsity team within a few weeks into the season. And as long as Dakota keeps working hard and improving, he could find himself on the varsity team sooner than he thinks, too. However, I'm not going to get too excited about this yet because it's very rare for a freshman to wrestle varsity unless he's a lightweight.

On the way home that night, Dakota is very excited about an awesome fireman's carry/throw he hit on one of his teammates during live wrestling. I wish I could have seen it. What I do notice though, is that Dakota is continuously coughing almost all the way home… That dang cold doesn't seem to want to go away... Dakota goes to bed almost as soon as we get back...

As the week progresses, Dakota's cough continues. Every night I tell him to go to bed early. And he says that he is, and it isn't helping. Somehow, Dakota also managed to tear up his knee, and now the minor injury is bothering him, too. I think I'll have to buy him some knee pads. Hopefully, that helps.

Regardless of the obstacles, the changing dynamics, and that I haven't been able to see Dakota wrestle this week, he tells me he is battling hard with the captains, and his coach, too. I have to tell you that I'm pretty happy to hear that.

I know he's working hard and I know he's improving every day underneath someone else's supervision and tutelage. I just wish I could see more of it like when I was with him at John Knapp's preseason practices at KT KIDZ. I also want him to get well, and get rid of that cold he has. Until that happens, though, he'll keep going to bed early every night. Hey, like Ben Franklin said, "Early to bed and early to rise, makes a man healthy, wealthy, and wise."

I wonder what good ol' Ben would have said if he was a wrestler...? Well, I don't think we'll ever know because I don't think Ben Franklin wrestled. But George Washington did, and he was pretty good, too. And so did Abraham Lincoln. Honest Abe was very good. And perhaps the most enthusiastic of the wrestling Presidents is one of my favorite Presidents, Teddy Roosevelt. Sounds like Dakota is in good company. Wouldn't you agree?

Well, we're now at the end of another week. And I'm driving Dakota over to wrestling as Tom Petty is singing one of my favorite songs on the radio, I Won't Back Down. I turn up the radio some more, and we listen to Tom, and me, too, of course, belt off the lyrics:

Well, I won't back down

No, I won't back down

You can stand me up at the gates of hell

But I won't back down

No, I'll stand my ground

Won't be turned around

And I'll keep this world from draggin' me down

Gonna stand my ground

And I won't back down...

Midway through the song, I explain to Dakota that this song is the perfect song for wrestling and for real life outside of wrestling. When he gets used to not backing down when things get hard on the mat, which he's doing a pretty good job at right now, he'll also then be able to carry that skill and courage over into the real world.

I explain to him in the parked car in front of the gymnasium of Windham High School that life will get hard when he gets older. And when it does, he's going to feel like backing down. But something inside of him just won't let him back down and hide from his responsibilities as a good man because he's a wrestler now... And that means something!

We enter the building, and I can't believe my eyes. I feel like Dakota has brought me back to my old wrestling family. The first person

I see is Coach Gary Alford. Gary is a former All-American college wrestler who has a great lateral drop. 20-years ago, I used to wrestle with him and then coached the Junior Olympic wrestling team with him. Today, my son and his daughter will be wrestling together. Precious and priceless. Gary and I embrace like only old warrior friends who haven't seen each other in a long time can.

Right next to Gary is Rocky Urso. Rocky was a standout Berlin High School and Central Connecticut State University (CCSU) Wrestler. Rocky and I used to battle hard also back 30 years ago on the same Junior Olympic Wrestling Team. And then again, after high school when I used to visit him at CCSU for a workout. We share a few moments remembering our great coach, the late Hall of Famer, Jim Day. And then Rocky and I also embrace as only old warrior friends can.

I finally got some time to watch Dakota wrestle today. There are multiple schools and a lot of kids wrestling at Windham High School on this Saturday morning. Once again, I see my old buddy, the Windham head coach, Pat Risley. My son's two coaches, Coach Torres and Coach Rogers are also there. I'm just finding out that a lot of schools no longer pay assistant coaches. So, Coach Rogers is a voluntary assistant coach for our team. I'm shocked by this news. Has support for wrestling and our schools really dwindled that much in our state?

Dakota wrestles some pretty tough kids today, including Coach Gary Alford's daughter, and he does well. He's getting better. Dakota cradles a few of his opponents. He also now has a new hip-heist move that seems to be going well for him. I'm proud of Dakota, and very impressed with him. The fine men in his life now who have been coaching him are obviously doing a great job with him.

While watching Dakota, I finally noticed another one of my old wrestling/coaching buddies, Coach Steve Merlino. I make my way over to say hi to him. Coach Merlino is one of the original guys who founded and ran open-mat wrestling in northeastern Connecticut at Windham High School. In the old days, all the best wrestlers used to go there to work out.

Coach Steve Merlino, Coach John Bennet, and Coach Shirzad Ahmadi ran those Windham open-mat sessions for years. And Vinny Knapp used to drive his sons John, Jude, and me to these wrestling sessions whenever he could. Coach Merlino is now the top guy in Connecticut Wrestling as the President of the CIAC Wrestling Organization. Very cool, huh? I introduced Steve to Dakota. And Coach Merlino talked about when he used to wrestle with me, Dakota's Dad. Very cool again. Finally, I mentioned to Coach Merlino that I'm going to write a book on wrestling when I get done with the football book I'm writing. I tell him how I would love to consult with this legend of wrestling on that book. He full-heartedly agrees to block off some time for me.

The practice and the wrestling week finally ends. Dakota goes off to the side to pop off some extra push-ups. Coach Alford, Coach Urso, Coach Rogers, and I take pictures together. We shake hands, hug each other, and talk excitedly as we all wish each other and our kids well out on the wrestling circuit this year. And we can't wait until our paths cross again…

Brian Preece: A lot is swirling in my head as I read about Daniel's and Dakota's week. I thought about how my Dad was good at telling us that he loved us. I remember I didn't answer back sometimes but started to in my adult life. I wish I would have done it sooner and been more like Dakota.

My Dad wasn't macho in a typical way, but nobody doubted his toughness. He was from a ranching family, and he and his buddies liked to fistfight when they were in high school. But at the same time, he would cry like a river at a sappy movie. And in his legendary motivational talks, there would likely be tears by everyone in the room, including him. His favorite movie was "Dr. Zhivago." He was a romantic. Let's just say I saw my Dad cry a lot more than my Mom. She came from a ranching family too and she is tough. But I'm glad I lived in a family with two supportive parents who weren't afraid to tell me that they loved me.

I think that's one of the biggest lessons I learned from them is to say to your kids that you love them. I try to do that every time I part ways with my daughter Lizzy, or with my son Zach, my child now at home, before he goes to bed. I would like that to be the last words just in case. Those were the last words my Dad and I said to each other before he had his stroke and never regained consciousness. I am so grateful that when we parted ways on this Earth, these were our last words to each other.

As I read about Dakota's weight class situation, it made me glad that I coached wrestling in Utah. In the mid-1990s, Utah became the second state to allow jayvee (or second-string) wrestlers a chance to go to region (league) tournaments and qualify for state. I think a few other states have followed suit, but unfortunately, the concept doesn't exist in the majority of states. My Mom and I debate still to this day whether this is a good thing, but I maintain my Dad would have loved this. His jayvee wrestlers were often the second best wrestlers in the state. One year, it was arguable that his entire jayvee team was the second-best team in the state.

Also, one year, because of scheduling difficulties and the region unwilling to work with him on a scheduling request, he had to split his team and wrestle in two places. He sent nine jayvee wrestlers and three varsity wrestlers out to the rival school, the team that ended up taking second in state to him. He kept nine of his varsity wrestlers back home to wrestle one of the top teams from Idaho that was coming down to the tournament he started called the "Tournament of Champions." He was actually fined by our state association for not fielding a jayvee team and sending his assistant coach to coach his team (I know it sounds ridiculous). He was personally fined $500, which was about a month's salary in the 1970s while the school was fined another 1K. The mostly jayvee team won handily, the mostly varsity team lost by three points. It might have been the first time in our state's history that a school wrestled two "varsity" meets in two different places.

I think allowing jayvee wrestlers a chance to compete at regionals with a chance of going to state has many positive benefits. It has definitely toughened up the field of wrestlers at state. Some people might find that counterintuitive, but as I say, a jayvee wrestler from School X that beats a varsity wrestler from School Y will make the tournament tougher. But another big benefit is that it helped to end weight cutting.

See, in Dakota's case, he could just wrestle 126 and try to qualify for state there. And most of our tournaments in Utah allow coaches to enter multiple wrestlers in a weight class. Dual meets, and dual meet tournaments do present some problems, but in the end, if Dakota's coach thought he would do better at 126 than at 120, he could have him compete at 126. And in my third year of coaching, we had two wrestlers from our school wrestle for the state title. It was an interesting coaching experience, to say the least. It was a pretty competitive match, and the varsity wrestler won by two points.

My main assistant and best friend, Darren Hirsche, actually never wrestled varsity except in one tournament where the other coaches insisted he wrestled varsity because he was so much better than the other jayvee wrestlers. He placed second to his varsity counterpart, his only loss in his senior season. But in his natural weight, he was behind a great wrestler who would later become a state champion wrestler (and WAC champion at BYU). The wrestler in the weight below was a state placer from a family that was really into wrestling. Darren did wrestling mostly as a way to get better for football and because he really liked the head wrestling coach. But it wasn't something he was passionate about, and he often felt as a senior he should just quit the team. He challenged the wrestler and beat him the first time. The rule in his program was that you had to beat the established varsity wrestler twice in a row. This is where my friend Darren decided not to wrestle-off against this wrestler again because they were good friends, and he knew how crushing it would be for his friend to get beat out as he was a senior himself.

If you are wondering if this story is B.S., ask his coach. His coach said all of it was true and that he thought Darren was the most selfless person he knew. When Darren was in college, this coach asked him to be one of his youth coaches. And although Darren would get a Juris Doctorate and could have done many things, he decided to become a teacher and a coach instead. A decision in which I am truly grateful. So I know Darren really loved this decision by our state association to allow jayvee wrestlers a chance to go to state. However, I know he regretted it not being around when he was a high school wrestler.

Our state has struggled with the issues of how to seed jayvee wrestlers in region tournaments, and how to score them. Currently, our smallest classifications (1A-3A) only score the highest-scoring wrestler in the weight. The jayvee wrestlers can still help the team by stopping other wrestlers from scoring points for their teams, though. But in our larger school classifications (4A-6A), both the varsity and jayvee wrestlers can score points directly for the team. It has made the richer programs richer in some respects, but at the same time, when I came to Provo High School, I wanted to work the system to my advantage.

If you want to contend for a state title, you really have to think about covering all 14 weights with two wrestlers. It might sound weird to many out there in the wrestling world, but Pleasant Grove High School won our state's largest classification in 2019 by qualifying 26 wrestlers to state and placing 16 of them in the tournament. I think when Utah instituted the two wrestlers qualifying for state approach, it actually increased participation and maintained their numbers better throughout the season. Some wrestlers quit, especially when they are juniors and seniors, when they can't be the "varsity" wrestler. It had curbed a lot of the weight cutting that was happening even before the National Federation started the hydration/weight-cutting procedures. I think the issue of weight cutting often discourages participation, especially for football athletes and those new to a sport. It is comforting as a coach to tell parents that if their child can make jayvee, they can wrestle at their natural weight and still have a chance to go to the state tournament.

The other thing that came to mind when reading Daniel's story this week was coaching my first meet as a head coach. In Utah, we can start competing the first Tuesday before Thanksgiving. We begin our season a bit earlier than in Connecticut. We scheduled a double dual. What was weird about it, now that I think about it was that one of the dual meets was against a school we would wrestle in our region later in the season. But I also scheduled a meet with the returning state champions from the largest classification. They were a traditional rival that had grown into a larger school and had emerged as a powerhouse. Placed in a different region and classification, our schools hadn't wrestled each other in a dual in a few years. Bottom line, our team was crushed like a grape. I think we won two total matches. They were in the lightweights, so we held a 9-6 lead before losing 66-9. We did win the other dual by just a few points in which I was grateful. But I was also thankful to be drubbed because it was humbling and showed me where we were at as a program and where we needed to improve. In my third year, we tied them 28-28 in one of the best dual meets ever. There was no criteria back then, so it was just a tie. But our heavyweight won by pin, and it brought our fans to our feet, so it felt like a victory. We also won 8 of the 14 weights. It was a huge stepping stone for our program.

CHAPTER SIXTEEN

CUTTING WEIGHT

Dan Blanchard: Monday night, after a pleasant conversation with Tony the doorman and former state champ, I headed into the school's back gym to catch the last few minutes of Dakota's practice.

I noticed two things when I got to the back gym. First, the basketball team wasn't waiting to use the gym, and Coach Torres had his wrestlers working very hard through some intense spinning drills.

The boys were grunting and groaning doing their best to push through the pain, dizziness, and oxygen deprivation. At one point, Coach Torres yelled, "Look at the freshman Dakota go! Now that's how you spin!"

Surprisingly, the basketball team still hadn't come in, so Coach Torres took the liberty to use some more time and line the boys up for sprints next. Once again, he pushed the boys to pass the pain barrier to do better and better. He yelled at them a few times that they are just going through the motions.

Finally, he blew the whistle as loud as he could and yelled at them at the top of his lungs, "LIFE IS HARD! AND IF YOU JUST GO THROUGH THE MOTIONS, THEN AS YOU AGE LIFE IS GOING

TO BECOME VERY HARD! YOU NEED TO DO MORE THAN JUST GO THROUGH THE MOTIONS! NOW LINE BACK UP FOR SPRINTS AND LET'S DO THEM FOR REAL THIS TIME!"

As a parent off to the side, I could see the extra effort the boys now put into the last few sprints. Coach's little speech worked. Coach Torres finally blew the whistle to stop and pulled everyone in for the end of practice ritual.

Then, all of a sudden, something amazing happened... As the high school wrestlers formed a circle around Coach Torres, Dakota dashed off alone to run an extra sprint all on his own.

Coach Torres again yelled, "LOOK AT THE FRESHMAN! YOU ALL HAVE TO WANT IT THAT BAD!"

As a father, I'm impressed with my boy, Dakota. I'm silently standing off to the side, beaming loudly...

The practice is finally over, and on the way out, Dakota dropped and did some extra push-ups in the school's hallway. A few student-athletes on other sports teams who didn't fully understand what Dakota was doing looked at him with confused looks. But none of that mattered because Dakota was determined to forge his own path through pure effort and not worry about being a try-hard. He's going to change the paradigm of a "Try-Hard" to a badge of honor and a coat of steel that will help protect him out on that wrestling mat. It will also protect him and help him later in life, too, as a good young man.

On the way home in the car that night, we talked about Dakota making weight the next day for the official minimum weight class certification test. Dakota has never had to watch his weight or what he ate before... So this is going to be interesting to see how it all plays out.

There is definitely going to be a learning curve here. Right now, he's a bit obsessed with making weight, and he can't quite fully hear me yet when I talk to him about weight management for wrestling.

Hey, maybe I'm a bit of an outlier. But, after all, many years ago, I won my first state championship in wrestling after jumping up two weight classes. So my wife and I are not fans of sucking weight for wrestling. I believe a wrestler should stay in shape all year long. When wrestling season comes around, he or she should already be in shape. And now the wrestler only has to lose a few pounds to make his or her optimal weight class to compete.

So far, Dakota seems to be following much of my formula, too. But, only time will tell if it works for him as well as it worked for me…

We were nervous about how Dakota would do and feel making weight in two nights from now for his certification test and then again for his first match the very next night. My wife shared how it pained her to see Dakota hungry and barely eating for those two days. He's a growing boy, and he usually eats us out of house and home.

The good news is that he made weight for his certification test on Tuesday, and again for his first match on Wednesday. He even had two pounds to spare. He weighed in at 124 pounds Wednesday night for the 126-pound weight class. I'd like to see him hang out at 126-127 pounds. And then the night before the competition, be a little more disciplined and come in at 125.5 pounds the next day to wrestle the 126-pound weight class. I know this is not an easy thing to do, and it will take some time for Dakota to figure it out.

Well, guess what? For Dakota's first wrestling match of his life, he had to go against a varsity returning state place winner. His first match ever was against a tough and outstanding wrestler. And on top of it all, it really bummed me out that neither my wife nor I would be there for him. My wife had to bring one of our daughters to her music recital. And I had to be at parent-teacher conferences for my job in New Britain, an hour away.

Thankfully one of my sisters showed up for him. She drove an hour to be there. Unfortunately, he lost against the returning state place winner. But he refused to be pinned. So that's a good thing. And when I finally arrived near the end of the night, my younger sister had a smile on her face as she told me she missed this life. My sister was one of our wrestling managers when I wrestled.

Dakota also had some additional support in some friends from school that showed up, as well as some of his teammates' families who were there, too, rooting for Dakota. I was bumming it that I missed Dakota's first match ever. But I found comfort in the community and feel that wrestling tends to bring out in the wrestling families. I did, however, share some of my expertise with a few of the families sitting around me on what to tell their sons on how to improve.

To my surprise, near the very end of the night, Dakota went back out to the center of the mat again. Another boy came out from the opposite side of the mat. I couldn't believe my eyes. The whistle blew. And Dakota took him down. Threw in a half-nelson, and would not let up until that other boy turned to his back. The referee's hand slapped the mat. And then Dakota's hand was raised in victory.

Wow! Baptism by fire, I thought. On his first night ever of competing, he wrestled a returning state place winner, and then got back out there and pinned his second kid. Dakota was the only kid to wrestle twice that night.

There were a lot of hugs, handshakes, and conversations in the gym after the wrestling meet was over. It was pretty cool that night. While parting, my sister asked me to send her his schedule so she could try to be at the next one, too. Just like old times… but only different… I thought…

Thankfully, I got to record Dakota's second match on my phone, so my wife could see it, too. But when I tried to show it to her, for some reason, it had only recorded for two seconds and then stopped.

Dang… It's tough and so humbling to be a parent sometimes… You should have seen the look on my wife's face… as Dakota laughed in the background at the look his mother was giving me… Life is never easy… is it?

Saturday came quick. Dakota hopped on the team's bus to head up to Waterford, the town in between two rivers, for his first varsity tournament. Unfortunately, I had to head the opposite direction to Avon in the Farmington Valley. I had to go to a holiday party for the Association of Publishers for Special Sales, in which I am the President of. I really enjoyed the holiday party and great company. But my mind was occasionally drifting to the fact that I knew I was missing at least my son's first match that day. Thankfully, his mom, aunt, and cousin were there to support him in my absence.

I got up to the tournament as fast as I could, and thankfully I only missed one of his matches. Sadly, he had come up against a fantastic kid who was beyond technically sound. According to Coach Rogers, every time Dakota had his opponent in some trouble, the kid methodically worked his way out of it and scored on Dakota instead. It was a tough loss for Dakota. But a good learning experience.

Dakota was really mad that he lost and wouldn't talk to anyone for a while. His mom was concerned. The coaches and I were happy. It's good to see a kid mad that he lost. If he doesn't get a bit mad at losing, then losing becomes easier and easier in the future to do… And that's the exact opposite of what we're all trying to do in raising up a good young man.

Dakota was soon up for his second match. My wife recorded it on her phone. She wanted to make sure that we didn't have any technical difficulties this time if you know what I mean… Right away Dakota got a takedown with a move he learned at KT KIDZ Wrestling with my old buddy John Knapp. Then Dakota cradled up his opponent with some of the techniques that Coach Torres and Coach Rogers have been working on him with. I'm yelling out moves to Dakota from about an eighth of a mile away up in the stands. There is no way on earth he can hear. Everything is going exactly the way it's supposed to go in this match, and Dakota wins 9-1.

Not too long after, Dakota is up for his 3rd match of the day. It is still early afternoon, and it has already been a long day. Dang… I know this kid Dakota is about to wrestle. He's one of John Knapp's wrestlers from KT KIDZ Wrestling. This kid is good. And he has been wrestling a long time.

Dakota battles hard, and on several occasions, it looks like Dakota has him. But this kid's experience is just too much as he continuously finds a way to navigate out of trouble and sails out front to a 9-2 victory over my boy. The next time they meet, Dakota will be more ready for him...

Unbeknownst to me at the time, one of my former co-workers in the educational world is in the audience on the opposite side of the gymnasium taking pictures of Dakota to send to me later. When I do get the pictures, I'm grateful and don't know what to say. She tells me that there is no need to say anything. And that's just what the wrestling community does for each other. No thanks needed. At this point, I get it because when I gave a wrestler a ride home that same night, his mom thanked me profusely, and I thought the same exact thing. No thanks needed. That's just what we do here.

Well, speaking of that being just what we do here. I can't wait to see what Dakota is going to do next week in wrestling... This raising a state champion or at least a good man someday is an amazing journey, wouldn't you agree?

Brian Preece: As Daniel pointed out, the wrestling community is awesome, and sometimes it even comes from parents and coaches from opposing schools. Two examples come to mind.

I wrestled in the era of videotape, so much of my career is on videotape. I suppose I can get this on "the cloud" in some shape or form. But why bother? My wife isn't interested in watching my wrestling matches, let alone other family members and friends. Every once in a great while, I will watch my old wrestling videos because I just want to hear my Dad's voice again. I was shocked to see how few photos there were of my wrestling, especially in high school. Most of the photos I have were when, as a senior, my team went out to wrestle the high school in which my Dad started his career and where I grew up until I was nearly 12 years old. Several days after the dual meet, somebody sent out the local newspaper, and there were several pictures of my match. I thought that was really cool, and I cut out the article and photos and put them in a scrapbook.

In 1998, I was blessed to coach three state champions, but personally, I didn't have any photos of them on the podium. The next year I was at a tournament, and I noticed in the school's trophy case there were photos of two of my state champions on the podium. The school coincidentally had wrestlers that placed in their weights. I mentioned to somebody I would really love to have copies of those photos. And about six weeks later at the state tournament, a parent from the school gave me an envelope containing pictures of those weight classes.

There are so many cool things about wrestlers. In my senior year, my friend and I were in the finals of a tournament. I was a 145-pounder, and he wrestled 185. It wasn't the best situation for drilling. But I remember always being able to find a friend from a rival school who might have been in a similar predicament that would drill with me. All these years later, I am now Facebook friends with three of the other five state placers in my weight class from my senior year. So as you can see, the community of wrestlers and so forth can stretch beyond your own team or school. Wrestlers, and wrestling families, are just great people, and friendships and relationships are built that last for years.

I'm not sure how much weight I cut growing up in this sport compared to others in my era, or before, or after. In youth wrestling, I skipped a meal here or there to make a certain weight class, but nothing extreme. As a sophomore I cut about 15 pounds to make the 105-pound weight class, and it was hard for a while. But over time, I was able to manage my weight and maybe had to lose ten pounds only once. This was a time before the hydration program of course. My most extreme was one time when I was a junior my Dad thought it might be best for me to cut down from 126 to 119 pounds. But my regular walking around weight was closer to 135. I think we might have had a two-pound allowance that meet, so I lost 14 pounds in two days.

It was sort of ridiculous. I think I went without food entirely for that time, didn't drink anything for 24 hours, went down to a gym and exercised in "plastics" in a dry sauna (to the incredulous stares of others). I was so obsessed with making weight I even drove down to their school during the school day to check my weight on their scales. I remembered I accidentally stepped on their school seal and a bunch of students wanted to beat me up. It was what wrestling was in that era. I won my match, but after the meet was over, I threw up my pre-match meal that I devoured in a matter of seconds. After that, losing a few pounds to get to 126 was okay with my father, my mother, and myself.

In my senior year, I wrestled 145. In the fall, I weighed about 165 pounds, but it wasn't a huge problem once I started working out a bit harder in the fall to get in the low to mid 150's. My only problem was that I hit a growth spurt during the season and grew about two inches from November to February. It was getting a bit harder to lose the weight, and like Dakota, I was pretty tall and lean for my weight class. I wouldn't count calories, but I did track the weight of my food. For example, I loved ice cream sandwiches, and they weighed about two ounces. I knew that was one-eighth of a pound. That was usually my lunch at school. I'm grateful that I never used diuretics or ever forced myself to vomit or other extreme things wrestlers did to lose weight. I figure pumping out push-ups in a dry sauna in plastics was crazy enough.

The scariest moment I had was that I was two and a half pounds overweight at our region (league) meet. But back then, you could throw on the plastics and work out. My biggest challenger was about a half-pound over. He just sat in the corner and spat in a cup while I furiously drilled or all-out wrestled with a teammate who was in a weight class above me. I tell people hard drilling and hard wrestling will get the weight off faster than riding a stationary bicycle or running sprints. Well, just before the final bell, I made weight. I was very nervous about my weight for State's the following week. And when it finally arrived, I was more than two pounds under.

As for my Mom, if you were wondering, she never got too worked up about it. She was, after all, a wife of a wrestling coach. I can't say she went out of her way to plan nutritious meals. We just ate what we ate, and if I didn't eat, she didn't make much of a fuss. But Moms, when the sport is new to them, often worry about all of this losing weight. It's perfectly natural. So as a coach, you have to be careful about this weight cutting.

I started coaching in 1986, and my last year as a full-time wrestling coach was 2016. A lot has changed. And for the better, in my opinion. But I won't say that I didn't have some wrestler that cut a substantial amount of weight. But over time, I evolved to the point that I discouraged it. If a wrestler weighed 123 naturally, I wouldn't say having them lose weight to get to 119 or 120 pounds would be cruel and unusual punishment. But I was more apt to have it be their idea, and I would never encourage Jayvee wrestlers or novice wrestlers to lose weight.

When athletes come out for wrestling, there will be some degree of natural weight loss in the first two weeks of wrestling. Even if the wrestlers are eating and drinking normally, they will still lose some weight. Extreme exercise changes metabolism, and the amount of calories a teenager usually burns is enormous. So with me, yes, I entered my senior season weighing 165 pounds, but I was "fat and sassy" as they say. After two weeks of working out hard, I would say my "natural weight" was more like 155 pounds, maybe slightly less. So, for me, my real weight-cutting was going down from 155 to 145.

By the way, we usually weighed in at 4:30 p.m. for a typical dual meet. The varsity matches would start at 7:00 p.m., and I figured I would be on the mat by 7:30 p.m. I usually ate yogurt and drank a can of sprite. Sprite, I thought, settled my stomach pretty well as I was always nervous. I might eat a few graham crackers.

My brother, who took State, always had a Wendy's hamburger, small fry, and a Coke before his dual meets. When I had him talk to my wrestlers before State to motivate them, he joked with them about his pre-match meal and joked that at least "he didn't 'Supersize' it because it was the state tournament." His point was, if something worked, don't change up before State and throw off your body. He told my wrestlers that if a pre-match meal makes them feel good and prepared, and doesn't upset their stomach, then to stay with it whatever it is.

But for young wrestlers like Dakota, they'll have to figure this all out. They have to learn not only what to eat or drink, but in what amounts, too. I told my wrestlers straight out that water is probably the best thing to drink. I also told them drinking soda would be way better than milk or orange juice, which could work over your stomach pretty good. And I would say overeating after weigh-in is more of a problem for wrestlers than not eating enough.

CHAPTER SEVENTEEN

DAKOTA'S BIG WIN

Dan Blanchard: The former state champ wrestling doorman, Tony, was the same as always. He was pleasant and wore that million-dollar smile. However, when I entered the back gym's wrestling room, something was different… The coach was really pushing the boys hard tonight, even more than usual. He kept yelling at them that life is hard, and you can't just keep going through the motions. He was also screaming that if you don't let wrestling break you, then you'll be better equipped not to let life break you either.

Unfortunately, tonight one of our wrestlers just couldn't take the demands of wrestling anymore. And he walked out of the wrestling room to escape his coach's whistle. I know this may sound cold, but wrestling really is Darwin-like. It's survival of the fittest in its rawest form in a very tough world of combat training.

I really hope this young man regroups and resets his mindset so he can come back even stronger. But, who knows… maybe he won't… I've always said that wrestling is a sport anyone can do, but… it's not for everyone…

If there is one thing wrestling does for our boys, is that it forces them to "Man Up" very fast, or they're not going to make it through the next practice. For those who do find a way to "Man Up," a bond, a brotherhood, and a life-long alliance forms between them that will last forever. No amount of time, nor no amount of miles put in between these brothers-in-arms will ever break this bond.

On the car ride home, Dakota is pretty excited. He tells me that he's beginning to understand the real difference between wrestling and other sports. He then rubs his legs to try to get the feeling to return to them. He also tells me that the talk we had over the weekend after his second loss really helped him. Against Coach today, Dakota tripped him and took him down for two points. He's not sure if Coach was taking it easy on him, or if he just got lucky...

But, regardless, he listened when I spoke this last weekend after his loss, and now he was able to use my advice this Monday night to achieve one of the greatest goals of all... taking down your Coach. Isn't it funny how we all tend to listen better after a loss?

I'm beaming and can't wait until I can park the car and run inside the house to tell my wife that Dakota listened, remembered, and implemented my advice to perfection. And he even took down Coach! Pretty damn cool, huh?

The next night I picked up Dakota from a basketball game that took place after Tuesday's wrestling practice. As I figured, Dakota didn't get so lucky today with Coach in the arena of takedowns. However, Dakota weighed-out just a little bit under his weight class, so I'll happily take that as our good thing for today.

What's not so good, though, is that even though he's on weight right now, he's really struggling with his learning curve on a wrestler's weight management. He barely ate anything tonight because he's worried about making weight the next day for his Wednesday night match. I explained to him how he can eat a little more than he is because he'll lose some weight sleeping that night.

Well, Wednesday morning, on my way to work, my wife called me upset again. She doesn't like seeing our boy always hungry. My wife tells me that for breakfast he had less than a quarter of a cup of chicken and some carrot sticks. And for lunch, he refused to bring anything at all because he's worried about making weight... I promised my wife that I will talk to him again about how he has to eat something for every meal.

Like my wife, my heart breaks too thinking about what my growing boy must be going through, even if it is slowly making this young boy become a good man someday... Back in the day, it was much easier for me to punish myself with my grueling work ethic with super intensity than it is for me to watch my boy go through it to make weight... and then also to have my wife in my ear, too...

Well, the good thing is that Dakota made weight for Wednesday night's match. And the really good thing is that he won 7-0. The bad thing is that his older sister told me that she saw Dakota a couple of times in school that day and he looked really hungry. On top of that, my wife called me on my way home from work. She concurred with my daughter that Dakota didn't look good. As I said earlier, it really bothers her to see him hungry.

When I got to his wrestling meet, I asked him how he was feeling, and he said, "Fine." Even though he went on to win his match that night 7-0, I noticed in the second period after Coach told him to pick down, he didn't seem to have the energy to get out. When I asked him about it later, he said to me that his leg was still hurting him, and he didn't have much energy.

This dragging butt is the kind of thing I'm trying to have him avoid with his wrestling weight-management. But, I guess like everything else, it's a long, arduous process before one can get it right.

Pushing weight aside, a pretty cool thing happened in Wednesday night's wrestling meet. The opposing team's coach came up to me to say hi. He is a former East Hartford High School wrestler, just like me. Then two other guys came over who are brothers. Both of them are also former East Hartford High School wrestlers. One of them I used to referee with many years ago. And the other one was actually a teammate of mine back in our glory days when we were ruling the mats for East Hartford High School.

It was really cool to have this meeting of the minds, which consisted of several former East Hartford High School wrestlers. During this catching up, I found out that Dakota will be wrestling one of their sons. In union, a few of us say, "The East Hartford connection!" Who would have known all these years later, and all these miles east of our old stomping grounds, we'd be here watching our sons wrestle each other…

Dakota and the other boy with the East Hartford connection actually didn't end up wrestling each other due to the other coach's team strategy for that night. He bumped the other boy up a weight class.

However, regardless, it was really cool to have us all back in a high school gymnasium at the same time watching and rooting for our teams and our boys.

During Dakota's match, I realized that I need to work with him on a few things. He needs to learn how to drag out of a front headlock. Also, he's not hipping in and arching enough to lift his opponents and bring them back to the mat when they attempt to stand up and get away from him. Finally, in Dakota's attempts to go for what now seems to be one of his more favorite moves, the far side cradle, he's missing a golden opportunity to get a nearside barbed wire/butcher. He had his kid's arm sucked in deep tonight, and he could have used the barbed wire/butcher instead of the cradle he attempted, which ended up not working at that moment anyway.

Another really cool thing happened tonight, too. I've been trying to teach Dakota how to fight back and even make his opponent pay for throwing the legs in on him by pinning the kid. But as you already know, that's always easier said than done. Well, thankfully, one of Dakota's teammates found himself in the exact scenario I've been speaking to Dakota about during his match that night. And he perfectly executed the move I've been trying to teach Dakota that pins your leg-riding opponent.

As the crowd went wild due to the unexpected pin from our wrestler, Dakota and I made eye contact. We both knew exactly what the other was thinking… Thank God for teammates… And thank God for the village busy at work again, helping my boy learn, grow, and become that good young man that we all want him to be!

In the latter part of the wrestling week, while watching Dakota's wrestling practices, I got to meet Robby. Robby is the first and only State Open Wrestling Champ from Dakota's high school. This young man was visiting because the college he wrestles for is on holiday break. Robby is a fine young man of good character with a great work ethic. And I was thrilled that he was watching Dakota and trying to give him some tips. I'm extremely grateful when the village expands. And I love it when another high-quality person comes in my son's circle and invests some time in helping him grow and become a better man.

Saturday morning, Dakota woke up overweight. It wasn't much. But he has to do something he's never had to do before, which is losing some weight right before he wrestles. To Dakota's credit, he was down in our basement, working out at 5:30 in the morning to rev up his metabolism. This helps him burn more calories during the next few hours, so he could make weight. Thankfully it worked. I brought him to the high school, he checked his weight, and it was good. Then I watched him board the team bus and said goodbye to him through the window. I couldn't help but notice how intense he was looking. It was as if he was headed off to some kind of battle of good versus evil, or at least something like that...

During this incredibly long day of wrestling, my wife and I watched Dakota win by a forfeit for his first match. Then the second match he went up against a kid from John Knapp's KT KIDZ wrestling program who has been wrestling all over for many, many years. This kid beat Dakota by technical fall, but at least he didn't pin Dakota. I considered this a great learning experience for him, and at least a small victory because he didn't get pinned.

Dakota's third match was very exciting. He took the early lead and almost pinned his opponent. Then his opponent came roaring back and practically pinned Dakota. The match was fast-moving with lots of action as it went back and forth, and back and forth. During one particular scramble, I was yelling for Dakota to pick up his head from the stands as loud as I could. If Dakota had been able to hear me and just picked up his head, I'm sure the kid would have fallen over to his back, and Dakota would have pinned him. But it was not to be. Dakota dipped his head a little bit more, and his opponent was able to use that to roll him to his back instead where he held Dakota down and pinned him. Dang... so close...

It was the first time this season that someone had pinned Dakota. The nature of that match was that someone was going to be pinned with all those big moves that were flying around. And now my job was to convince Dakota that it's okay that he got pinned. It very well could have been the other kid just as easy because even though Dakota got pinned, he didn't get out-wrestled. Dakota was just as good as that varsity kid, but it just wasn't in the cards on this particular night. I'll work with him on picking up his head in certain situations, and the next time these two meet, if the stars are aligned right, it just may be the other guy falling and crashing to his back.

The last match of the night, Coach bumped Dakota up a weight class to wrestle against the other team's varsity captain. This will be a very hard and a very good test for Dakota. And if he can win this one, it would be a huge confidence booster for him.

The match starts off well. Dakota doesn't seem to be out of his league with this kid, even though he is only a freshman in his first year of wrestling. After some missed shots, the other boy gets in deep on

Dakota's legs. Dakota then whizzered hard, buries his opponent's head underneath him, and uses his long arms to reach for the kid's ankle. Dakota then works his way to the side of his opponent to drive him off his base and secure the 2-point takedown just like I have been trying to get him to do when kids shoot on his legs.

He's now up two to nothing over this kid, and I really think Dakota can win this match. After a flurry of moves, Dakota lands a deep half-nelson on his opponent and drives him over but can't seem to pin him. From the top of the stands, I'm yelling at the top of my lungs for Dakota to settle back and look up. People in the stands are turning to see who the crazy guy is that is yelling so loud… and I don't care. I continue to scream louder than I've ever yelled before, and then something amazing happens… Dakota settles back, looks up, the other kid's shoulder goes down, and the referee slaps the mat. Dakota has done it! He went up a weight class and pinned their varsity captain as a brand new freshman wrestler. What a great way to end the night! What a great way to boost his confidence!

Later I will ask my battered and bruised boy who is sporting what looks like two black eyes if he heard me yelling for him to settle back and look up, and he'll say no. Then I'll ask him how he knew to settle back and look up, and he'll say he just knew to do it somehow…

Life can be crazy sometimes, can't it? Well, regardless of whether he can hear me or not, I'll keep yelling from the stands and embarrassing my wife. Hey, what else do you expect me to do? As a father who is no longer a coach, I can't scream from the mat for my own boy like I have done for so many years, for so many other parents' children… It really does take a village to help a young boy to grow into a good man someday, doesn't it?

Brian Preece: It was fun to read about Daniel's and see his excitement when Dakota won a big match against a top wrestler from another school. Dakota has been working hard, doing the extra work to get better, and it paid off. Daniel's story of the pure joy of Dakota's success brought back a flood of memories.

My Dad wasn't my first high school coach, but he certainly was present when I wrestled. I credit Daniel for yelling his support from the stands. My Dad always found his way to the side of the mat, and even the coaching chair itself. Now that I'm older, I understand that he should have deferred to the actual head coach and his staff.

My parents didn't miss too many matches. But they did miss my first ever high school tournament in which we traveled to Las Vegas to wrestle in the El Dorado Invitational. This was a dual meet tournament, which was really rare in those days. I believe at that time, Jimmy May, one of the great Nevada coaches, was at El Dorado, and they weren't just a Silver State powerhouse, but a national powerhouse. It was a 32-school tournament that had a mix of good teams and some not so good teams. We had a "tournament" team, which means we were better in tournaments because we had some elite wrestlers that could penetrate through a bracket. But in a dual meet format, we weren't as good because most often we would forfeit three or four weights. So being down 18 or 24 points before the dual meet even started where there were just 12 weights was hard to overcome. But if the elite wrestlers all won, or yet better won by pin, we could win a dual if a couple of us other guys could pull out a win. We would end up the year having two state champions and two third place finishers. I won two matches at state my sophomore year just missing placing by one match. All nine of our guys were pretty decent wrestlers and capable of winning.

So we would win some dual meets, which we did so in this tournament. I remember getting thrown on my head a bit at this tournament. It was grueling. We had six duals over two days, and I went 2-4 in my matches.

The next tournament was called the Granite School District Tournament of the high schools that made up our school district in Salt Lake, which at that time was the largest school district. It was an individual bracketed tournament. We had eight schools and about all of them were actually in our region (or league). This meant that it was a good preview of what would happen down the road in the postseason. My season was not off to a flying start as I was 3-6. My Dad wanted me to wrestle JV for this tournament to get my confidence up. But my head coach Alan Albright insisted to my Dad that I would be fine, and he wanted me to wrestle varsity.

I won my first match and then got pinned by a wrestler who was a returning state champion. I won my next match and was now battling for third place. It was the wildest match I was ever in, and the first and only time in my wrestling experience, I had no idea what the score was. We took turns going to our backs, it was just crazy. Then we went into overtime, which was a different format then. You just wrestled three one-minute periods, and if you were tied after that, it was up to the official to decide a winner. I think I won the match 16-14.

My head coach was extremely thrilled that he was "right" and my Dad was "wrong." I had actually contributed some critical points to our team and placed in my first varsity tournament. My Dad was glad to be wrong and very pleased with my victory. It was sometimes hard to listen to my coach over his yelling, but it was great to get his approval and a big hug after the win. What is funny is that I see Coach

Albright all the time. Coach Albright would later become the BYU head coach and coach me in college. Eventually, he returned to coaching high school and became a school counselor. My wife got a job at the same school. Coach Albright loves to tell my wife, my son, and anyone in earshot this story of how he believed in me and how I came through. We even did a community television broadcast together, and he fit the story in. I roll with it because he's always my coach and I love him. And I respect him more and more as I think of the whole situation he had to deal with in coaching the son of a famous coach who didn't want to just sit in the stands.

I do know it's hard sometimes for fathers who know wrestling to take a back seat in the stands and let the actual coach do his job. My Dad didn't do all that well. At region and state, Coach Albright let my Dad be in the coaching chair because it became too hard to coach over my Dad, and it was confusing to me. I think back, and I should have been stronger and spoke to my Dad about this. He should have been in the stands and been more supportive of my coach. I see a lot of Dads in coaching chairs who have never even attended their kid's practice. I am not against fathers coaching their sons. But I think they need to commit to be at practices first and become a part of the staff next. They also need to be willing to coach other kids than their own. But as it turned out, my sophomore year coach would become the assistant coach at BYU. Thus then leaving my Dad to become my official head coach for my junior and senior seasons.

The joy of parents after the victory of their offspring can lead to exciting and surreal moments. In 1998, I coached three state champions. The last of the trio that won, my 215-pound wrestler, was indeed a special moment for athlete, coach, and Mom. He was wrestling the undefeated returning state champion who had won all of his matches, except his semifinal, by pin. He had pinned my wrestler twice in the first round, including the week before at the region meet. But when this other boy had to go the distance, I noticed something. He got tired.

So, I told my wrestler, "get through the first period, and you'll win the match." Well, he got through the first period. Then by the third period, my wrestler had built up a big lead and then pinned his opponent. And you won't believe this, the head coach of his opponent was Coach Albright. The twists and turns of life. When the referee raised his arm in victory, his mother leaped over the arena rail, sprinted past security, and gave her son a hug right on the center of the mat. And yes, I was pretty excited myself and did absolutely nothing to derail her efforts.

This state meet was truly special to me, but it was also a bit hard. It was the first state meet since my Dad had passed away in April of 1997. He wasn't there in person to give advice, but I did feel his spirit with me that night. My Mom, my sister and my new bride were all there in support as well. My best friend, Darren Hirsche, was in the corner with me, and I was so happy for him because he was this young man's primary workout partner. Another good friend, Steve Oliverson, the school's assistant principal, made the trip and got a front-row seat as well. It was great to share this as a coach with so many people who I loved and admired. But I'm sure my happiness was far less than that of his proud mother. The bond between parent and child is truly special.

CHAPTER EIGHTEEN

KNOWING WHEN A WIN IS NEEDED

Dan Blanchard: This is a different kind of week. It's Christmas vacation, and we're all surrounded by delicious weight-gaining food. And the wrestlers, including Dakota, are not exempt from this holiday phenomenon. Dakota is really struggling with his weight this week. I bet the rest of his teammates are too. Thankfully, all the wrestlers have just been given a two-pound growth allowance for the rest of the season.

This two-pound allowance means Dakota can now weigh 128-pounds or less for the 126- pound weight class. However, he's been weighing in the 130s all week long. And we can see it on his face that he is worried and stressed about it.

However, the positive spin to eating all that extra holiday food is that we get to visit with family during this school break. And while we were visiting with family, my wife's Aunt Judy approached me with how happy and impressed she is with Dakota. In the past, he ran away from her like a little boy when she tried to talk to him. This holiday though, Dakota stood his ground. He actually had a conversation with her as a young man should do. It looks like he's growing up. And I'm pretty sure wrestling has something to do with it.

Speaking of wrestling having something to do with it, the practices have been very tough this week. And Dakota is really banged up. Subsequently, he's beginning to get to know the school's athletic trainer now, too. Dakota has a banged-up collarbone and forearm to go along with his sore elbow, and both bruised knees. He also has two bruised eyes. And he says he is sore all over.

It's not all pain and no fun this week, though. The wrestling coaches have implemented some conditioning drills based around The Twelve Days of Christmas. Dakota has done so much spinning to The Twelve Days of Christmas that he now knows this Christmas Carol by heart. Hey, that may not sound like a lot of fun to us ordinary people, but wrestlers are a different breed if you know what I mean.

Three other cool things happened this week too. First, Dakota told me on the way home from practice one night that wrestling really has changed him for the better. Second, I opened up a very cool email the day after Christmas. It was a Happy Holidays email from Dan Gable. Gable is the greatest wrestler and wrestling coach the United States has ever known. Also, my wife's uncle Lenny, from North Carolina, unexpectedly rolled into town on Thursday. He was a pretty good wrestler himself back in the 1970s for Windham High School here in Connecticut. Uncle Lenny said he can't wait to go hang out at his alma mater to watch Dakota wrestle at the Windham Duals this weekend.

Friday's practice was the first high school practice that I got to see in its entirety. Just as I had enjoyed watching the entire practices at KT KIDZ this past fall, it was great to finally see a full practice at Dakota's high school. I was the only parent there. Thankfully, the coaches didn't seem to mind.

However, while I was there, I spent a lot of my time strolling down memory lane with my old Junior Olympian teammate, Coach Scott Rogers. I did peek over at Dakota from time to time. Once in a while, I saw the college wrestler, Roby, who was in town for the week, spending some time helping Dakota out with wrestling techniques.

Near the end of practice, the boys did a lot more spinning. Boy, they really like to spin around here. It seems like they're always spinning. And the coaches are always yelling at them to go faster. Finally, at the end of the practice, they finished up with the game of Sharks and Minnows. Coach Rogers even jumped into the fun. Eventually, he was dragged down by the wrestlers when the 5th or 6th kid jumped on him.

Dakota left practice still a pound over… I'm not too worried about it, though.

Saturday, the morning of the Windham Duals, Dakota wakes up early. He comes downstairs to visit me while I'm working on one of my columns. Dakota tells me that he's still a half of a pound over, even with the two-pound growth allowance. I can't say that I'm shocked that he weighs 128.5 pounds. But he sure looks caught by surprise and extremely stressed over it.

He's going to have to lose some weight before he wrestles this morning. I don't think it's a big deal. But we can tell by the tell-tale signs on Dakota's face that he is feeling that it is a big deal. He even asks me what happens if he doesn't make weight.

I tell him, "That is his coach's concern. It's not his concern about what happens if he doesn't make weight. His only concern right now is just to make weight."

I dropped Dakota off at Windham High School for him to go make weight while I run out to the mall to go buy him some better knee pads that will stay up while he's wrestling. I almost didn't make it back in time to see Dakota's first match. As soon as I walked through the gymnasium's door, I could hear Mrs. Rogers, Coach's Rogers wife, singing the National Anthem. It was really cool to see one of our own, leading us through our country's National Anthem as she belted out one high note after another. It was also cool that I didn't miss Dakota's first match. Also, the first wrestler that saw me told me Dakota made weight. Very cool. I knew he could do it.

It was a long, tough day full of some excellent wrestling for all those wrestlers in that gym. Dakota ran into the returning state champ wrestler in his weight class for his first match of the day. He looked like he had two opportunities to take the other boy down, but then the State Champ prevailed and took Dakota down right to his back and pinned him. It was a great learning experience for the 14-year old who has never wrestled before this year.

Dakota won his second match by collecting a forfeit. His third match went back and forth. Dakota had the boy pinned, but time ran out in the period. Later in the match, Dakota found himself on his back right near the out of bounds line and was pinned. His fourth match, he won by collecting another forfeit.

I came down out of the stands and approached Dakota about how he could have won his third match. But I could see in his eyes that he wasn't ready for it. So I asked him if he'd like to go over this later, and he said, "Yes."

I accepted his answer and then turned to the team's captain and explained to him just a little nuance of wrestling strategy that would have helped him win his first match of the day. This older wrestler listened with interest and thanked me for helping him. It really does take a village to raise a kid.

I think the coach could see that Dakota was feeling a little down, and he made arrangements for Dakota to get one more match that day. It would be an exhibition jayvee match against a kid who was closer to his age. Dakota went out there and dominated the boy and then pinned him in the first period. It was a great way to end the night. Great call, coach! It really does take a village to raise a boy into a good young man.

Brian Preece: As I read Daniel's stuff, I couldn't help thinking how as a wrestling coach, it is extremely important to know when to test a wrestler and when to make sure the wrestler has every opportunity to win. I've seen a lot of coaches, and maybe I've done this a few times, not be careful with their athletes in regards to this. Many coaches will throw out a wrestler in a varsity meet because it is the only wrestler they have in a weight class. But the wrestler is by no means a "varsity wrestler." And the losses, and sometimes losses by pin along with injuries and such, start to mount up. It is important to gauge your athletes, and as I said, I wasn't always perfect.

So I'm glad Dakota's coach was in tune with what Dakota needed- a win. I don't think Dakota was going to quit the team or anything, but his coach knew he was getting discouraged. My Dad always thought it was better to learn by winning versus losing. One thing an athlete inherently learns by winning is the awesome feeling that winning brings. And then they'll crave it. They also learn what techniques and strategies were successful. When an athlete loses, they learn what didn't work, but they still don't necessarily understand what does work.

I also appreciated how Daniel was in tune when it was appropriate to coach his son. I generally thought immediately after a loss was not the best time to tell any athlete what they did wrong. Maybe with some athletes at certain times, it was okay, but with most athletes, this is not the best time to instruct. I thought it was best to teach after a wrestler won his match. They are happy, and for the most part and happier people listen better. So it's just a good idea generally, after a loss, for a Dad or a coach to let it sit for a bit. Maybe it needs to be a whole day, or perhaps even after the next match, when a win is obtained. It's best to wait.

My Dad never had team meetings after meets. If they won, which was usual, he let his team celebrate with family and friends. If they lost, he felt it was better to wait until the next practice. At this point, he could better assess what went right, what went wrong. Then he could present the best solutions to improve the team. I know my sister, a very successful volleyball coach with six state titles, generally uses the same approach. I would often use the same approach, too. But, when I didn't, I had the rule to start with a positive, do the bad stuff, and end on a positive-win or lose. My sister also has a 24-hour rule in dealing with parents after games. Her reasoning was simple. If the team won, she wants to feel good about it and celebrate the victory and not deal with any negative things. If the team lost, she might not be in the right frame of mind to deal with an angry parent, and she might say something she might regret. The same thing for a parent. Give it a night's rest, clarity in regards to solving any problem will usually surface given enough time.

In regards to Dakota's concerns about his weight. Teens do make mountains out of molehills. But it is important to realize this molehill is a mountain in their eyes. So as a coach (and parent), I always tried not to minimize teen angst. Sometimes just listening is enough, sometimes presenting solutions is needed. And as Dakota found out, he has more strength than maybe he gave himself credit for.

I might have done things a bit differently than many coaches in regards to Christmas break. I always had some workouts over the break, but I usually gave my wrestlers some additional time off. Our state association always had dates when practices and meets weren't allowed. It was usually December 24-27 and January 1. But it could also be December 23-26 and January 1. Every once in a while, especially after I was married, I would take a vacation myself, like in leaving town. Rest is needed by coaches and wrestlers alike. So instead of four days without formal practice, they might get five or six.

I also had a workout plan for them on the days practice wasn't allowed, but I never had them do anything on Sundays or Christmas Day. But I did, however, encouraged them to run, lift weights, do push-ups, pull-ups, sit-ups, etc. If they went away for Christmas break, I would even encourage them to contact the high school in the area and see if they could workout with their teams. I had a few grapplers that did, and every once in a while, I had some athletes visiting Provo come workout with our team. I always thought that Christmas break was a crucial time. I think by maybe giving them an extra day or two off, they might work harder on the days we were practicing.

But I also think rest is part of the game itself. I also used Christmas break to really emphasize technique, maybe over hard drilling and wrestling. And I tried to make the technique sessions fun. This is where I might have introduced more funk wrestling. I often brought in some guest clinicians, which included my brother. I also brought in my friend, Dan Potts, who was an assistant coach at the school where I coached at before or some other former wrestlers. It was also a great time to give my assistant coaches time to shine a bit. For conditioning, we would often do games, and dare I say it, we sometimes played some hoops.

CHAPTER NINETEEN

MAKING WEIGHT: CONNECTICUT VS UTAH

Dan Blanchard: We're finishing up Christmas vacation, and beginning the New Year. This has been a rough vacation in some ways. Early Sunday morning, while I was busily working on writing my next book, my boy Dakota came downstairs. He greeted me, wearing an anxious and troubled face again. He told me that he weighed 134-pounds.

That's six-pounds over his weight class. And ten pounds heavier than his lowest weight was a few weeks ago. Did he have a growth spurt? His pediatrician did say that he was going to be a big man someday. Or, is it just the holiday season that is causing the weight problems right now with the missed workouts and the extra eating?

The next few days didn't go much better. Monday, Dakota was 132-pounds after practice. That's still four pounds over for Thursday's match. Our family usually goes with another family out to a buffet on New Year's Eve. But we're not going to go now. We stayed home on New Year's Eve and had a quiet night. Tuesday was New Year's Day, and we didn't have practice, so I took Dakota out running. When we got back, he weighed himself, and he was still at 132-pounds or four pounds overweight, even with the two-pound growth allowance they have given us.

In a moment of frustration, Dakota asked me if he could wrestle up in the 132-pound weight class, instead.

I told him that I personally don't have a problem with that. But him bumping up would depend on a bunch of other factors. He has to consider his teammate who is already in that weight class and what his coaches thought, too. Also, did he really have a growth spurt? Or is it just the holidays?

During the exchange, my wife Jennifer joined in and told Dakota that this is the sport that he signed up for. This is part of wrestling. And he shouldn't be trying to take the easy way out...

I'm really hoping that he can make weight this week. And I'm going to have to start working with him again at night before we go to bed to see if I can help him maintain his weight. I guess then I'll know if he's going to have to go up a weight class. However, that will probably mean no more varsity for him. And it will most likely also leave the team another wrestler down where they will have to forfeit again.

These days the kids wrestle at seven percent body fat. That is the lowest the CIAC Wrestling Board will let them go. The part that is a little frustrating for us older and former wrestlers is that Dakota's coach, Coach Torres wrestled at six percent body fat. And his other coach, my old warrior buddy, Coach Rogers, wrestled with me on that Junior Olympic team at five percent body fat. It would seem that there is wiggle room there for today's kids, and they should be able to make weight. But, times are different today and so are the kids.... as Coach Rogers' wife keeps reminding me that she just doesn't see the focus in kids' eyes today like she used to see when my East Hartford team and I used to show up in Windham to wrestle against her future husband and his Windham team.

To tell you the truth, I have mixed emotions about Dakota's weight. Dakota is only a freshman, and wrestling varsity is hard enough without the extra stress of trying to make weight every day, especially for a new kid. However, because he's just a freshman, I'm also concerned about him bumping up a weight class too. He will have to go against kids who are now not only older than him, but also bigger than him, too. Then, of course, we have to take the team's welfare into account as well. If he bumps up because he can no longer make weight, it will hurt the team. There's no easy way out of this one… I'm not sure what we're going to do about his one if Dakota can't find it in himself to do even more, and the extra nightly workouts don't do the trick…

This week's Wednesday match got pushed back to Thursday night because of the holidays. Dakota and I did a 20-minute workout in the basement on Wednesday night to help him make weight for his match the next day.

During the 20-minute workout with Dakota, I was sucking wind and had to face the fact that I'm out of shape. At one point, I told Dakota that he is going to have to help me get back in shape with these regular nightly workouts. I also thought it might help him take his mind off of his own problems if he was trying to help someone else.

He responded that I'm going to have to help myself get back in shape.

I really wasn't expecting that answer. But, it was a straightforward and honest answer. So, in a way, after the initial shock, I'm kind of happy that he said that. It showed some maturity and how one is supposed to take responsibility for themselves

Thursday, after school, Dakota checked his weight and found out he was still two pounds over his new 128-pound weight class thanks to the two-pound growth allowance. It was panic time. Dakota ran nonstop for over an hour, trying to make weight.

When I got to his match later that night, Dakota told me that he made weight by one-tenth of a pound.

"Awesome!" I thought.

Then he told me that after weigh-ins, he ate only a muffin and a granola bar because he was worried about making weight for Saturday. My heart sank because I was more concerned about him wrestling tonight on a low fuel tank than him making weight on Saturday. We can cross that Saturday bridge later.

Dakota was the first match of the night. He did okay. His match against an older boy went back and forth. One of the times when it looked like Dakota could have pinned his opponent, I yelled, "STEP OVER" so loud that the people in front of me in the stands moved their seats because I blasted their eardrums out.

Oops…

Unfortunately, Dakota didn't step over. He probably couldn't hear me. And his opponent rolled him to his back and pinned him. Rookie mistake… or maybe I should say mistakes… We'll have to learn from it and do better next time…

The rest of the night was just as eventful as our wrestling team battled back and forth with the other team. At one point during the heated competition, though, Coach Torres had to tell Dakota to wake up. Yeah, as crazy as that sounds, Dakota, while sitting on the team bench in the middle of the ruckus, somehow fell asleep. I'm assuming he was sleeping because of his weight loss and lack of food that day.

Later in the night, when I was mingling among the wrestlers, showing them some moves, and encouraging some who were getting ready to wrestle, I was approached by a fan wearing the opposing team's sweatshirt. It was my old buddy, Paul Diaz. Paul was our heavyweight wrestler back in 1988 at East Hartford High School. Paul and I also played together on East Hartford's State Championship football team that same school year.

It was wonderful catching up with Paul, who retired a few years ago as a correctional officer. We left that night saying that we'd have to meet up sometime for a cup of coffee, as my wife commented that she can't take me anywhere without someone knowing me there…

Saturday morning, Dakota woke up one pound underweight. Yeah! Maybe now we can get back to some normalcy and put the holiday weight problems behind us. Now, let's hope the wrestling scale that Dakota has to weigh-in on later this morning is calibrated exactly like our home scale.

I dropped Dakota off at school at 6:45 A.M. for him to catch the bus for the hour-plus ride. My wife and I soon followed the team up in our car after making sure that our other four children were all set for the day.

At 8:45, my wife Jenn and I enter the gymnasium and find out that Dakota made weight with a pound to spare. Very cool! It looks like our home scale was correct, or at least the same as theirs. We're so relieved. However, what we hear next isn't so good.

While Dakota was a pound under, our team's 132-pound captain was a pound over. He didn't make weight and won't be allowed to wrestle at the 132-pound weight class today. And that stinks. But, that's how wrestling goes sometimes. And that's also how life some-times goes, too. We don't always get what we want. And we don't al-ways get what we think we worked hard for and what we think we deserve.

The day's wrestling starts off at the 126-pound weight class again, and Dakota steps on the mat ready to wrestle when his weight class is called. At the center of the mat, the referee raises his hand immedi-ately. Dakota looks a little confused. It turns out that Dakota won by forfeit because the other team didn't have a wrestler in his weight class. Dakota would face the same exact scenario again later in the day for his second match and fourth match as well.

"What the heck is happening to the sport of wrestling?" I wonder. Is the sport just too hard for kids today? Or do they have too many other options to choose from now? Or is it something else? We never had forfeits like this when I wrestled. Heck, we were three deep in most weight classes. And so were most of the teams we went against.

Dakota was awarded three wins today without wrestling those three matches. I mean three wins is a great thing to have on your rec-ord, but I don't think anyone really wants to see him win like that if it can somehow be avoided.

Thankfully, there was someone for Dakota to wrestle for his third match. Although it wasn't exactly a regular match. For his third match, they didn't have anyone either. So, they gave him an exhibition match against a jayvee kid who also needed someone to wrestle. Dakota dominated his opponent and quickly pinned him. At the end of the match, I spoke with Dakota. I told him that it's nice every once in a while to wrestle a kid his own age. This way, he can see that the varsity battles and the varsity beatings that he has been enduring on a daily basis are paying off.

At the end of the day, the referee, Dave LeBlanc, who is also an old buddy of mine from East Hartford, congratulated Dakota for wrestling so well. Dave had another referee with him who I didn't recognize immediately.

The other referee was Dave's son, Tyler, who I used to watch him wrestle for East Hartford when I was coaching New Britain. I shook hands with Tyler and exchanged greetings. I then told him that the last time I saw him, he still looked like a boy. Now, he certainly doesn't look like a boy anymore. He's obviously developed into a good young man who shook my hand, looked me in the eyes, and was very polite.

Tyler is taller than his Dad, Dave, just like my son Dakota is already taller than me. As I look at Tyler and Dave, I think how cool it is that they are refereeing wrestling together. I then wonder as I stare at them together as father and son, if in some ways, they represent what Dakota and I will be in another decade from now...

What a great day of wrestling! Our team won all their matches today. And so did, Dakota, too. Also, my wife and I got to know better some of the other team parents who were in the stands with us. I even got to show a few wrestling moves to some of the wrestlers in between matches. And when the wrestlers' bus finally pulled back into our high school's parking lot, Jenn and I took Dakota out for an early dinner. He even got to eat something besides egg whites, oatmeal, and carrot sticks. Don't worry. He'll be doing some extra workouts during the upcoming week with me. So, as I just said, it was a great day of wrestling!

Brian Preece: As I read about Daniel's week and all the forfeits, it makes me curious about the state of wrestling in Connecticut compared to Utah. I think maybe wrestling is a bit healthier here in Utah. It fits in well with the culture of the Church of Jesus Christ of Latter-Day Saints (more commonly called the Mormon Church). The church's founder Joseph Smith was a prominent "catch wrestler" in the early 1800s. He was nominated for the National Wrestling Hall of Fame by 1984 Olympic gold medalist Mark Schultz, who converted to Mormonism and led the BYU program for several years.

And a good share of people who love wrestling knows that Cael Sanderson prepped in Utah. So it doesn't hurt having arguably the country's greatest-ever wrestler, and certainly, today's top college coach, hail from your state. He is basically Utah's Dan Gable. And his father Steve is one of the legendary high school coaches in our state. And he is still going at it developing state champions and All-Americans.

Our USA Wrestling Utah organization is solid right now. We went to a unique model that most other states don't use, an actual business model. Most states, and Utah until recently, relied on volunteer Dads (and Moms) to lead the organization. But, it was decided, and admittedly we had a wealthy benefactor to help get things started, to make the USA Wrestling Utah president a paid position. There are other paid positions in our organization as well. And when I said paid,

I mean paid as in a career. This is their full-time job. One aspect of their pay comes from running events. The Executive Director, Jeff Newby, runs all sorts of events all year long from youth events, girls-only events, and high school events. Newby is fantastic. He is brilliant, and his energy seems boundless. Through his efforts, our youth numbers have really grown. And we've been able to organize a lot of national teams for our youth and high school wrestlers. We have two youth clubs that are in the top ten in size in the country.

But at the same time, Utah isn't immune to the things Daniel is seeing in Connecticut. We have plenty of high school programs that can't field complete teams. And we do have a wealth gap. Those programs that have developed youth programs are doing great, others can't fill their squads. And since Utah does allow jayvee wrestlers a chance to go to state, those programs that can attract numbers and quality athletes to fill these slots really have an advantage. I think our state tends to cater to the elite wrestlers very well but comes up a bit short in helping our struggling programs. And I have challenged USA Wrestling Utah to reach out to some of our struggling urban and rural programs with clinics and camps, and whatever other ideas they might have to recruit athletes to our great sport. Also, while our youth wrestling numbers are high per capita, there seems to be a drop off in numbers between youth and junior high wrestling. And then there is another drop off between junior high wrestling to high school wrestling. Many theories abound, including the idea that maybe we're burning out athletes with too many ultra-competitive experiences too soon. Who knows?

The school I coached at until I retired last school year, Provo High School, has undergone a substantial demographic transition. In 1950 the school was generally all White students. In 1994-95 when I started teaching there, the school had maybe five percent ethnic minority students. Now in 2020, it's nearly 45% ethnic minority (mostly Latinx), and if the trends hold, the school will have more students of color than White students by decade's end. Our school generally didn't/doesn't integrate these minority students well into our sports and clubs. Thus, our successes in sports started to taper off.

However, I do give credit that our most recent administrations have made a huge effort in this area. They are making the school more inclusive, but these efforts to change the general trajectory of things will take time, of course. In 1999-2000, we were named the top school for 4A sports, but for the last several years, we have been near or at the very bottom. Between 1997-2000, our program attracted around 65-70 wrestlers. Now we have about 20-25 wrestlers, and four of them were female wrestlers. (It should be noted that girls wrestling in Utah has exploded and our state will sanction girls wrestling for the 2020-21 school year.). The good news is that the wrestling program now truly represents the ethnic make-up of our school and that we did have a wrestler become a 2X state champion.

That 2X state champion wrestler was our 285-pound wrestler who had to lose 20-25 pounds the past three seasons to make the weight. He is also a Polynesian or Pacific Islander and was a great football player who signed to play for the Air Force Academy. Our school does have a significant Pacific Islander population. So it is hoped that his success can help attract more athletes from the football program and Pacific Islander population.

I bring this up because our more diverse and less affluent high schools are generally struggling. The Latinx population isn't integrating as well in the dominant (religious) culture of Utah, as they might in surrounding states. This means that a far lower percentage of Latinx students participate in high school sports (and wrestling) in Utah than Arizona, California, or Nevada. And perhaps there might be a double-edged sword to the success of USAWrestling Utah. To really participate at its fullest levels, it does take a bit of money.

Also, the concept of the high-school teacher/coach is dying. More and more programs are led by paraprofessionals (non-teachers). The turnover of high school coaches is enormous. Teaching itself has become so overwhelming that it is hard to get teachers to coach anything, let alone wrestling.

I feel as a coach I was blessed because several times, I had two assistant coaches that were also teachers. And I think this is a much better model. When schools can't find a teacher to coach, then many times a wrestler's Dad becomes the head coach of the team. And even if they know wrestling, they are not apt to last past their son's time in the program. Also, while there, they usually don't have the connections in the school to build up numbers and track their athlete's progress in school and other things coaches have to do these days. And now, our state makes all coaches go through a certification program. This is easier for teachers who are coaches versus Dads because they are more readily available to the school's athletic director.

Utah is also pretty laissez-faire about transfers, and parents can "choice" their students into any school they want for their ninth-grade year. There is no "play where you live" rules in Utah. So naturally, in any sport, athletes tend to end up at a select few schools, especially in the urban areas. So our state has "football schools", "baseball schools", "basketball schools" and of course "wrestling schools". My All-American wrestler was openly recruited by three different schools. And none of the schools were ever sanctioned by our state association.

And lastly, our high school wrestling coaches association has really waned in recent years in both numbers and influence. Back 20 or so years ago, the organization held clinics for wrestlers and coaches, and it was a much closer community. It was a community of coaches that worked hard for the best interest and growth of the sport. And again, I think the reason for this is too many head coaches are paraprofessionals, and the coaching turnover is so high right now. I believe Utah wrestling has a solid foundation. However, it's more potent at the younger levels. Unfortunately, our high school wrestlers haven't performed as well in national tournaments as they did the previous two decades. Whether this is a trend to be concerned about or just a lull remains to be seen.

CHAPTER TWENTY

MAKING MEMORIES

Dan Blanchard: Dang! Another crazy weekend that was overflowing with a ton of stress from things that were outside of the regular family issues and sports. Unfortunately, Dakota and I didn't do any night workouts at all this weekend.

However, even though we had an overwhelming and stressful weekend, it still kind of ended on a positive note. My wife, Jennifer, and I decided that we needed to have a family movie night consisting of a Star Wars movie. Yeah… that would be a nice way to end the crazy weekend. Our family of seven cuddled up together on our over-sized couch with popcorn and snacks could be just what the doctor ordered, if you know what I mean?

Dakota was trying to show some restraint with snacking because he didn't get in any extra workouts this weekend. He's been having a lot of trouble making weight lately. But, about ten minutes into the movie, he asked if he could have some snacks anyway.

I told him, "Sure! Just show some self-discipline because whatever you eat now, you're going to have to run off later."

He ate some snacks, and he did show some restraint at first. But… not a whole lot of control in the end. A couple of times, my wife and I looked at him and said, "Well, I guess you're going to be doing some extra running this week!"

He did his best to ignore us.

About halfway through the Star Wars movie, which we had just bought new from the store, the film lost its picture. We could hear the characters speaking, and the weapons firing, but the picture was gone entirely.

Go figure… I guess it was just one of those weekends…

However, I think the movie going out on us was a blessing in disguise because with the film unexpectedly ending early, so did all of the snacking. And it's a good thing the eating ended prematurely because Dakota woke up on Monday morning at 132- pounds. Now he needs to lose four pounds to be able to wrestle in Wednesday night's match…

This week continues with some challenges and stress. Dakota has trouble finishing up all of his homework for school. He doesn't seem to have transferred the success principle of working hard in wrestling to working hard everywhere else, too, yet. However, Dakota does have the beginnings of knowing how to work hard now, thanks to wrestling. And if he continues to work hard in wrestling, then I'm convinced that eventually working hard will become ingrained in him. And ultimately, his habit or working hard will transfer over to other areas of his life as well. These things take time though…

In addition, we don't always succeed by just working harder or working longer. Sometimes we have to use skill and strategies, like time management tricks. I've spoken to Dakota about doing some of the things I do in keeping up with my enormous workload. Just do a little bit of work every time you get a chance. Maybe you get up earlier. Perhaps it's while you're waiting for the bus. Maybe it's on the bus. Perhaps it's during lunchtime. Maybe it's right after school before sports start.

Dakota shook his head and said, "I can't do homework on the bus. How would I even balance my notebooks and textbooks?"

To tell you the truth, I don't care if he does homework on the bus or not. I just want him to steal whatever little moments he can throughout the day to get his homework done, or whatever else he has to do. It's called time management… and it's important if one wants to be successful...

Wednesday night, I stay late at work and head over to Dakota's match from New Britain. This worked out well since the wrestling meet was just the next town over from where I work, which is an hour away from home. My wife couldn't make it to the wrestling meet because she had to bring our daughters to soccer.

When I finally get to wrestling, I can't believe my eyes. Standing at the scoring table is the Connecticut refereeing legend, Ray Mainville. Ray has been around the sport of wrestling in Connecticut for 52- years. He was one of the two referees who refereed my State Championship match over 30-years ago. The other referee that called my State Championship match was Dr. Abraham Chamie. Unfortunately, Abe wasn't there on this particular night. But, I have been lucky enough to reconnect with Abe, too, over the years. We go out for coffee about every six months or so.

Tonight, it was great to see Ray Mainville again. My boy Dakota has so enriched my life by bringing me back into the wrestling fold. Here I continually find myself once again among my old wrestling family from the good old days.

After catching up with Ray, and finding out that Dakota made weight by one-tenth of a pound, I head toward the team and see Coach Torres' million dollar smile once again. He informs me that we're wrestling the #3 team in the state. They also have ten wrestlers ranked in the Top 5 in their weight classes!

"Dang!" I think to myself. This is going to be one heck of a night for the boys.

Carrying on with that million-dollar smile of his, Coach Torres then tells me that every single one of our wrestlers has a winning record right now. "Even the freshman, Dakota, has a winning wrestling record so far," as he smiles even bigger. This is the first time every single wrestler of his has had a winning record since he has been the coach there.

However, tonight, even after a valiant effort, many of my son's teammates won't be raising their hands in victory.

When Dakota finally gets his chance to wrestle, he earns the first takedown of the match against an outstanding wrestler. Our fans liven up. Some yell, "Pin him, Dakota." However, this kid Dakota is wrestling is too good to be held down for long. He eventually reverses Dakota to tie up the score 2-2.

In the second period, the other kid picks the top and immediately throws in the legs on my freshman boy, who doesn't really know how to defend himself from leg wrestling yet. Dakota hangs in there tough, but the other kid cranks on his shoulder with a power half-nelson and turns Dakota a few times for back exposure points.

The third period Dakota picks neutral. Even though he's a bit worn out from battling those legs and power half-nelsons, he almost gets the takedown. But the other wrestler hits a sweet maneuver and managed to get to the side, and then eventually behind Dakota to secure a takedown.

Again, the other wrestler throws in legs and punishes Dakota with that power half-nelson some more. I find myself rubbing my own sore shoulder that I had surgery on as I watch him turn Dakota a few more times for more back exposure points. On the positive side, though, he couldn't pin Dakota. I'm really impressed.

Dakota lasted the entire six minutes with an excellent wrestler from an outstanding team. And Dakota only lost 14-2. As far as I'm concerned, that is a victory of sorts for my 14-year old boy who is new to wrestling. Dakota doesn't see it that way, though. After the match, he is so upset with losing that he can't even talk to me when I approach him. He just turns and walks away.

It would have been easy to be offended at that moment as a parent. But, because I spent so many years as a coach, I know anger is the inner-workings of a champion in the making. I must admit, though, that it was a lot easier to see and handle it from other parents' sons while coaching than at that moment as a parent just trying to help my own boy.

Thursday morning Dakota woke up at 130-pounds, which is two pounds over his weight class again. It looks like the cycle continues. I'm trying to get him to hang out at a bodyweight of 128-129 pounds, so making weight won't be so hard. But, we haven't gotten there yet... Oh, well... I suppose it's better than the 132-pounds he was on Monday morning. However, anything can happen before Saturday's weigh-ins if Dakota isn't vigilant... And if he isn't, he'll be doing a lot of running before weigh-ins again.

I get to see the very end of Friday night's practice as I chat with the coaches a bit. After practice, I see something that I've never seen before and then something else that I've seen a lot of over the years. First, these guys come out of nowhere with this very mysterious mist spray that they apply to the mats. They look like they should be wearing Space Martian suits, but they're not. I ask the coach what that is, and he tells me that they are fogging the mat. I've never heard of that terminology before. But I guess they were disinfecting the mats with their new really special mist spray... Times have changed... As the kids are checking their weight after practice, I hear something familiar from the old days. The coach is talking about how one of our wrestlers has ringworm, but he should be fine to wrestle the next day because he has a doctor's note.

Unfortunately, I did not get to see Dakota wrestle in Saturday's tournament. One of many side jobs pulled me away for the entire day. My wife, Jennifer, kept me informed though. Mid-morning she texted me that Dakota won his first match 9-1. I showed everyone at work the text. I was pumped. Later, my wife texted me that Dakota's next kid is very good. I texted her back, "Damn," and told everyone at work about it. They all said, "Damn." Too.

In the early afternoon, my wife, Jenn, texted me that Dakota got pinned. I once again shared that with everyone at work. They all said they were sorry, and that maybe he'll get the next one. He'll have to win the next one if he's going to make it to the semifinals to wrestle for 3rd and 4th place. If he makes it to the semifinals, then I'll have a chance of seeing him.

Late afternoon, I and everyone I work with at the American Federation of Teachers in Rocky Hill, Connecticut are holding our breath for the next text message from Jenn. The text finally comes… Dakota was losing 7-0, and then came storming back to take the lead in points. He then tried to hit a move and missed it, causing him to land on his back and get pinned while he was ahead in points.

We're all heart-broken for Dakota. I guess I won't get to see him wrestle tonight because he is now out of the double-elimination tournament. However, even though I'm sad my freshman boy lost in the varsity tournament, I'm glad he went down swinging for the fences. You have to give it your all in life. You can't always play it safe. Also, my wife, Jennifer, said that this was probably the best she has seen Dakota wrestle so far.

When I do get out of work and drive the hour to get to the wrestling tournament, I get to watch the semifinals and finals and support some of Dakota's teammates. Several of the parents tell me that they can't believe how well my freshman boy wrestled in this varsity tournament today. I'm beaming as a proud father should be.

Also, Coach Crudden, another Connecticut wrestling legend, came out of the stands to talk to Dakota and me. He shared that he was watching Dakota and he was very impressed with how well Dakota wrestled. That means a lot coming from Crudden.

To cap the day off, my old heavyweight teammate Paul Diaz from the old days was there too, and we got to talk again. As we were chatting, Coach Flynn, the Enfield coach, came up to me and said that he has been really enjoying my wrestling blog. I remember watching Flynn wrestle for Fermi when I was coaching New Britain many years ago. He was tough and one heck of a wrestler. And it felt wonderful to hear him say that he's been following my blog. I'm pumped that he is really enjoying it from the parenting side of raising a boy into a good young man through the sport of wrestling.

Finally, at the very end of the night, I walked by the referee from East Hartford, Tyler LeBlanc. We both stopped and shook hands. I said that it was a nice day of wrestling. He agreed and responded with, "I like wrestling." Me too, I thought...

Brian Preece: For some reason, Daniel's writing this week reminded me of a funny story when I wrestled a 2-time state champion from one of our region league rivals. I went out and shot a bad double leg, which was just a set-up for my outside Kelly fireman's carry. And whoa and behold, I scored the takedown. Then we went out of bounds. As I took the referee's position, I hung my head on the side instead of being in the legal position of resting my head in the middle of the back on the bottom wrestler. The referee didn't care and blew his whistle. My opponent while executing his stand-up took his elbow and threw it back right into my face. I was seeing stars. He then reversed me and pinned me within seconds. I was still stunned as the official raised his hand and directed me toward my bench. Then according to my teammates, I asked this fateful question. "Did I win?" Everyone, including my own coaches, busted up laughing. Then one of them said, "No, Preece, you didn't win." But then I said somewhat proudly, "Well, at least I took the state champ down."

Because my Dad was a coach, I got to know a lot of the referees over the years, even before I actually started wrestling. Some of the high school officials also worked the junior high meets. One of my Dad's favorite officials was a guy named Jerry Pace. He was a former state placer from a rural town about thirty minutes east of Salt Lake. I think he was a rancher like my Dad was and certainly a cowboy too. My Dad considered him one of the best officials in the state. And when I started officiating right out of high school, he told me to observe Pace closely.

In my sophomore year, I placed third in the Granite District Tournament. So, in my junior year, when I found myself in the semifinals at the same tournament, I wanted to do better this time than the year before. My opponent was pretty tough, and he was from a good program. He would also be the wrestler I would end up wrestling for the region championship two months later. But in this particular match, my sense of fashion as a wrestler played an interesting role.

I wore long socks a lot and sometimes no socks at all because a lot of the college wrestlers were doing that back then. And I wanted to be cool like them. But this particular day at the Granite District Tournament was a long sock day. And I had rolled up two dollar bills and stuffed them in my left sock. I forgot all about them, and while wrestling, they came out of the sock. When we went out of bounds and came back to the center to restart, Referee Pace asked us if any of us lost some money. I sheepishly affirmed that I did. Then Pace, with a dead-pan expression, goes, "Geez Preece, trying to pay me off?" He then stuffed the money in his back pocket and blew the whistle. I ended up winning the match 3-2 to go to the finals all on my own without paying off the ref. I think Pace joked with my Dad and told him, "Tell your kid to take better care of his money," or something to that effect.

This ended up not being a good tournament, in the end, for me, though. In my next match, I was wrestling my Dad's "favorite wrestler," or who he often told people was his favorite wrestler. After coaching at Uintah, my Dad took a job at Cyprus High School located in Magna in Salt Lake County. He coached there for four years. In his final year of coaching, in walked a wrestler named David Vialpando. David was of pure natural talent. And in a dual meet, he upset the top-ranked kid in the state from Uintah, where my Dad formerly coached. In fact, the wrestler he beat wrestled with me in my Dad's little league program. And David won the match in Vernal, the other kid's home turf.

I remember seeing a photo of David jumping into my Dad's arms after that match. It's perhaps my Dad's favorite coaching photograph. The picture of them is a bit out of focus, but the crowd isn't, and in the back row of the audience were some of the "old-timers" as my Dad called them grinning ear to ear. Later, in the state tournament, the Uintah wrestler would win the rematch, and David would finish fourth in the state. But not bad for a first-year wrestler. David loved my Dad and had total faith in his coaching. I think that's why my Dad really loved David. But my Dad got out of coaching the next season to sell insurance. David was having a great year and even beat the wrestler that made me see stars. He would win the region, but then he got a kidney infection and couldn't wrestle in the state tournament.

Now, here at the Granite District Tournament, we were both in the 126-pound weight class. When the 112-pound matches were called up, I started heading down the bleachers from the top to get warmed up. I was in mid jog and then I tripped and tumbled a few steps down landing on the floor to the ovation of everyone in the crowd. It was embarrassing. And to add insult to injury, minutes later, David pinned me. Thankfully, and he didn't need to do this, later in the season, he went down to 119-pounds and took State with an undefeated record. With him at 119, I was able to win the region title by beating the same guy I wrestled in the semifinals of this tournament. I wonder if David went down a weight to please his old coach, my Dad. He would have easily won the 126-pound title too. But I'm grateful he did go down because I then won the region title and managed to place sixth in State that year. I think it was a joke, but my Dad said, "It was really tough to coach me against David."

CHAPTER TWENTY-ONE

ILLNESS, INJURY, AND OBSTACLES

Dan Blanchard: Dang! Just as Dakota was starting to turn the corner and really step up his game! This last weekend might have been his best performance in a varsity tournament so far... But here we are again running into some very frustrating obstacles at the beginning of this Week Eight of his regular high school freshman season.

Dakota woke up Sunday morning four pounds overweight. The cycle of his distressed weight management continues. And not only has that, but his knee problems and neck problem continued as well. And now a swollen, black and blue, puffy ear has also finally arrived on the scene. I let Dakota know that he needs to wear his headgear in wrestling practice, or he's going to get a cauliflower ear. And it will hurt, along with everything else.

My wife, Jennifer, suggested that perhaps I shouldn't be telling the whole wide world what is hurting Dakota. This might be unnecessary information that maybe his opponents shouldn't have. After thinking about it for a moment, I replied with, "All wrestlers are hurting from something. That's just how this game is played. It's just a fact of life for a wrestler."

During the day, Dakota asked me a few times about working out so he could lose some weight. But I tell him he has to wait because I'm buried in my responsibilities of a father of five children who works multiple jobs. Yes! Even on a Sunday! The good Lord might have rested on the 7th day, but unfortunately, I can't.

Eventually, Dakota told me he's going out for a run on his own, instead. He also mentioned that his knee is sore. I told him not to run. And that maybe later I can hopefully get him to the gym to ride a stationary bike, which will be easier on his knee.

He decided instead to go for a run anyway. And in a way, I can't blame him because he's still an impatient teenage boy who wants things right away, and his father has an overgrown to-do list. Plus, I also know that running is one of the better ways to improve one's conditioning and lose some weight when you're not wrestling or drilling, as long as you bundle up.

Later, Dakota returned from his run. And the first thing he said was, "Dad, my knee hurts." From across the room, I could see that it was swollen. Once I got close to it, I could see that it was the size of a softball. Dang! He looks like he's going to miss some wrestling now. And I don't know how he's going to make weight for Wednesday night's match. I should have looked at his knee before he left for his run. I'm kicking myself for this one.

Dakota wakes up with his big puffy knee still there on Monday morning. He can barely walk. I followed his old man walk into the bathroom, where he checked his weight. This is becoming our morning routine. Crap! He's 134-pounds. Now he's six pounds over his weight class, and he can barely move. This is not good.

Now I'm very concerned about him making weight for Wednesday night's match. I honestly have no idea how he's going to wrestle, or how he's even going to make weight if he can somehow compete. I also know that this must be tearing my 14-year old boy up on the inside, too.

My wife, Jenn, and I go back and forth on what steps to take next. I keep insisting that he sees the school's athletic department trainer. Jenn keeps insisting that she take him to the doctor's office, and then she'll bring him into school later to see the trainer.

I assume most of us out there already know how this is going to go down when a mother bear has a hurt child. Jenn wins this one, and Dakota goes to the doctor's office with his Mom that morning, and then the orthopedic specialist later that afternoon. Then he finally goes to the athletic trainer at the school.

It doesn't look like he'll wrestle on Wednesday... Maybe he'll be ready to wrestle on Saturday...

Wednesday comes and goes, and Dakota doesn't wrestle. He sits on the team bench, and I sit in the bleachers showing other parents pictures of Dakota's knee to help explain why he isn't wrestling. All the parents are very nice. They all say that he's just a freshman, he's got plenty of time to wrestle still. So it's not a big deal. The important thing is for his knee to get healthy so he can compete again when it's the right time.

I fully agree with them. But, I also know that it was not easy for Dakota and me to just sit there and not have anything invested in our team's win that night. And win they did. They won big. It was a bittersweet night though. And Dakota is still four pounds overweight...

"WHAT! What do you mean Dakota is being rushed to the emergency room?" I hear myself asking my wife, Jennifer, who had just called me at school on Friday afternoon.

"I will meet you at the Hartford Children's Hospital as soon as I can get out of here," I say, trying to soothe Jenn.

When I arrive at the hospital, I see Dakota is in the most pain he has ever been in before. He's holding his stomach and squirming around while his waves of heavy breathing fill our ears and tug at our insides.

"How long has this been going on? I ask Jenn.

"For about four hours now. And this isn't even the worst of it. The pain was way worse earlier."

"Have they given him anything for the pain?" I ask.

"No. The doctors haven't because they might have to operate," Jenn lets me know.

Oh, my gosh! As a parent, you all can imagine how the worse is going through my mind. They're going to cut my little boy open. He's going to be in crazy pain for a long time! His wrestling season is over. He may never wrestle again… He's going to miss a bunch of school. He's right in the middle of midterm exams. The medical bills are going to be crazy expensive. I have what used to be good medical insurance as a public employee teacher. But, they have been chipping away at my coverage a little bit every year. It's a disgrace what has happened to our medical coverage that I pay good money into every week. Jenn and I try not to even go to the doctors anymore if we can help it. And that's an injustice none of us should have to face.

Life shouldn't be this way. Just like so many of you out there, we're just middle of the road, middle-class people, who work hard every day. We try to raise our children the best we can so they can go forth someday and do their part in making this world a better place. But, obstacle after obstacle appears in our paths, and as all of you out there already know, life is just plain hard. It's never easy. And it's never a straight road from point A to point B. And that's a fact, isn't it?

We're worried stiff over what's going to happen to Dakota. And then something amazing happens… Do you remember that scene in the Forrest Gump Movie where Forrest, played by Tom Hanks, just stops running for no reason at all, and says, "I think I'll go home now? Well, believe it or not, while still squirming in pain, Dakota, all of a sudden, sits up and says, "I think I'll go home now." Out of nowhere, the crippling, debilitating pain just stopped. And now he was ready to go home.

How weird…? What the heck just happened? Soon after, all of Dakota's medical tests returned negative. But the doctors kept Dakota for a couple more hours of observation just in case he relapsed. After a few more hours of laying in one of those little beds in the emergency room, they told us that it might be viral, and to go home. Call them or bring him back if it starts up again.

I let Coach Torres and Coach Rogers know why Dakota missed wrestling practice. They responded back that I should keep Dakota home from Saturday's wrestling. We all obviously have mixed emotions. Dakota wasn't going to wrestle anyway because of his huge knee, but it would have been nice to at least sit on the bench with the team. And now throw into the mix this whole mystery viral thing, too... And once again, life is a mixed-up bag of tossed around emotions, thoughts, and dreams.

Maybe this is a blessing in disguise... Maybe Dakota needed a week off... Let's all hope for the best for Monday... And for the team today. Since I am not at wrestling today, I thought I'd at least write about wrestling today. And after I do a bunch of snow shoveling this weekend, I sure would love to see Dakota healthy and back out there on the mats on Monday as he continues his pursuit of someday becoming a State Champion or at least a good man... Speaking of a good man, he's going to have to help me shovel some snow this weekend, regardless of his knee or this mystery viral thing...

Brian Preece: As I read about Daniel's week, I too was anxious about whatever it was that was ailing Dakota. I was guessing maybe an appendicitis. I had my appendix removed in January of 1977 when I was 11 years-old. I remember, it was a Thursday and I felt sick the whole day. My Dad had lined up an exhibition match for me before a dual meet with a coach's son from a team from Idaho, or maybe it was Colorado. This team was coming in the night before for a dual meet before the big Tournament of Champions that weekend. I felt the pressure to go wrestle but was sick all day.

My Mom called my Dad, who was teaching, and told him that I shouldn't wrestle that night. I got sicker and sicker and missed the meet. I was worried I was letting my Dad down. The next day I got worse and my temperature soared. My Dad was at school as the tournament was on its way. Meanwhile, I stayed home from school, and after my temperature spiked pretty high, my Mom rushed me off to the hospital. Our family doctor served as the surgeon, and my appendix was about to burst according to him. Also, the anesthetic didn't work properly. I guess I woke up in the middle of the procedure and exclaimed, "Dr. Stringham, this really hurts!" They put me back under, and I got through the surgery. But as I regained consciousness, I guess I cussed like a sailor, and my Mom was pretty embarrassed. I cussed at everyone, I guess, and used a lot of foul language that my Mom didn't know I knew.

Now remember this was way before cell phones, so it was hard for my Mom to communicate with my Dad about the surgery and so forth. Then the next day, the second day of the tournament, I was anxious to know what was going on. My Dad visited the hospital after the championship finals, and I had to know how they finished. He told me they lost to Montrose (Colorado) by a half-point. I was bummed out more than he was. Now this was before Track Wrestling and as it turned out a scoring mistake was made and Uintah had actually won the tournament. But my Dad said he was never going to call up their school and tell them to give the first place trophy back. He was the host school and he felt responsible for the mistake. But he did count it as one of the 50 tournaments he won as a coach. By the way, my Mom was usually the head scorer of the tournaments, and she was very good at numbers. But she wasn't there that day because she was with me. So maybe that's why the mistake was made.

Things have changed over the years. Now you hear about athletes in our current time that have appendectomies, and they are back competing in less than 24 hours. But back then, it was a bit more serious procedure in the sense that you were actually cut open, and there were stitches. Or, in my case, a long six-inch stitch. The stitch wouldn't be taken out for at least a week, and my parents were told to have me take it easy for the next month in regards to wrestling and such. To be honest, I didn't mind as I wasn't really enjoying wrestling that much at that time in my life. I didn't like the weekend trips to Salt Lake or other places that were several hours away that required us all to get up at 4:00 in the morning. But by the end of February, I was back at it.

Oh, by the way, if you want to know how much of a wrestling town Vernal is versus say basketball, I won the Shoot, Pass, and Dribble contest for my fourth grade year. The winner of the fifth-grade division was Pat Jenkins, who would become a 3X state champion wrestler. So wrestlers even dominated the basketball scene too in Vernal. The Shoot, Pass, and Dribble is the basketball version of the Punt, Pass, and Kick. You shoot from different spots, see how many wall passes you can do in a certain amount of time, and then dribble through cones for speed. And I won against kids from five other elementary schools from the county. Of course, the local paper, the *Vernal Express,* covered the event, and my photo was taken with the winners of the fifth and sixth grades.

I was pretty pleased with myself. My Dad got ribbed pretty good from his coaching friends and even some of his wrestlers, but he was actually very proud of me. I still have the plaque somewhere in my shed. My Dad was actually a pretty good basketball player in high school, so I guess having some ability in the sport isn't totally shocking. I was probably in the top ten or so in my high school class as a basketball player, not really good enough to make the team as no coach is going to take ten seniors, but maybe if I worked at it I could have made our team.

My younger brother Scott was better than me and actually played basketball and wrestled in junior high. The basketball coach in high school really wanted him to play and was willing to work with my Dad about making a schedule work so he could be part of their program. He was a pretty darn good point guard. What was weird was that my Dad didn't mind either of us playing church basketball. Mormons are known for their love of the round ball. And their church leagues at this time were legendary for opening with a prayer, followed by some pretty competitive hoops, and plenty of fights among the saints. While most of Dakota's meets were on Wednesday nights, our dual meet night was typically Thursday. Wednesday was church basketball, and I would play all the time. It was a good way to cut some weight. I remember scoring 32 points in a game once and wondering why I was wrestling.

Believe it or not, my Dad was also not against his athletes skiing. I think he wouldn't have allowed it while at Uintah. But at Skyline, where I went, was a different story. My high school was generally in an affluent area, and many students liked to ski. And I was introduced to it in junior high. Our school had a ski program where they took students up skiing. Can you imagine public schools doing that in our day of lawyers, liability and lawsuits? So forbidding skiing with his wrestlers was not going to go over well for my Dad. And if other wrestlers were allowed to ski, I wanted to ski too. I did wise up my senior year, though, and didn't ski after Christmas break. For some reason, somebody told me that six weeks was "the normal recovery time for a blown-out knee," so I figured it would be safe to ski over Christmas break. I could be back by region in early February if the worst were to happen. When the wrestling season was over, there was no freestyle for me. I was on the slopes until April. Then on to golf. And I did all of this around my job at a grocery store.

Unlike Dakota, I was pretty fortunate with the injuries in high school. In fact, I only missed one practice. Well, I actually went to practice but didn't work out. It was in between region and state my sophomore season where sometimes different schools liked to get together and work out. Our team drove about 30 minutes to work out with Viewmont High School, who was coached at that time by Steve Sanderson, the father of legendary wrestler Cael Sanderson. Oh, by the way, Cael's brothers, Cody, Cole and Cyler, are pretty tough too! My back hurt and I was urinating a bit of blood over the weekend. I probably had a kidney infection. So I sat on the side and watched intently the Viewmont wrestler who I thought I might meet at the state meet. We didn't meet. He finished third in the State, and I was knocked out the round before we would have met in the consolation semifinals. Oh well.

But as a coach, I've had plenty of wrestlers that have had to sit out because of injuries. You can really feel Dakota's and Daniel's frustrations with the injury situation. As a coach, you have to see the big picture, and of course, Dakota needs to see the big picture too. I've seen a lot of coaches push things too much, and they have injured wrestlers compete and even practice when they need to be resting, or at the very least just working on cardio. Knee injuries are always interesting because ACL tears are season-enders, while sometimes the damage is just fluid in the knee, and a few days rest can do the trick. I had a wrestler, a senior, wrestle his last three weeks with meniscus tears in both knees. But as he told me, "I'm a senior, and I'm not planning on going out for track or soccer." In my heart, his knees cost him the state title, but he's a champion in my eyes.

CHAPTER TWENTY-TWO

THE "WHAT IFS"

Dan Blanchard: Well, we survived shoveling our 640-foot dirt-driveway in the frigid cold, snow, and ice this weekend. But, outside of doing what we had to do to survive another New England storm, there wasn't much else going on.

The weather kept the kids out of school, so there was no wrestling practice. The weather has also kept Dakota pacing in our living room and dining room. He's filled with mixed emotions. With every day that passes without any wrestling, his knee and other injuries are getting better. And thank goodness he hadn't had another stomach episode since Friday when we had to rush him to the emergency room for what we thought was a ruptured appendix.

But… and it's a long but… It's also now Tuesday, and Dakota is getting rustier by the day. He's falling more and more out of wrestling shape. And he's also five pounds overweight for tomorrow's match. Getting better or getting his weight down… How do we choose? This sure is a tough sport! It's a maker of men! It forces one's hand almost on a daily basis. There is no sitting on the fence in this sport.

Well... it turns out that Dakota and I aren't going to have to choose, after all. The trainer just let us know that he examined Dakota's knee and that Dakota will stay on the sideline as just an observer for the rest of this week. Another week out. And another week for Dakota to pace my living room and dining room floor... Is this another one of the blessings in disguise? Well, right now, it doesn't feel like it... However, I suppose time will tell...

On the car ride home, Dakota shared with me how frustrated he was with the whole unfortunate situation. The other kids are getting better, and all he can do right now is just watch and hope his knee heals soon.

Wednesday night finds me again in the stands watching our high school wrestling team wrestle. My eyes wander over to my boy Dakota sitting on the bench injured. Yeah... you've guessed it. This is a real bummer for all of us. The good thing is that Dakota's knee seems to be getting better every day, and his team wrestled a great match tonight. They pulled out a great victory even though they had to give up several forfeits that gave the other side six points for each one.

Also, as I was watching the other team wrestle, I noticed that two of their wrestlers were kids that Dakota wrestled with over the summer at John Knapp's. So, that was kind of cool. And even cooler... their coach was Paul Myers, another guy whom I've known for a long time.

Back when I was the New Britain coach, Paul was one of the Hartford wrestling coaches. I also wrestled with his younger brother, John Myers, many years ago in the Junior Olympics out in Iowa. And come to think of it, their father, Dr. Ed Myers, used to be my gym teacher in my old high school in East Hartford. The whole Myers family was filled with great wrestlers and was a real force to be wrecking with. Paul and I had a great time catching up some at the end of the meet that night.

On the short seven-minute ride home from Dakota's school, we talked about wrestling, and he told me that his knee was all of a sudden, hurting badly again. I took a look at it when I got home and saw that it once again was the size of a softball. What the heck happen? It was getting better. How the heck did it blow back up? We were all figuring he'd be wrestling again on Monday. How long would he be out now? This whole thing was driving Dakota, his dad, and his coaches crazy...

Now the balancing act of my life-responsibilities is getting even trickier. Thursday night, I have to leave for a speech I'm doing in Red Lion, Pennsylvania. It's a six-hour car drive, and I'm going to be gone for a couple of days. Dakota is going back to the doctor's office on Friday to get his softball-size knee drained. And since my wife is with me, neither of us will be there for him. Thank God, grandma will.

My first speech in Red Lion, PA. is for the Superintendent Scott Deisley and his administration team. It goes very well, and Superintendent Scott Deisley really makes me feel like part of their family. After the speech, we went over to Red Lion High School to watch a colossal college wrestling match between Lock Haven and Arizona State University.

The Red Lion School District really goes the extra mile. Superintendent Scott Deisely and Athletic Director Arnie Fritzius make sure that my wife and I are having a great time at the match as their special guests. And I can't thank them enough for this special treatment. Scott,

Arnie, and the rest of the Red Lion School District staff, students, parents, and community are doing some amazing things over there.

Sadly, during this incredible night at their fantastic facility, my wife Jennifer is going back and forth on her phone with grandma checking up on Dakota's status. Eventually, the final verdict is in from the doctor. Dakota will be out four to five more weeks. If it's five weeks, his season is over.

Our goal is four weeks for him to get healthy. Then somehow, we have to get him in shape again and enter him in the States. As bad as this may seem, especially to Dakota and his coaches and teammates, there may still be some light at the end of this tunnel. The Red Lion night ended on a very positive beat with Lock Haven University, who was ranked #22 in the country upsetting #12 Arizona State in a thrilling match. There's just something about those Pennsylvania wrestlers…

The next day was a busy one. Saturday morning, I woke up very early to give an amazing speech to the Red Lion School District coaches and athletes. They were a fantastic group. If I lived closer, I think I'd somehow find myself over there a lot.

Right after the speech, Jenn and I jumped into the car and sped back to Connecticut to try to catch some of the wrestling tournament that Dakota and his team were at. Jenn and I got there just in time to see the finals and semifinals. Our team did awesome. We only had nine kids wrestling out of the fourteen weight classes. And out of those nine wrestlers, seven placed. It was a fantastic day for our wrestling team. And we just got inched out at the very end from placing in the top three as a team. Everyone said that if Dakota hadn't been hurt, we absolutely would have taken 3rd place as a team... Oh well... what are you going to do...? That's life... That's just how it goes sometimes... And that's what wrestling teaches you.

Now for a bit of nostalgia. The wrestling tournament was held at Rocky Hill High School, and the head coach Paul Myers. Yeah, he's the same one from this past Wednesday night. So, it was good again to see him and talk to him once more this week. This tournament is called the "Doc Myers Tournament. It's named after Pauls' father, my old high school gym teacher in East Hartford, Dr. Myers, who is a legend of sorts in the Hartford County of Connecticut. I believe Dr. Myers even refereed the 1968 U.S. Wrestling Olympic Trials.

Today's winner of the Doc Myers Tournament was Avon. They had an outstanding performance today. One of the parents told me that Avon is undefeated so far, and it's the best team that they've had since 1986.

I told him that I can still remember that 1986 team of Avon. He smiled big and said proudly that the coach who they presently have was a wrestler on that team. And I responded with, "I know. I wrestled Coach John Mclaughlin in the 1988 semifinals of the Connecticut State Open Championships. Everyone was anticipating that it would be the match of the night! John was the undefeated Class L State Champ, and I was the undefeated Class LL State Champ. It was a great match between two teen titans of the day in which I can still vividly remember every moment of that victory for me."

Wow! Do these blasts from the past ever cease in this amazing sport of wrestling.

Now somehow, we have to keep Dakota's spirits up for the next four weeks. It's not going to be easy, but on the positive side, Dakota is still part of the team, and we will be at all of the wrestling practices and events. And I'm sure we're going to see some excellent wrestling along the way and spend some real quality time with the people who love this sport, too!

Brian Preece: In Utah, theoretically, a team can qualify 28 wrestlers to state. I think a couple of schools have done that. But the 2004-05 team I coached qualified just six wrestlers to the state tournament. Somehow, we finished fifth in the state tournament. We had one state champion, three second-place finishes, one third-place finish, and one wrestler that went 2-2 and just missed placing in state. My "super six" as I called them went 20-6 at the state meet, which made this coach very happy. So I could relate to Dakota's team being small in number but being able to compete well. Quality can often win out over quantity in the wrestling scene. And of course, my high school teams always had "holes" or forfeits.

In 1975, my Dad had his own Super Six. He only qualified six wrestlers to the State tournament but they still won. Five of his grapplers took state and the other wrestler placed fourth going a combined 17-2 in their matches. Pretty impressive!

In my sophomore year, we usually wrestled with eight or nine guys out of 12 weights. I think we had nine full-time wrestlers, but it seemed like somebody was always injured. Regardless, we were able to win some dual meets. We actually qualified eight wrestlers to the state meet, but only five of us ended up winning matches. However, we still placed fourth as a team with two state champs, two thirds, and me going 2-2 and missing placing by one match.

I remember my sophomore year we beat the team that won our region and placed just ahead of us at state in a dual meet. We were able to fill a full squad for that match recruiting some guys literally out of the hall to fill the weights. They probably all got pinned, but it did prevent the other team from shifting wrestlers around for strategic purposes. One was a pretty good athlete, but he was a senior and basically hung it up after his one and only dual meet. I remember pulling off a huge upset over a ranked wrestler, which pleased my head coach (Coach Albright) and teammates very much. My victory proved to be the difference in the dual as we won by three points. I was able to carry a bit of confidence into the region meet where I placed fourth. At state, I got a bit of a break as David Vialpando, the region champ in our weight, had to pull out of the state meet because of a kidney infection. It moved everyone up a position on the bracket.

I became the "third" place wrestler from our region. However, I still had to beat a wrestler that only lost four times that season in the first round. But somehow, I did it. That was truly the highlight of my season. It was the best match I wrestled that year. Then I went against my old youth wrestling nemesis Todd Norton who pinned me. He ended up taking state. I won my next match before losing to a wrestler from Granite High School, the team we beat in that dual but placed ahead of us in state. But I wrestled a different wrestler this time who had cut down a weight class. I lost by a couple of points. I just couldn't escape from him. I feel bad because if I had won that match, we would have taken third place in the state. But so it goes. Hey, I did better than most people expected.

It is frustrating as a coach not being able to compete with a full team or have some devastating injuries. I feel I have some bad luck with all of that. Even the year where we had three state champions mishaps still happened. I had another wrestler that took second place in state the previous season who decided that year to drop out of school to join the Army. The possibility of a fourth state champion, who would have shot us up to a third-place finish in state as a team, still gets to me 20 plus years later. Instead we finished seventh. A couple of seasons later, I had a wrestler tear out his knee in football. He would have definitely been a state title contender. However, his backup did place second in state. Another promising wrestler that year, who was just a junior, broke his leg in a match. It was gruesome, as in Joe Theisman gruesome. I felt this young man had the potential to go to state for us and win a match or two. Oh, the "what ifs…"

But the saddest situation was a wrestler who I had that placed fifth in state as a freshman. Then he suffered a neck injury in football. His career seemed over as he missed his next two seasons. I had to watch wrestlers he dominated throughout junior high and his freshman year take state. He would have been on the super six team, and with him, we again probably would have cracked the top three in state.

However, there is a positive here. Halfway through his senior season, he was somehow cleared to participate. And though he missed two and half years of wrestling, he won region for us and placed fifth in state, which helped us to a fifth-place team finish. But I can't help but think that with more time on the mat, he might have won it all. He would have at least placed second in state as he lost in the quarterfinals to the eventual runner-up in sudden death overtime. He was a teammate of our wrestler that placed second at the NHSCA Senior Nationals held in Pittsburgh (now Virginia Beach). If he stayed healthy, he might have been right up there on the All-American podium as well with his teammate. He was that good of an athlete and wrestler. I mean, who places in state in a middleweight class after missing two and half years and wrestling, with maybe competing in just 15 matches before the state tournament.

But sometimes it's not injuries (or grades or joining the Army) that derail a wrestler's career and a coach's dream of what might have been. When I was an assistant coach at West High School, in the fall before wrestling season, we had one of our top football players shoot someone in a gang-related killing. We had got him to wrestle the school year before, and we figured him and his first cousin would have manned our 171 and 189-pound weight classes. I thought they definitely could have placed at state for us. This was one of my toughest days as an educator because I coached both the shooter and the victim. Another tough day was when another young man who we had got to wrestle was shot and killed, also in a gang-related situation. I think he was a sophomore or maybe a junior, a real natural athlete who I felt could have developed into a good wrestler. This was also a young man who particularly touched my heart as I recruited him to the sport personally. He was beginning to make some strides in the classroom and in life, too. But sometimes it's just too hard to run from your past.

Then there are the athletes who just quit the sport. Sadly, I've had some promising athletes make that decision. In some cases, it was when I recruited a top-notch athlete to wrestle. But when they didn't have the immediate success they expected because they were a good football or baseball athlete, they got a bit frustrated and quit. A couple of times I had wrestlers quit who were so close to turning that corner and becoming contenders to place at region and state. In fact, there are three that come to mind that would have been on that 2004-05 team. In their freshman and sophomore seasons, they beat guys that ended up placing in state. Maybe if they stuck with it, and we didn't have that injury, we could have won state. These wrestlers just needed to trust the process and their own abilities. Oh, the what-ifs! Each case or mishap is unique and always painful. And I realize sometimes injuries drive wrestlers out of the sport. I even one time counseled a wrestler to hang it up. He was a great baseball player and was having shoulder problems. My own desires to have more team points in a tournament, or to win a dual meet, wasn't worth his baseball season and possible scholarship opportunities.

In the end, I hope Dakota can get healthy and doesn't get too frustrated. High school athletes have to balance their commitment to the team, academics, and home responsibilities. Some also have to work. And there are those injuries. But all of this builds character and builds boys into men.

CHAPTER TWENTY-THREE

THOUGHTS ON GABLE VS. OWINGS

Dan Blanchard: It's been tough. Real tough. Dakota has spent his entire life so far as the only boy in a family of seven. He even has a female dog. But recently, he felt like he finally found his place, his sport, his team, and the right group of guys to hang out with, learn from, and become a better man with, too. But now his knee injury is causing him to feel like it's all been taking away from him.

He made varsity as just a freshman. That's a big deal! And he did it as a freshman who hadn't wrestled before. And that's a very big deal. That's something he can be really proud of for the rest of his life. Furthermore, when he steps on those varsity wrestling mats in a tournament as just a freshman, everyone there knows that he's going to win at least a couple of matches.

If a few things go right, he literally has a chance of placing somewhere in almost every varsity wrestling tournament that his team enters… And now, sadly and unfortunately, he's seeing all those amazing experiences not materialize for him because of something that is out of his control, his knee injury. One of the hardest working freshmen wrestlers out there, can't outwork this injury. Rather, he has to sit back and let fate and time take its turn…

Now, as Dakota's Dad, a special education/history teacher, a fellow wrestler, former coach, want-to-be wise man, and aspiring Great Dad, I still don't believe that a dream deferred is a dream denied. It's just a dream on a different time schedule. Furthermore, I also know that if, for some reason, that dream doesn't eventually materialize, then maybe not getting that dream gives one their destiny instead.

For example, Dan Gable, not getting his dream of an undefeated college wrestling career at Iowa, gave him his destiny of eventually becoming the greatest wrestler and coach there ever was. It also gave him the destiny of being named the Athlete of the Century, as well as having his own Dan Gable Wrestling Museum.

You see, in Dan Gable's last match in his final season, he lost to Larry Owings of the University of Washington. Up to this point, Dan Gable had never been beaten. And believe it or not, Gable says that this loss to Owings helped him refocus on wrestling. It got him to step up to the next level, where he'd eventually become a legend that the whole-wide wrestling world will never forget. He went unscored upon in the Olympics!

Pretty cool story, huh? Pretty awesome lesson, too, right? Now, if I can just get my boy to stop pacing my living room floor with that limp, depressed look, and sour demeanor, and see the big picture as I do…

I know… I know… easier said than done, especially when one is right in the middle of it. And, yes, he's still just a boy… Hey, someday my boy will know that his Dad was right… But that moment is still a long way down the road… As I'm sure a lot of you parents out there already know that…

Now back to Dakota's knee. On this Monday night, shockingly, we discovered that Dakota's knee was bigger than ever. And now it has some discoloration, too. And to add to the storm, he's also now ten pounds over his weight class. Things are not looking good at the moment here in the Blanchard household.

"What the heck is going on here?" I'm wondering… He had his knee drained on Friday. It should be getting better. Not worse! And we're losing control of his weight, too.

This must be another test, trial, and tribulation from the Gods of the Wrestling World. The greater forces want to see if Dakota really wants to be that State Champion, or at least a good man someday. But to do this, first, he needs to overcome disappointment and frustration, as well as things that don't seem fair, and still do the right thing…

I've been trying to get Dakota to do some alternative workouts where he doesn't use his knee like core calisthenics and boxing in the basement. But, he is resisting it saying that it doesn't help him lose weight, he needs to run and wrestle. But he can't. I'm working non-stop with all the things I do, so I haven't been able to get him to the gym for some bike riding. Although, Dakota doesn't think that will work either. He wants to run and wrestle… I get it… Sometimes that's all I want to do, too. And I can't do it either.

Our midweek match was Senior Night. And Dakota is once again riding the team bench, and I'm up in the stands watching his team. They only have nine varsity wrestlers to fill the fourteen weight classes. They wrestle well but come out on the short end of the stick again because of all the forfeit points they have to give up.

The boy who steps out from the other team who would have wrestled Dakota if he wasn't injured is a boy named Tommy. Dakota met Tommy over the fall and made friends with him at John Knapp's KT KIDZ Wrestling in Rocky Hill. Me and the boys' father, who I now also consider a friend, conversed about how it would have been awesome to see these two wrestle each other. But, unfortunately, it wasn't going to happen that night.

Saturday's tournament was a long one. However, there were a lot of bright spots, even though Dakota didn't wrestle. His team did very well. A bunch of them placed in the top four. Also, Dakota's friend Tommy, who he was supposed to wrestle on Wednesday night, placed 3rd. Dakota was very happy for him and his own teammates.

It was a long day, however. But, in the late morning, I was approached by a woman who asked me if I was Danny Blanchard. Whenever someone calls me Danny, I know they must be from the days in my youth in East Hartford. She then shared with me that she was Kim Miller.

Kim is the sister to Connecticut fallen Trooper Kevin Miller. Kevin was my dear friend, teammate, and brother in combat from the good old days of the 1980s when we both wrestled for East Hartford High School. We kicked a lot of butts together out there on those mats. If you want to learn more about the amazing story of my old teammate and friend Kevin Miller, please read this blog I wrote about him: http://granddaddyssecrets.com/old-buddy-kevin-miller-ct-state-trooper/.

A short while later, another guy approached me to say hello. It was Chris Grant. I had met Chris many years ago back in the wrestling world. Thanks to social media, over the last several years, we have been able to stay abreast of what each other has been doing. However, it has been a lot of years since we have seen each other in person. We did some catching up, and it was great.

I love it when people from the old days are brave enough to come up and just say hi. I don't always recognize everyone right away. And I'm not always good with names either. But, I am always grateful and happy when I do get to talk to people who I shared a history with. So, thanks Kim Miller and Chris Grant, for stopping by to say hi and sharing a moment with me again and for saying hello to Dakota, too.

Late in the day, I got a special treat. The referee from East Hartford, Dave LeBlanc, approached me right before taking the mat to tell me that my old coach had entered the building. On the other side of the gymnasium, my old East Hartford High School wrestling coach, Steve Konopka was sitting with the legend Windham coach Brian Crudden.

I had to say hi. Together we sat, and together we laughed. We told stories. We had a great time together. Referee Dave LeBlanc eventually joined us, too. And then so did former East Hartford wrestler and former RHAM wrestling coach Kevin Kanaitis. And to make the moment even more awesome, while we were all laughing over old wrestling and coaching stories, Chris Grant walked up upon us and snapped a picture. Chris knew that this was one of those special moments that should be captured in an image so that it could live on forever...

Well, as I said earlier, it was a very long day, as most wrestling tournaments are. However, even this tournament eventually ended. The wrestlers collected their trophies. And old friends and new friends together made their way toward the door to go back to the places they all came from before. On the way out the door, however, I bumped into Coach Crudden again. He asked me where we were wrestling on Wednesday night because he wants to go watch us again. He also mentioned something about maybe doing some kind of summer picnic or something with the team.

Well, I'm not sure how the stars are lining up like this, but anytime a man like Crudden takes an interest in your team, that can only be a good thing. As a matter of fact, it's a really good thing. Because Coach Crudden is a very good man who has a way about him that helps other young men learn how to become good men too... I'd be proud to have some of his character, kindness, and generosity rub off on my boy Dakota...

Now we just have to wait and see what happens next with Dakota's knee... and the fast-approaching state tournament...

Brian Preece: The wrestling world is, in some sense, a small connected world. During my coaching days (and currently), I was/am a freelance sportswriter, mostly for the *Daily Herald*, the rag that covers Utah County and nearby Wasatch County, where Cael Sanderson wrestled. I've also written some for the two Salt Lake papers (*Deseret Morning News* and *Salt Lake Tribune*). I bring up Cael (forgive me for calling him by his first name, but I've known him since he was a tyke and he's always been Cael to me) because I went out to the NCAA tournament twice when he was wrestling for Iowa State, including the time he won his fourth NCAA title. Part of my piece on his historical achievement led me to do a short interview with Dan Gable. I asked him about Cael finishing his NCAA career undefeated, and Gable was gracious. A former coaching colleague and friend Scott Schulte did a book on Dan Gable, and he got the legend to sign it for me. Scott told Gable about what I have done in Utah wrestling, and Gable's note reflected my efforts, which I appreciated.

I am a member of the Church of Jesus Christ of Latter-Day Saints or a Mormon, and there are some famous wrestlers among our flock, including three Olympic gold medalists in Cael Sanderson, Mark Schultz, and Rulon Gardner. But another famous Mormon wrestler is Larry Owings, who was the only wrestler to beat Dan Gable in a competitive match.

I guess it's okay to be somewhat proud of your church that produced the wrestlers that won multiple NCAA titles, as well as, the wrestler to beat the Russian great Alexander Karelin, and the grappler that denied Gable his third NCAA title and undefeated career.

I haven't met Owings personally, but we are Facebook friends. I bump into Gardner here or there as he coaches at Herriman High School in Salt Lake County. I have somewhat lost contact with Schultz after he left BYU. However, I did do a review of the movie "Foxcatcher" that he appreciated. I was a clinician two years at the BYU wrestling camp when he was the head coach there. It was fun to hang out with him and Ben Ohai, another great Mormon wrestler. Ben placed second in the NCAA tournament in 1974 wrestling for BYU. He also trained and competed against the Peterson brothers, who also won Olympic medals in 1972 with Gable. Ben was one of my Dad's closest friends and spoke at his funeral.

Indeed, as Daniel pointed out, the loss to Owings fueled the fire within Gable. It helped him become an Olympic champion and become the winningest coach in NCAA wrestling history. However, it seems like Sanderson is fast on his tail. For Owings, his own story is fascinating. In a short interview on Youtube for Trackwrestling, Owings said he was naturally a bit introverted. So, "being the guy that beat Dan Gable" was challenging. He didn't enjoy the notoriety that came with it, Owings eventually became a school teacher and never really embraced his achievement until after he retired. Nearly 50 years after their epic bout, the two came together to talk about the match and how it shaped their lives. After he retired from being a school teacher, Owings became an assistant high school coach in Oregon. Then there was another documentary done on him. It's also available on YouTube (KC Films). In this film, Owings talks about his own three rules of success: 1) believe in yourself, 2) don't quit, and 3) look for ways to help other people.

I have to say I really appreciate Daniel's interest in Dakota's team beyond his son. A lot of parents only really come to see their sons (or daughters) wrestle. Daniel gets to every meet and cheers on Dakota's teammates while also sharing his own wisdom to help them get better. This is truly admirable and fits into that Owings' ethic of looking for ways to help other people.

Gable has talked about how the loss to Owings was painful, but it made him a better wrestler and eventually a great coach. I think of how defeat shaped my own career path. I'm convinced of a few things. If I had taken state, I'm not sure I would have gone into teaching and coaching and been the successful coach I was. And I think successful coaching isn't just about winning and losing but also the ability to positively shape young people and help them get through defeats and trials. I think it is also about mentoring other prospective coaches. And I am proud of the fact that I have mentored a few to become successful high school coaches and contributors to the sport. Most wrestlers don't become state champions, and I only coached about ten in my entire coaching career. Most wrestlers one will coach won't even get on the podium, but regardless, you can still teach them the life lessons to become great men (and women).

CHAPTER TWENTY-FOUR

A TRIP DOWN MEMORY LANE

Dan Blanchard: The beginning of this week has been a blur, and I have barely been able to even notice the wrestling season that is winding down. Sadly, wrestling has taken a back seat lately since Dakota has been injured, and I've been running myself dizzy with all of my responsibilities.

Early in the week, I had several meetings to attend after work for my part-time side jobs with the American Federation of Teachers. While I was at one of these meetings, I got a text from my wife that my daughter was having trouble breathing, and my wife was rushing her to the hospital.

I met them at the hospital in Hartford. And we sat there until the next morning. I was so frustrated and tired, but at the same time, grateful that my daughter did finally receive medical care. Unfortunately, she has the flu. Twelve hours later, her little sister came down with the flu also. And in about another twelve hours, her older sister also started showing symptoms of the flu. Hmm… Humbug…

It looks like another obstacle, the flu, has just been added to the mix in the Blanchard home that could keep Dakota from wrestling in the States next Friday night. Oh, yeah, his knee is still swollen, and he's also still ten pounds overweight. And I won't even talk about the whole get back in shape thing here… Dakota has a monumental challenge in front of him that's uphill the entire way. Only time will tell how this one is going to work out.

Speaking of time, time continues to go on as time will go on. None of us can stop it. And regardless of the chaos, this week brings, I once again find myself lacing up my shoes at 5:00 P.M. on another Wednesday night. I'm heading out the door to my son's wrestling match, which he won't be wrestling in because he's still injured. We're crossing our fingers for the State tournament.

As I was exiting the house through the garage on Wednesday night, I couldn't help but notice the sunlight shining into the garage through the far side window. I was instantly transported back to my youth and wrestler career at that moment. Back then, practices ended at 5:00 P.M. every night. Most of the season, when we came out of the East Hartford High School wrestling pit, it was still dark outside. But, when we exited the pit and finally saw sunlight beaming through the glass doors, we all knew that our season was just about over. The same realization hit me hard in my garage tonight. This first season with my son Dakota was nearly over, too. The sun coming through the window says so. It's been a long time since I thought about sunlight peeking through a glass window during the wrestling season. It kind of seems like a lifetime ago…

Wednesday night's match was Dakota and his team's last meet of the season. It was against East Catholic High School in Manchester, Connecticut. This was bittersweet from me because East Catholic was my first coaching job. Eric Gremmo and I were the wrestling coaches there from 1990-1994. We were the two twenty-year-olds who took over a team that was collapsing. We only had seven wrestlers on the team in 1990. And no one from East Catholic had qualified to wrestle in the State Open Tournament in about a decade.

Eric and I worked very hard with those wrestlers, and because of the small numbers, we were able to give them a lot of individual attention. I wrestled a lot with every single one of them, every single day during that season. And three months later, when the States did finally come around once again, we placed and qualified four of the seven of our wrestlers for the Connecticut State Open Championships. What a great victory that was! What a great season that was! After that season, the East Catholic wrestling team did nothing but grow. Within a few short years, we had 35 wrestlers.

However, as time continues to move, and seasons continue to change, I had to move on, too eventually. I left East Catholic to take my first teaching job at an international preparatory boarding school far away from Manchester, Connecticut. While living and teaching at Saint Thomas More, I also started a wrestling team for the school. After that, I landed at New Britain High School, where I coached wrestling for eight more years until my son Dakota was born. Upon Dakota's birth, I gave up coaching New Britain, USA, CT Wrestling, and several other wrestling gigs as well, so I could spend time with my boy. I had done the same thing three years earlier with coaching football when my daughter was born.

As I was driving to East Catholic this last Wednesday night, I noticed that I was traveling on the same exact roads I drove in college. When I was a student at the University of Connecticut, I used to drive these same exact roads to go coach at East Catholic. While tracking down Route 44, I couldn't help but think about all the great times Coach Eric Gremmo, and I had. I also thought about how we would eventually go on to coach the Connecticut National Team. I now remembered again all those late-night drives we had in those big vans bringing our wrestlers back from home from somewhere else in our country. Those were some great memories of Eric and me taking turns driving and chatting while the wrestlers slept in the back of the over-size van. Tonight, my memories are especially vivid when I drove by Eric's old house. The Shady Glen's Restaurant, where we used to get cheeseburgers with extra crispy cheese, is right across the street from Eric's old house. Eric lives out in Idaho now.

A little bit after Eric's old home, I drove by Manchester High School, and it caused me to think about Coach Barry Bernstein. He was like a father-figure to Eric and me. He did a lot to help us two twenty-year-olds new coaches who shared his town of Manchester and coached right down the road from him at East Catholic. Several years ago, a retired Bernstein just happened to be at a cross-country meet, watching his granddaughter that Dakota was also running in. Of course, Bernstein watched Dakota run and had some excellent advice for me to give him about his running.

As my car neared the entrance of East Catholic High School, the late and great Coach Jim Day from Berlin High School crept into my mind. He, too, was like a father-figure to Eric and me during those early days. Coach Day often drove all the way down to East Catholic from Berlin to help Eric, and I rebuild the wrestling program. He was a great mentor and a great friend.

And of course, I can't forget Tom Malin, the East Catholic Athletic Director during those years. Tom was always there for anything

we ever needed. And if there ever was a father-figure, Tom was undoubtedly it. Tom got to meet my oldest daughter several years ago
when she had a volleyball game at East Catholic. Unfortunately, he
has never met Dakota, and now he's retired and gone...

I really miss these three great older men who helped the young
Dan Blanchard, and Eric Gremmo become better men and coaches.
They helped us do a better job of helping the next generation become
better men, too. Their positive influence will be felt for generations to
come. And Dakota will be one of the indirect benefactors of their good
character and good deeds.

When I walked into East Catholic for the match tonight, I couldn't
help but take a quick walk around. I saw the cafeteria that we used to
practice in, and the stairs we used to run on. I walked by Tom Malin's
old office and saw a beautiful plaque with his name on it, hanging up
outside his old door. This made me smile. Walking back to the gym, I
saw the Athlete's Prayer hanging up on the wall. As I read it, my son,
Dakota, appeared and gave me a hug like he always does. I shared with
him that back in the old days, the priest who worked at this school used
to recite this prayer to our wrestling team every night right before we
went out to battle on those same wrestling mats that his team will be
on tonight.

For some strange reason, it saddened me that my son wasn't there
in those days and that he can never honestly know what it was like. I
felt like I really wanted to share this special moment with him, but
would never be able to find the words to share it with him ade-
quately... Hopefully, someday he'll create some memories of his own
in this sport that will be just as special to him. And his son probably
won't be able to fully understand, either...

As I walked into the gym with Dakota, I was really hoping that I'd see at least one familiar East Catholic face from the old days of about a quarter of a century ago. Unfortunately, that didn't come to fruition, though. I really wanted to introduce Dakota to them… but it wasn't to be on that night…

Thoughts and feelings were whirling all throughout me. I thought about how I left there 25-years ago. And I thought about how over time, I had traded my muscles and my amazing ability to wrestle during those days for something else. The trade-off was for fifty more pounds of body weight, a career as an educator, author, and speaker, as well as a wife, children, and a whole new set of friends in a new town that I now live in. Hmm...

One of the first present-day friendly new hometown faces I saw as I approached the bleachers was Val Rogers. Val is Coach Scot Rogers' wife. You might remember me talking about how we wrestled in the Junior Olympics together. Scot and Val have a son on the team who is a very good wrestler, and who is having a great season.

I've really enjoyed getting to know Val this season. The great sport of wrestling caused our paths to cross, or otherwise, we probably would not have ever met. Val is a great person who believes wholeheartedly in raising good young men. She's well-read, well-spoken, confident, and friendly. She even sings the National Anthem before our matches. Val and I have had many great conversations about things that matter while watching our sons wrestle. I'm glad that I, Val, the coaches, the wrestlers, and their families are all part of the same wrestling family now in our hometown of Mansfield, Connecticut.

Well, the night ended on a high note. And even though I used to coach East Catholic, and thus they will always have a warm place in my heart, I still wanted my son Dakota's team to win. Fittingly, the meet came down to the last match of the night. All the weight fell on the shoulders of one of our wrestlers who had been struggling some this season.

Well, I don't know if he read the Wrestler's Prayer or not, but he didn't struggle this time out. As soon as the whistle blew, our kid took it right to the East Catholic wrestler. And he never let up until the other boy's back was flat on the mat for a pin and a win for his team. What a match! What a night! What a bittersweet nostalgic night it was strolling down memory lane. It even kind of got me wondering where my abs and my double leg takedown disappeared too… I seem to have lost them. Does anyone know where they went? Oh, look. It seems like maybe Dakota has found them. He has great abs and an excellent double-leg takedown of his own now. Hopefully, we'll get to see them next week in the States.

The rest of the week was, I guess you could say it was uneventful. Dakota was still sidelined with his knee injury. The coaches were a little concerned with the low energy and enthusiasm in the wrestling room the last couple of days of this week, so they did a pretty cool thing about it. Since we didn't have any wrestling that Saturday, something we haven't had in a long time… The wrestling coaches took the team up to American International College in Springfield, Massachusetts, to watch them wrestle against Norwich University out of Vermont.

It was the perfect day, and perfect timing to do this sort of thing. It gave the boys a break and hopefully fired them up for next week's practices, which will be the last four practices before we head out to the States on Friday night. And we still don't know yet if Dakota will get to experience the States as a freshman wrestling in this massive varsity tournament, or just be an observer again in the stands...

Brian Preece: A few years back, I took a road trip with my son to my old neighborhood up in Salt Lake. I showed him the house I grew up from age eleven through my high school days, my old junior high (Churchill Junior High, "Go Chargers!"), and my old high school Skyline ("Go Eagles!").

We went into the main gym area for a bit. We then traveled to the auxiliary building, which, when I was in high school, housed another small gym and the swimming pool on the lower level and the wrestling room on the upper level. The wrestling room was no longer the wrestling room but a fitness/dancing room. But it still contained "some" of the wrestling history, placards of the state placers hung on the south wall. I showed my son my name and my brother Scott's. We both placed sixth in the state in our junior years. My weight was incorrect as they had it at 135 pounds, which was my brother's weight. I actually wrestled 126 in my junior year. Then the placard for fourth place and I was there at 145 pounds. However, some of the state champion placards were nowhere to be found.

We then made our way back to the main gym. The wrestling room was moved back to the location it was before I was in high school, an upstairs area in the main gym. However, the room wasn't fully enclosed so you could hear the basketballs in the main gym and the weights pounding in the room directly below. We did peek at the weight room on the way up, football players were at it working out. I actually bumped into the adopted son of two of my former classmates. I had actually taken his mother to Homecoming and had had a crush on her in high school. We had a nice short chat.

Eventually, I found a state champion placard. I pointed out to my son, how his Uncle Scott was a state champion in 1991 at 145 pounds. This was my Dad's last year coaching. However, my brother wasn't the final match my Dad would coach as his teammate Jake Marshall took state at 171 pounds. He would also wrestle in the second-ever NHSCA Senior Nationals in Pittsburgh (now Virginia Beach). Jake placed eighth, becoming my Dad's last All-American. One thing I brag about is that my Dad and I are the only father-son combination in the history of Utah to coach NHSCA All-Americans. But my wrestler placed second, so it is one thing I one-upped my father as a coach (haha). In the old but now new wrestling room, back in my days competing, it had a real hard wrestling mat, probably something from the early 1970s or maybe even before. On occasion, it was used to warm up on before dual home meets. So we didn't have to go to the auxiliary building, which required going outdoors. That wasn't preferable in Utah winters. The wrestling room area also provided some students opportunities during school hours to mess around and make-out.

As far as the wrestling room we used in high school, it was more than big enough for our small squad of wrestlers. I think in my junior year, we might have had close to 20 guys for a New York minute, but most of the time, our numbers struggled to get into double digits. Our wrestling lockers were in the main building. We walked through ice and snow in the winter months to get to the practice room. It was a short walk, like going across a street, but your shoes and socks could still get soaked. We didn't have wall mats, which aggravated my father because he had a couple of drills (a stand-up drill and a double leg shot drill) where he liked to use the wall. We just did what we needed to do against the brick wall. On the double leg drill, it really taught us to keep our heads up. The longer east and west walls were glass. The west glass wall overlooked the swimming pool. And the east glass wall overlooked the small auxiliary gym used by the girls' basketball team and drill team, which was called LaNaches. Our team captains invented the "LaNachees Stretch." The stretch was just an Achilles Heel stretch, but we always did the stretch overlooking the girls practicing. I think their advisor/coach didn't like us leering at the girls, but what can I say, we were teenage boys.

I know I was a strange cat, much like Peter Brady from the *Brady Bunch* looking for an identity. My Dad gave us all workout singlets but none of us were going for it, except maybe for one wrestler we had that moved into our school from Wyoming. They wore singlets in practice at his old school. But for us affluent suburbanites, not cool. These practice singlets were yellow, not gold, which was our school color, and went down to your mid-calf. Not a good look. In my senior year, I took to wearing scrubs, as in surgical scrubs, as my preferred workout gear earning the nickname "The Surgeon" from some of my teammates. Again, my Dad put up with it so I would wrestle. He wanted us to wear tights for competition, but I refused. Unlike Emilio Estevez's character's quote in *The Breakfast Club*, it wasn't the "required uniform" but completely optional.

For my style of wrestling, I wanted my knees to stick to the mat and not slide. So even if I got a sore knee or mat burns, I would never wear a knee pad. The reason I wanted my knee to stick was it was my pivot point for my outside fireman's carry. It was the fulcrum for my move, and it needed to be planted firmly in the mat surface. I know some wrestlers (and coaches) prefer knee pads and tights because your legs could slide if attacked while sprawling, but I rarely was ever shot on. So some of us wore tights, some of us didn't, and that probably bugged my Dad, who again gave into me a bit. In his Uintah days, practice gear was uniform; what you competed in was uniform. Everybody wore the same thing. He even got matching blazers for his wrestlers for travel and match days.

My Dad didn't work at the school as a teacher. He was a driver education instructor for the district and a "roamer." He drove students from the eight different high schools in the school district. This made it harder for him to coach. One of his best talents as a coach was as a recruiter. And being a roamer made it hard, if not impossible, to get to know the students because he was not teaching directly at the school. Our school's dismissal was at 2:20 P.M., which made it hard sometimes for my Dad to get to practice on time. However, he wasn't big on stretching and calisthenics. So as soon as Dad arrived at practice, we immediately began technique and drilling. All stretching was to be done on our own before my father showed up. "He had no time for that." When a wrestler said they needed to stretch, he would just say something like, "what the hell were you doing for all the time before I got here?"

I bring up this visit to my old school because when Daniel reminisced about his first coaching gig. It brought up these memories and the whole concept that people forget that changeover happens in a school's staff. At that time, only one teacher from my old days was still there, my Data Processing teacher. And yes, we had computers way back then. But you had to get to class early to get the "colored" monitor. Like Daniel's experience, no one was there that day who personally knew who I was, or who my brother was, or even who my father was. The volleyball coach that works there does know my sister, but I didn't bump into him that day. The trip down memory lane sort of made me a bit melancholy.

Once in a while, my family and I travel through Vernal. This is where my Dad began his coaching career and where I was born. I have shown my children my old house, my elementary school, and the old high school building, which is now the junior high. The new Uintah High School was built on a hayfield that my Mom and Dad once owned. My children were a bit embarrassed when I went into a couple of places and asked people if they knew who my Dad, Dennis Preece, was. I didn't get any answers in the affirmative. It was a small sample but also discouraging.

The Uintah wrestling teams still do well, though the school hasn't won a state title since 1999. But the town seems a bit more "urbanized" now, and the high school wrestling teams aren't quite the hub of interest as they were "back in the day" with students or the townspeople alike. Instead of bringing thousands to the Wasatch Front to watch the state meet, maybe a couple of hundred fans make the trek. This year the team has a brand new coach, Phillip Keddy, who wrestled at Uintah then went to the University of Iowa, where he became an NCAA All-American. There are hopes that he will take the Utes back to their glory days of when my Dad coached. For some in the old guard, the glory days mean only one thing--championship banners!

CHAPTER TWENTY-FIVE

STATE TOURNEY TIME

Dan Blanchard: This is it! Dakota's last week. Do or die. Right here. Right now. No second chances for him to end his freshman wrestling season on a good note.

I've been bringing him to the gym when I can for him to ride the stationary bike lightly, so he doesn't hurt his knee anymore. And hopefully, get him to burn some calories so he can bring his weight down from being ten pounds over his weight class. The car rides to the gym and back home have given us some time again to talk in the car like we used to in the fall when we were driving back and forth to and from KT KIDZ Wrestling in Rocky Hill with my old buddy Coach John Knapp.

During one of our recent car rides, I shared an experience with Dakota when I was a young coach. I was entirely against something that some of the older coaches in the state were doing. They were making their wrestlers lose a massive amount of weight, and they wanted me to do the same. When I protested, they all looked at me like I was a naïve young green coach who didn't' get it yet. They said, "Everyone does it." And then to make matters worse, their wrestlers had a lot of success, which then just reinforced the wrong that they were doing to somehow be right. I remember responding to those coaches, "Just because everyone is doing it, doesn't mean it is right."

After that story, I shared with Dakota another similar experience I went through many years later as a newly elected local politician. I was the only one in a particular public hearing protesting and arguing against a specific action that was about to take place. Some of my counterparts felt they needed to educate me on how this sort of thing happens all the time. Even though I was green to the political game, I responded with, "Just because it happens all the time, doesn't mean it's right."

I'm hoping from these talks, and hopefully the many more still to come with my son, Dakota, that I'm positively influencing him when he's called upon to have some moral courage of his own. Hopefully, he'll remember some of these conversations and find a way to dig deep and do the morally right thing. I want him to protect the little guy who doesn't have a voice or a vastly diminished voice.

I know wrestling and how it builds physical, emotional, and psychological courage. This is an excellent base to work from to have moral courage someday in the adult world, too.

Now on another note. Dakota's doctor's appointment was scheduled for Thursday this week. Unfortunately, regardless of whatever decision the doctor makes, Dakota won't be unable to wrestle in the State Championships. He won't be able to get in any practices before States. So, we took a chance and moved his appointment up to this Monday. This, in itself, is risky because it gives his knee three fewer days to heal before he sees the doctor.

However, somehow, on Monday, Dakota gets the go-ahead from the doctor to wrestle again. Obstacle defeated! Now he somehow has to make weight and get back into "wrestling shape." Two very tall orders...

And you know how life can never be easy or straight forward? Well, a snowstorm rolled in on Tuesday that canceled school and wrestling practice. And it's also threatening to cancel school and practice the next day as well. Right before the flakes come in, I tell Dakota to get into my Subaru, which is excellent in the snow, because I'm taking him to the gym again.

He's frustrated and says, "What the heck? I can't seem to catch a break here," as he's getting into the car. While driving down the road, I share with him that it's not about what happens to you that matters, but what you do about it that counts the most. It's how you respond to adversity that makes or breaks the man or woman.

Now, we're responding by driving in a snowstorm to the gym for a workout. Then later, we'll squeeze in another workout through some drilling in our basement. And then we'll do the third workout tonight when we're shoveling the snow off of our 640-foot dirt driveway. As for tomorrow, we'll cross that bridge when we come to it.

Wednesday does come, and we find another obstacle in our way. His school opens with a delay. But that is not the problem. The problem or challenge is that because school and sports were canceled on Tuesday, the school needs to make up a basketball game today. The boys' basketball game that is scheduled for today will be played in the front gym. The girls' make-up game will be in the back gym. The wrestlers don't have a gym to practice in today. This is really bad timing considering it's the week leading up to the States. This is a vital practice that Dakota cannot miss.

Luckily, Coach Torres and Coach Rogers commandeered a small yoga room for the wrestlers to literally squeeze into and squeeze in a quick hard practice. It got really hot in there. They fogged up all the mirrors. And it sort of felt a little bit like those old Windham wrestling practices of the old days in their tiny pit. A fact that I'm sure wasn't lost on my son's two coaches who both are former Windham wrestlers.

Thursday, the last day to squeeze in a practice before the States competition, and we have just received an early morning email that we're back in the yoga room again today… Hmm… On the week leading up to the Wrestling State Championships… we don't have our gym still… Does that sound right to you?

Dakota's alarm went off at 5:30 this morning as it does on every morning that he has school. However, something is different about him this morning. He looks like he's in really rough shape. He looks exhausted, banged up, and scratched all up. What he's trying to do is no joke. He's trying to get back in wrestling shape in less than a week, while simultaneously losing ten pounds so he can make weight on Friday, and then again on Saturday.

Dakota has been seeded #10 for the tournament. That's a great accomplishment for a freshman wrestling in the varsity States to be seeded or ranked in the top 10 in his weight class. If my memory serves me correct, my freshman year at his weight class, I was seeded #7, and I knocked off the #10 guy on the Friday night of the tournament. If things haven't changed since I wrestled, Dakota will not have an easy match Friday night. He'll be on the other side of that 7-10 equation and have to wrestle better than what I did by beating the #7 kid to survive and get to the next day.

Friday morning, I didn't get a chance to see Dakota before I left for the gym and then work. When I finally do get a chance to see him on Friday night right after weigh-ins at Bristol Central High School, I find out he somehow made weight. But now he looks even worse than he did on Thursday morning. He looks exhausted and battered as if he had been in a low-grade Rocky Balboa fight before this State Wrestling Tournament has even started.

At the States, I find out many things have changed since I wrestled and coached so many years ago. Multiple times, parents asked me questions where I gave them outdated answers from the old days. After a while, I had to preface each response I gave with, "Back in the old days…. but we better check with Coach to be sure…"

Another thing I got wrong was that Dakota wasn't seeded or ranked 10th. He was actually seeded 11th, which is even worse news because instead of going against the #7 guy, he now has to go against the #6 guy. And the #6 wrestler is from Bristol Central, and he's outstanding. Dakota gets out there and does his best on Friday night versus this guy. But Dakota is rusty from not wrestling over the last six weeks, and this wasn't the first match we wanted him to have for his comeback. The Bristol Central guy is too much, and he defeats Dakota. I am extremely sad for Dakota because after all he did to make it back, he's now he's done. Just like that.

However, something really cool happens next. I find out I'm once again wrong and using outdated information. Dakota will be back in the morning to wrestle again. I am so relieved and happy that I was wrong this time. Another cool thing happens, too. As I'm walking around the gymnasium, I bump into one of my oldest East Hartford friends, Pat Moynihan, who I hadn't seen in a very long time. It turns out that his son is a wrestler, too. Right after I leave Pat, moments later, I bump into another old schoolmate of mine who I also hadn't seen in a very long time, Jeff Oken. He, too, has a son who is a wrestler there. Wow! How cool, I think. When I was a boy, Jeff was on my wrestling team. And I used to work out with Pat from time to time. And now we're all here watching out sons wrestle.

Saturday morning Dakota made weight. And as I was watching Dakota wrestle his first match, Pat Moynihan slid up next to me and said, "Dakota is going to win this one. He's a grinder. He'll grind this one out. He'll wear that kid down and win." Pat was right. Dakota grinded the whole match and would not let up pressure on his opponent for one moment. Dakota won 5-0. Great match. So cool to have Pat, one of my oldest friends, there to share it with me. Later, Jeff told me he had watched it from the stands.

Next, Dakota had to wrestle the #5 wrestler from Bristol Eastern, the team that will go on to win this State Wrestling Tournament. Dang… why did he have to get this guy? On top of it, Dakota is at the trainer station with a big bag of ice on his arm. He injured it in his last match.

Dakota is concerned and doesn't know how he's going to wrestle his next opponent.

I say, "Dakota, everyone here is hurting from something. Every-one here has some kind of nagging injury at this point in the season. Now it just comes down to mental toughness. You have to put the pain behind you and go to war with this next kid. You have to have one mission right now. And that is to make this next kid respect you. Make him believe that he was just in the fight of his life. You do that, and I don't care if you win or lose. Let the chips fall where they will. If you earn his respect, you have won regardless of what the score is."

I think my talk helped. Against this excellent wrestler, Dakota almost got the first takedown of the match. But great wrestlers find ways to land on top, and that's what his kid did somehow. At the end of the first period, the score was only 2-0. The second period was extremely close too. Dakota scored 2 points, and his opponent scored 3 points. Dakota went into the third period, only losing 5-2. I wanted Dakota in neutral, where he was strongest. His coach told him to pick down. And unfortunately, Dakota couldn't get out, and even got turned once for three back points causing him eventually to lose 8-2. It was an awesome match. And a great wrestler couldn't pin Dakota, or even beat him by a lot. That in itself is a victory. Later that night, at home, while eating ice cream with the family, I asked Dakota how he kept the score so close. He smiled and responded that he made the other guy respect him. His mom laughed and said, "Great answer!"

Although the weekend was a very long one. It was pretty cool watching Dakota wrestle again. It was also pretty cool watching several of Dakota's teammates place in the Class L States. One of Dakota's teammates who had been seeded #2 was feeling down a bit because he didn't make it to the finals. This kid Ben is a great kid, and there is no doubt in my mind that he will go off and be a very good man someday who will make this world a better place. I said, "Ben, you don't have to be a state champ. You have already won in life because this sport has taught you to be comfortable with hard work and taking responsibility. And that's all you really need. Take those two things forward in life, and you're going to do just fine."

During this long weekend, it was also very cool hanging out with Pat Moynihan and Jeff Oken again and watching their boys place in the States. Their sons are outstanding wrestlers and even had to face off against each other in the medal rounds.

Now that the wrestling season is over for Dakota... what's next? I heard Dakota's coach ask him if he wanted to work out with his teammates who qualified to wrestle in the State Open Tournament next week. He said, "Yes." However, I also heard that another snowstorm is coming, too.

Hmm... Maybe Dakota's season and my writing about it isn't entirely over after all... neither are his challenges... stay tuned for whatever is next... it should be interesting...

Brian Preece: I am glad Dakota got to wrestle in the state tournament and won a match. That is a huge accomplishment for a freshman. And working through the injuries and the cutting of weight speaks well of Dakota's character. I did wish Connecticut had Utah's rules on allowing two wrestlers per weight class a chance to go to the state tournament. I really think this would have taken some pressure off of Dakota a bit to make weight. Without this option, it does become difficult for the wrestler, coach, and parent alike to make a decision on what to do. But Dakota wanted a chance to compete at state, and sacrifices had to be made, and all credit to Dakota for getting it done.

Back when I wrestled, it depended on the school district you were in whether you even got a chance to wrestle high school as a freshman or ninth-grader. Unfortunately, my district didn't allow freshmen to compete. Our school district did have junior high wrestling, but it was somewhat lame. We got to do four dual meets and two tournaments before the postseason. Our school district had about twelve or so junior high schools that fed into the eight high schools, and they were broken up into two divisions. The top four wrestlers in each division got to go on to the district championships. In seventh grade, I was a district and divisional champion. But in the eighth and ninth grades, I placed second in both division and district. Each year I had someone that kept beating me.

Our district had a great wrestler named David Lucero who would have easily taken high school state as a freshman. But, unfortunately, he was unable to compete because of district rules. He then had some academic issues in his sophomore year that didn't allow him to compete in region and state. Finally, the stars aligned, and he won state his junior and senior years. In regards to high school wrestling, you might consider Lucero to be Utah's Dan Gable as he never lost a match in junior high or high school. (If you were wondering about Cael Sanderson, he actually lost three matches in high school, and I witnessed one of those losses.)

Lucero's brothers Enos and Frank wrestled for my Dad at Cyprus High School, the school where my father taught and coached right after leaving Uintah High School. Enos placed in state twice, fourth as a sophomore and second as a junior, but then dropped out of school to join the Army. That was a bit heartbreaking for my father, but it was what it was. However, Enos' participation in the sport led to Frankie and David being exposed to wrestling. David was the best natural athlete and wrestler I ever saw.

I started a web page, and I remember writing a piece calling him the Utah Wrestler of the Decade for the 1980s. We were sort of the same size briefly. David wrestled 105 pounds in junior high, and I was the weight below him. I did lose a few pounds to get out of his weight my ninth grade year, but I still lost to his teammate in the divisional and district championships anyway. Then about fifteen years ago or so, those regulations came to an end. Districts that had ninth-graders in junior high were allowed to compete for the high school in which their junior high fed into. It did change the landscape of high school wrestling. Before 1997, our state only had one 4X state champion, now about every season, we have two to three on the average.

In regards to the surge of 4X state champions, Utah athletics has six classifications. So besides allowing more ninth-graders a chance to compete in high school wrestling, the number of classifications has watered down the competition a bit. Our smallest classifications (1A and 2A) have about 13 schools each. Class 3A has just under 20 schools, 4A currently has 22 schools while the largest classifications, 5A and 6A, have 28 and 25 wrestling schools, respectively.

Utah has pretty good youth wrestling, so our ninth graders that have some experience come in ready to compete. But though that is definitely true, a good share of these four-time state champions wouldn't have achieved that in yesteryear when there were fewer classifications. Even Cael Sanderson, who was a 4X state champion in 3A (1994-97), lost to the 5A state champion as a sophomore. While you never know what would happen in a rematch, their meeting was decisive. Orem High's Todd Mitchell, who could be an answer to a trivia question on who was one of the last wrestlers to beat Cael in folkstyle, won by major decision. Mitchell is somewhat famous in our local wrestling circles for not only beating Cael, but also for gaining notoriety as an actor and model. It should be noted that Mitchell was a senior when he beat Cael, and was also a 2X state champion himself.

For a short three year or so span, we had what we called "Super State." It was sanctioned by our state association but not really sponsored. No team scores were kept, and it had to be run by USA Wrestling Utah. But the classification championships were really recognized as the state championships meaning that was the true climax of the wrestling season. It was the meet that communities rallied around. Winning those tournaments is what goes down in the official record books as state championship teams and individuals. Therefore, the amount of participation at Super State wasn't that great, and the tournament died out due to a lack of meaningful competition.

However, in Utah, we do something neat called the Dollamur All-Star Dual. It just had its 20th competition this year. At its inception in 2001, Utah had five classifications, and there were two teams, the small schools (1A-3A) versus the larger schools (4A-5A). The event also was a fundraiser for Utah's only college program, Utah Valley University, so it was decided to change the format and expand the number of teams and wrestlers. So six teams were created with each classification having their own teams and then a wildcard team made up of wrestlers from all the classifications. Since the top two wrestlers often come from the same classification, the wildcard team has actually done pretty well as team scores are tracked.

So when Utah expanded to six classifications three years ago, it did present a challenge because people really thought the wildcard team was a good idea. So they combined the 1A and 2A into one team. The event takes place in early January and is well attended with close to 3,000 fans. Though team scores are kept, the most important thing is putting the two best wrestlers against each other in each weight on center stage. The event takes place on three mats, so there is always something to watch, and in recent years, it has included some junior high and girl's matches as well. Of course, with any in-season all-star competition, there are wrestlers, along with their coaches and parents, who feel slighted by not being selected. But the committee, in which I am apart, really tries hard to make sure the most deserving wrestlers get the invite.

Usually, within a few days of the Dollamur All-Star Dual is The Rockwell Rumble or The Rumble, as most people refer to it, which was started by a friend of mine named Cole Kelley. It is one of the largest tournaments in the United States. The majority of Utah high schools will attend. But many schools will only enter their best wrestlers in the tourney because the competition is so keen. This year there were 77 teams and 820 competitors. Clovis, a powerhouse team from California, came up and won the tournament while Windsor, Colorado, was second. So there were about 20 teams from out-of-state, and these teams came from Arizona, California, Colorado, Idaho, Nevada, and Wyoming. In the past, the tournament has attracted teams from Montana, New Mexico, Oregon, and Washington. And one time, a wrestler came all the way from Canada to compete, though he had prior connections to Utah. It's a bit smaller, and less competitive than the Reno Tournament of Champions and Doc Buchanan, but it is still a great tournament that provides way better competition than our state tournaments.

For several years I ran the JV tournament associated with it. But I eventually turned that over to USA Wrestling Utah Executive Director

Jeff Newby. If you medal in The Rumble, you are definitely an elite level wrestler. Even if you medal in the JV Rumble, you are pretty tough. That tournament has better competition than many of our state's typical varsity invitationals. It is much tougher than the 1A state tournament. The Rumble, even though it happens about three weeks before the state tournament, will give diehard Utah wrestling fans a glimpse of what an all-classification tournament might look like. Although there are still a sizable amount of Beehive state teams that compete elsewhere that weekend.

Still, I dream of a pure state tournament that is fully supported and sponsored by our state association. My concept is to use the California model, where we still have our region tournaments (now called divisionals) that qualify for the classification championships. Here, schools of the same relative size can compete against each other. Then the top placers of these classification tournaments advance to the state championships. Our current state championships have 16-wrestler brackets except for 1A that uses an 8-wrestler bracket. Like California, I would like to use a 38-wrestler bracket. And though a decent amount of wrestling diehards like my concept, there is resistance among a fair share of coaches. And a lot of resistance from the administrators, who like to put state championship banners on their gymnasium walls even if it only means competing against a dozen other schools to do so.

CHAPTER TWENTY-SIX

ON TO NATIONALS

Dan Blanchard: The season is over, but it really isn't over yet. Sore, bruised, and scratched up, Dakota is back in my Subaru right in the middle of another New England snowstorm. We're heading out on this Monday morning to a neighboring town for Dakota to work out with a group of wrestlers that qualified for the Connecticut State Open Championships.

Dakota, who is only a freshman, didn't qualify to wrestle in the Connecticut State Open Championships. But, he told me that if this will make him better, then this is what he wants to do this week instead of letting his wounds heal.

Ironically, this particular day's practice is held at his mother's old high school. It was kind of neat for Dakota to see the inside of his mother's high school and to get a chance to do some wrestling there.

Dakota looked pretty good today, working out with some excellent wrestlers who were all older and more experienced. His knee was holding up, and I felt like he was wrestling more like an upperclassman rather than an underclassman.

Also, I stood near him, just off the side of the mat barking out moves and offering advice to him every moment I could in between wrestling. It kind of felt like he was training down at KT KIDZ again with John Knapp from this past fall as I was standing on the side of the mat again, helping him as a one-on-one coach. It also felt a little bit like Dakota was the one training to go to the Connecticut State Open Championships. It didn't really feel like he was just some kid squeezing in a workout.

After wrestling practice, I took Dakota out for a big lunch so he can put back on some of those ten pounds that he had to lose to wrestle this past weekend in the Class L State Championships. I also kept reminding him that his days of sucking-weight were over. The car ride to lunch and home was pretty long, so we had a lot of time to talk more about the lessons of life again. And one of those life lessons that kept emerging was how people talk about getting better at wrestling, but then don't take action to match their words.

Just look around. There aren't many kids working out this week that aren't mandated to work out because they qualified for the State Open. If one really wants to get better, then why aren't they taking advantage of the great opportunities this week is offering to wrestle with a small group of great wrestlers? Because the numbers are so low this week, and this is a group of advanced wrestlers as well, they are getting some tremendous individual coaching. What an excellent opportunity to get better, especially for the kids that don't have to be here… Which most aren't. Most have missed the boat.

Tuesday, I didn't have the opportunity to watch Dakota workout because I had to work. However, that night when I was asking him how he did, the first thing he told me was that the wrestling coach was very impressed with his work ethic. The second thing he told me was that he did very well against a kid that pinned him during the season. Boy, has he improved. And think about this, too. He didn't come to me and immediately tell me that he was beating a kid that beat him earlier. Instead, the first thing he told me was that the coach was impressed with his effort. He's been paying attention. And he still remembers that EFFORT is everything! It's not always about the wins. It's the effort. I'm so proud of him.

Wednesday, I shared Teddy Roosevelt's, "Man in the Arena" Speech with Dakota. Teddy was one of my favorite Presidents. During his lunch and dinner breaks as President, he used to invite in professional wrestlers and professional boxers to sneak in a workout.

Here is the speech. Notice the wisdom and how it entirely relates to wrestling.

It is not the critic who counts; not the man who points out how the strong man stumbles, or where the doer of deeds could have done them better. The credit belongs to the man who is actually in the arena, whose face is marred by dust and sweat and blood; who strives valiantly; who errs, who comes short again and again, because there is no effort without error and shortcoming; but who does actually strive to do the deeds; who knows great enthusiasms, the great devotions; who spends himself in a worthy cause; who at the best knows in the end the triumph of high achievement, and who at the worst, if he fails, at least fails while daring greatly, so that his place shall never be with those cold and timid souls who neither know victory nor defeat.

Thursday, the last wrestling practice of the season, I managed to get to the end of Dakota's wrestling practice. He's in another neighboring town working out with the really good kids again. I noticed Dakota's face. He looks like he has been through the wringer. And he's not even competing this weekend! I also notice that at the end of the practice the wrestling coach says how much he likes Dakota because he works very hard. He even tries to recruit Dakota to come to his school for next year. My son's coach shuts him down right away saying that Dakota isn't going anywhere. He's staying right where he is to wrestle.

The weekend comes, and I find myself somewhere I haven't been in a long time. I'm back at the Hillhouse Field House in New Haven, watching the Connecticut State Open Championships. However, this time I'm with my son Dakota and my wife, Jennifer. This is an entirely new experience from the old days of when I was there as a wrestler and then a coach. I see a lot of old friends there from the old days, and we have a great time watching some awesome wrestling and hanging out together.

The quarter-finals were great, and as always, the semifinals to determine who got to wrestle in the finals that night was super exciting. Sometimes I forget how much I really love the thrill of battle… The feeling of a hard-earned victory… The do or die moment… My mind also drifted to my own quarter-final match so many years ago when I teched my guy. And then to the semifinals. I was up by a good ten points on my way to another tech before I pinned my opponent. Coach Torres pulled me out of my stroll down memory lane when he asked me if I was going to march tonight in the Parade of Former Champions. Unfortunately, with four other children at home, I wasn't going to be able to stay for that parade or the finals. Maybe down the road when

Dakota is here placing in this tournament, I'll participate in the Parade of Former Champions.

However, while we were there watching some great wrestling, Coach Rogers yelled over to me to check my email. He had just sent some information on the NHSCA Nationals that he wants Dakota to wrestle in during March down in Virginia Beach. I coached wrestlers at that tournament in 1998 and 1999 when it was in Pittsburgh. And now Dakota wants to compete in that tournament. Hmm… maybe wrestling isn't over after all. Here comes the off-season...

Later, I asked Dakota what he thought of the Connecticut State Open Championships. He answered me in the typical teen boy fashion when he said…

"It's exciting."

That's it. It's not always easy to get these boys to talk, is it?

Brian Preece: I remember my first trip out to the NHSCA Senior Nationals as a coach. It was in 1999, and at that time, it was in Pittsburgh, and it was just for seniors. And no, I didn't know Daniel back then. Over time the NHSCA Nationals has added more competitions for different grades or ages of wrestlers.

It was a fun trip that I took with one of my wrestlers, who placed second in state, along with his father. We traveled with Mark Campbell, who coached at Taylorsville High School, a large school in Salt Lake County. He had coached Justin Ruiz in high school, who was an All-American at Nebraska but better known for being on several national teams in Greco-Roman. He placed second in the Olympic trials twice, I believe. Ruiz was part of the great Utah class of 1998, where we had three Senior Nationals champs in Ruiz, Aaron Holker, and Ryan Lewis. Holker would become an NCAA champion at Iowa State as a teammate of Cael Sanderson. Holker would also be BYU's last NCAA All-American before they dropped their program, so that's why he ended up at Iowa State. Lewis, who actually prepped at Uintah High School where my father once coached, wrestled at Minnesota finishing second in the NCAA championships twice. We had another finalist in Russ Brunson, who competed at Boise State, and two other placers in Gabe Vigil and James Spillett. Vigil also wrestled at Boise State and missed placing one year at the NCAA tournament by one match.

Utah finished third place out of all the states which says a lot for a state at that time that had just over two million people. Campbell wasn't taking out any of his school's wrestlers but came out with a young man from a neighboring rival school. We flew into Columbus, Ohio, and then we got a rental car and headed off to Pittsburgh. On our three hour drive to Pittsburgh, it got dark quickly, and we had an interesting "cultural experience" as we stopped in Wheeling, West Virginia. When we asked for directions to a place to eat, it was the first time in America, I was having a hard time understanding the English language. We arrived in Pittsburgh just before midnight and got settled in our Hotel for the night.

The next day while we checked in at the tournament, I marveled at the cool geography of the Pittsburgh area. The big hills and the coming together of those massive three rivers (Allegheny, Monongahela, and Ohio) gives Pittsburgh its nickname of the Three Rivers City. The competition was at the campus of Duquesne. At that time, you could only compete in the nationals if you were a senior and had placed first or second at some time in your state career. The only "problem" was that the wrestler Campbell had brought out had placed third in the state meet. I wasn't sure how much research the event organizers did and what was going to happen if they found out he wasn't a state finalist. But I wasn't going to rat him out. He got into the tournament without any fuss at all. By the way, he did great and finished one match away from placing in a bracket of nearly 80 wrestlers. Years later, by the way, they allowed states to bring wrestlers that weren't finalists, but they had to "petition" to get in. Campbell and I both figured the NHSCA would let him in anyway because they wanted the money.

As for my wrestler, he went 1-2. I think one issue you could come into in Utah was our state meet is usually in mid-February. The nationals were at the end of March. So it is imperative that wrestlers stay in shape and keep their techniques sharp for a long period of time. Finishing second in state is always hard to accept. However, I thought going to the Senior Nationals, even if he didn't place, would take some of the sting out of things. And it did, we had a great time. But my wrestler didn't train all that seriously until maybe a week before the event. And he had to go up a weight class.

He won his first match against a state champion from Washington, which was one of the most exciting matches in the first round of the tournament. The two grapplers created a buzz in a battle that ended up 18-15 or something close to that. There were a lot of throws, and it was just a fun match to watch. Next, he then got pinned by the New York state champion, who was ranked fourth then lost out to a wrestler from South Dakota. Other wrestlers came out from Utah, too, and we all had fun sitting together and rooting for each other. Rival wrestlers and coaches became friends. I even sat in the corner with Coach Paul Messersmith as his boy Andy took fifth in the event. His two losses in the tournament were to the same wrestler, Johnny Thompson, who became a 2X NCAA champion for Oklahoma State. As for Andy, he would become a Division II All-American, I believe, and like me, followed his father's footsteps into teaching and coaching.

As a head coach, I took three wrestlers out to this event. The second wrestler I took out two years later went 0-2. I was optimistic about a victory in his first-round match. He would be wrestling against a wrestler from South Carolina. The Palmetto state isn't exactly known for great high school wrestling. Well, this kid was the exception and then some, and he beat my wrestler 9-4 and then went on to take second place. The event had moved that year for some reason to Newark, Delaware. After he lost his second match, his family became more excited to see the sites versus watching wrestling. They actually wanted me to take them to New York City. I wasn't too keen on the idea, which was a two hour plus drive by car. I wasn't sure what we would do for parking. We looked into the railway, but that seemed expensive. I talked them out of it, and we actually went to Washington, D.C instead. We found a great parking spot right by the mall and saw the different monuments and visited the Smithsonian museums. It was just my third trip to D.C., so it was a lot of fun.

My third wrestler (Nathaniel Holt) I took to Nationals took a more serious approach. He went and worked out with a freestyle club that had some wrestlers also heading out to Pittsburgh. His twin brother Michael, who had taken second in state, but had torn both his meniscus a few weeks before that tournament, wasn't healthy enough to compete. But Michael, his father Matt, along with my assistant principal Jose Enriquez came with us on the trip. Enriquez was a former California state champion and had coached for a couple of years at our sister high school in our district before going into administration. I was hoping he would be in our room a lot, but that didn't materialize. But he knew the sport really well. Enriquez wrestled at BYU and went to the NCAA tournament three times. It was also great to have him come out not just for his expertise, but it also meant much of the expenses were on the school's tab. In the previous two times, I went out to the nationals, I personally picked up a good share of the expenses. We did fundraising to offset some expenses for the wrestlers. But, most of the money I earned through my coaching stipend went into paying for these for experiences. But I'm sure this is the case for many coaches.

Nathaniel was a 2X state champion, and he had won the Reno Tournament of Champions. It was at Reno where he got on the radar of several colleges, including Central Michigan. Tom Borelli, their head coach and his assistant at the time Casey Cunningham, actually took us out to dinner one of the nights we were there. Well, I should say we took them out to dinner because if they paid for it, that would be an NCAA violation, I guess. Tennessee-Chattanooga and Missouri were also showing a strong interest in Nathaniel. Chattanooga's assistant coaches at that time were Chris Bono and Sammy Henson. So it was cool to meet all these famous great wrestlers, now coaches, as they were recruiting one of my own. What was interesting was that Nathaniel would win the University Nationals to qualify to wrestle in the 2008 Olympic Trials. There he actually wrestled against Bono in the first round. Bono was one of the oldest wrestlers at the trials, and Nathaniel was the youngest wrestler in the freestyle tournament. Bono did beat him, but Nathaniel did take him down.

I remember the first day of the tournament, and I guess I just hate paying for parking. I dropped Nathaniel and company off at the arena while I went to park the car. I drove around and around and around looking for a place to park. Finally, I found a place on a very hilly street and successfully parallel parked. As I started walking up the steep hill to get to the arena, I bumped into one of the assistant coaches at Blair Academy out of New Jersey. In high school wrestling, Blair Academy year in and year out is one of the best, if not the best, high school program in the country. As a private boarding school, they literally recruit from all over the country. They had several wrestlers in the tournament, and one of them was in Nathaniel's weight. We had a friendly chat and parted ways.

Nathaniel's journey was far from easy. In his first match against a state runner-up from Florida, he was tossed to his back. But he fought off and won the match by a couple of points. He then in successive order beat state champions from Kansas, Oklahoma, and Michigan. I think the wrestler from Kansas was a 3X state champion, and the wrestler from Michigan would become an NCAA All-American. There are so many great wrestlers in this tournament.

Nathaniel gave up the first takedown in four of his matches in the tournament but showed incredible resiliency. I noticed that many elite wrestlers when they get scored on early in a tournament like this, they often can't bounce back. It's something that never happened to them in their high school careers, so they don't always know how to handle it. But Nathaniel had the ability to not get fazed by early setbacks. He was also a great mat wrestler. He couldn't be held down (except maybe once), and he was a bruiser on top with his leg riding.

In his semifinal match against his nationally ranked opponent from Blair Academy, Nathaniel again gave up the first takedown. But Nathaniel fought back and simply wore his opponent down winning 6-

4, I believe. I remember when Enriquez shouted out to Nathaniel that his opponent was tired. Then his opponent glanced back toward us in his chairs. We knew right then Nathaniel had him beat. I do remember how the assistant coach from Blair, in a very gracious way, shook my hand right after the match. He had remembered me from our short walk. I said to him, "I had no idea we would meet again like this." Nathaniel didn't wrestle the championship match he had hoped for, losing to Bubba Jenkins, who prepped in Virginia, in the championship finals. But as many know in the wrestling community, Jenkins was no slouch as he would start his career at Penn State, then transfer to Arizona State, and pin his former teammate David Taylor to win an NCAA title.

Nathaniel did wrestle for Central Michigan two seasons. He transferred to Boise State, but his career was ended by a neck injury in the fall of 2008. Before his injury, I got to coach him one last time when Central Michigan was out at the Reno Tournament of Champions. There is both a high school and college tournament run by the same people. I remember he placed in the competition.

During one of his consolation matches, somehow, his Dad and I got on the floor. Central Michigan had three or four wrestlers competing at the same time. Coach Borelli spotted me and motioned me over and asked, "Would you mind coaching Nathaniel so I can coach one of my other kids?" I joked with him by saying, "If you trust me?" He smiled and jogged off to another mat. Matt, Nathaniel's' Dad, sat down with me, and we coached Nathaniel to an easy victory. But there was some irony in the whole thing as his opponent was from Utah Valley University. For the past several years, I was one of their benefactors serving on the board of the Utah Amateur Wrestling Foundation, which was really a booster organization for the program. However, their head coach didn't get too worked up about it. So now I can say I have an undefeated record as a college coach.

Daniel and Dakota will have an exciting time at the Nationals. I know two other "national" tournaments have been created. Most of our Utah wrestlers now go to the one in Cedar Falls, Iowa, run by USA Wrestling. But there are still enough great wrestlers that go to Virginia Beach to make it just a fun meet to watch. There will be wrestlers there that will end up being college All-Americans and competing to represent our country on national and Olympic teams. And now that the tournament has expanded from its early days to feature younger wrestlers, this is a wonderful opportunity for Dakota! I can't wait to see what Dakota and Daniel do next year…

CHAPTER TWENTY-SEVEN

TERRY DAVIS –AUTHOR OF VISION QUEST

It's Not What I Did for Wrestling. It's
What Wrestling Did for Me

Way back in 1979 my little first novel Vision Quest: A Wrestling Story, about a high school wrestler, was published by the Viking Press and Bantam Books. There wasn't much fiction about sport wrestlers or wrestling then; there's not much now.

In 1985 Warner Bros. released a feature film based on the story, starring Matthew Modine as Louden Swain, the main character, and Linda Fiorentino as Carla, the female lead. It's fun to see them in movies now; they're right up there in the highest ranks of actors.

Speaking of the highest ranks of actors, the peerless Forest Whitaker was a minor player in VQ all those years ago. And so was Daphne Zuniga, who played Darby Granger, editor of the school paper. And how cute was she!

I wish I had a nickel for every time that little movie played on TV. The movie introduced people to the book. A few people over the years – wrestlers, mostly – have gotten hold of me about it, or asked me to sign a book, which I'm honored to do. The following touches me so tenderly that I'm thinking maybe I shouldn't say it, that saying it might spoil the beauty: twice over the years a mom or dad has sent me a copy of the book to sign for their new little boy whom they named Louden.

Sometimes a guy will send me a shirt from his wrestling program. It touches my heart that they care about elements of the story I cared so much about when I wrote the book, and – years before – when I wrestled in high school.

For a reason I can't fathom, more people have contacted me about the story in the past year. Mostly it's guys, but sometimes it's women about their guys. In the past few months, for some reason, the men – some of them coaches now, and all former wrestlers – have thanked me for "what you have done for wrestling." I'd be proud to think I'd ever done anything for wrestling.

What I think they mean is that the movie Vision Quest, based on my little book, treats wrestling as a respectable sport and wrestlers as decent guys and committed athletes rather than the moron bullies so many pop movies make wrestlers out to be.

The sequel to Vision Quest that I'm working on now is titled Son of Swain (again, Louden Swain is the protagonist in VQ)); Louden and Carla name their son Tim). In its first draft the book had the following subtitle: A Paean to the Ancient and Enduring Sport of Wrestling. I'd started out wanting the book to be a paean - a hymn of praise - to wrestling, but I couldn't reach that goal; I wasn't able to go deep enough into contemporary wrestling. My experience with wrestling is sixty years old, and I'm too ignorant about contemporary wrestling to write credibly about it. The new subtitle to Son of Swain is this: Further

Questing on the Mat Warrior's Path. Tim's story is like his dad's in that they both quest in their wrestling lives to realize their vision of the warrior.

As I've said, it would make me proud to think I'd ever done anything for wrestling. The truth – and the subject of this little essay, which I want to use as a foreword to the bigger story - is that wrestling did close to everything for me. Okay, give me a sec here to try to say what it means for a simple activity like the sport of wrestling to have done everything for a high school boy, now a seventy-three-year old fat man who can braid his ear and nose hair. Don't judge me too harshly here. You hang some battery-powered mini Christmas lights from the braid and it multiplies my entire festive aura.

My sense of it is that we humans aren't much, and certainly are not happy – and probably cannot be happy when we have no self-worth. If we have no self-worth, but then get some, we can be happy and join in the swirl of life with our fellow humans.

Earning self-worth in my years of wrestling did, in absolute fact, mean everything to me.

For some reason (it was a brain-chemistry thing, I'm told, a precursor to my bipolar disorder) when I was in grade school I always had to play with words when I spoke. I could not say the word shoes, for example; it had to be shoezels-woozels; same with shovel, shovelwuvel. Even later in life, (I remember this especially) when I heard on TV or read in an article about Egypt's government, the name Hosni Mubarak (president, I guess) always came out in my head Hosenose Mubarski.

I was in my glory when we would talk in class about Europe. I couldn't keep from saying to someone, "Hey, (someone), yer a peein'. And I would always work around to "Wer' a peein'!" Ther' a peein," and "I'm a peein'!"

Talking about a subject in class in fifth grade, I could not say the word without playing on it somehow. I was also out of control in terms of behavior; I couldn't wait to raise my hand to be called on. Other kids – and especially the teacher – got sick of me. I didn't blame the kids. Toward the adult, though, a first-year teacher named Dick Kegley, I do still bear a grievance

I don't know how intelligent I really was in fifth grade, although the label smart little shit that many adults gave me was accurate to a degree. I was a faithful reader of news magazines and National Geo-graphic, along with fiction and nonfiction narrative. I knew more about what was going on in the world than some of the adults around me, and I never hesitated to tell them when they spoke inaccurately. Okay, truth be told: I knew more world and national news than most of the adults around me. Yes, I was an obnoxious little shit.

Kegley took it upon himself to break me of this behavior. He in-structed the class to shout out when I spoke without being called on; he would say, "Young Mister Davis thinks he's smarter than the rest of us" when I'd lose control and shout out an answer in Current Events.

The first time I lost control and made myself obnoxious, and Kegley mad, was when he used the phrase "like comparing apples and oranges." I don't know how smart I was, but I wasn't a dullard. I had heard the phrase before and was knocked over by the thoughtlessness of it. What really got to me was that people who were supposed to be smart – like news anchors and members of Congress – used it. "I said to Kegley, Mr. Kegley, what does that mean, 'like comparing apples and oranges'?" And Kegley replied, "It means, Mister Davis that apples and oranges are so different that they cannot be compared."

"But they're both fruit," was my reply. "They're both roundish, both have a peel, both have seeds, they both get squeezed into juice, both grow on trees and have a stem." The look on his face suggested his head might be about to explode.

I remember one early winter when my mom bought me one of the new fleece-lined coats. I took it off, showed some kids, and Kegley told the class that "Young Mister Davis thinks he's better dressed than the rest of us."

Kegley was a popular teacher; he did things none of us had seen a teacher do before. At recess he'd put his arms around a couple kids, other kids would hook on, and they'd make a long line and walk around the playground singing title songs from old TV shows on the Movie Land network like Have Gun Will Travel. The guy knew a zillion of those songs. Everybody but me and Jim Bays, who was in a wheelchair, joined in the romping and singing.

At the end of fifth grade, Kegley moved up to teach sixth; all the kids who wanted to were allowed to be in his class again. He told my folks he wanted me to be there to finish some work on my behavior. My mom and dad wanted to do what was right for me, and they figured this new young teacher must be right; after all, he'd been to college, and they hadn't, nor had anyone in our family. I would be the first.

Kegley worked with me the same in sixth grade as he had in fifth. I wish I'd been tough enough to let it roll off my back, but I didn't have that much tough in me. The critical thing I didn't have enough of was self-esteem. I accepted his opinion of me as what I really was.

When I'd speak out of turn, he'd spring from his position in front of the class, grab the sides of my desk-chair and push me across the floor to a back corner of the room; then he'd blaze back to his desk, and from a top corner hoist the classroom's gigantic dictionary, blaze back again and drop it with a resonate thud on my writing surface and instruct me to start copying.

Maybe I should, but I give the man no credit for the broadened vocabulary I took with me to junior high. I'll never forget the scraping sound the metal legs of my desk-chair made on the uneven boards of our wood floor – and the sounds of splintering wood - while he pushed me across the uneven boards of our floor.

I developed a stutter that sixth grade year. Come fall, we moved into a new junior high. The stutter solved my speaking-out-of-turn. I didn't talk much at all, especially not in class or to the new kids I didn't know.

I'd been a good little athlete and played all the sports. In junior high, though, I couldn't make any of the teams. I did okay when the guys got together outside of school; guys wanted me on their team then, but I didn't play with them on the school teams. I lost track of a lot of guys in junior high.

Our high school in the northwest section of Spokane was huge. Shadle Park High School, enrollment 3,400. Needless to say, there was a lot of competition to make the teams, and I didn't make first-team on any of them. One of the things I'd liked about junior high was wrestling in Phy Ed. We'd had a school team, but I didn't turn out for it.

I see this in my mind now as I'm clacking the keys here. It was my sophomore year: some of my old pals from early in school were wrestling, and I was sitting with them at lunch, listening to them talk about it and envying them. I had a ton of pent-up aggression, and it dawned on me that wrestling just might be the way to jettison some of it. I skipped my afternoon classes, went home and grabbed gym shoes (wrestling shoes didn't exist then) and sweats.

I walked into the little, narrow wrestling room on the second floor of the gym. Green wrestling mats covered the floor and walls. I see that room as I sit here imagining a story, remembering my life and typing out the words. I see the room, I smell it, and I feel the mat surface on my forearms. At the direction of head coach Lyle Pugh the guys did pushups, sit-ups squat-thrusts and bridged on their necks. They were down on their foreheads with their legs supporting their bottom halves. They rolled their heads back and forth, then side to side.

I introduced myself to assistant coach Bill Via, whom I didn't know then, but in later years became one of my favorite baseball coaches for both school ball and American Legion. I asked if I could turn out. "You bet," Bill said, and I jumped in with the neck drill.

Our wrestling workouts were a physical challenge. I always kept up, but still I was always beat when we finished our strength work, chose a partner and began mat work, learning and practicing takedowns, moves and holds and counters to moves and holds.

The strength work was a challenge to my strength and endurance; it felt good to use what strength and endurance I had. I felt a measure of pride to work and sweat with these guys who were also committed to this physical, mental and emotional challenge. I probably couldn't have articulated it then, but I felt it.

Here's a word about emotional challenge: you're out there on the mat alone, no teammates to distract the audience from you or to share the responsibility for a loss. Here's something else to consider: people say play basketball, play football, play baseball, play soccer. Ever heard anyone say "play wrestling?" No. Nobody says it that way, and nobody thinks it.

I thrived on the discipline: never miss practice, don't let a day go by without running your miles, doing your pushups, sits, dips on the parallel bars, climbing the pole and the pegboard. There's a nice scene in the movie of Louden climbing the board. It's on YouTube. Check it out.

You run your miles, your heart grows stronger, and your lungs grow a greater capacity, and over time you run faster and farther. You do your pushups, dips, climb the pole and pegboard, and your chest, back, shoulders, top of your back, and arms all get stronger. This work comprises a Law of Nature: you put in the work, and Nature rewards you with growth.

It wasn't a huge measure of pride I felt, but even before I'd wrestled a match, much less won one, I felt proud to be doing this thing that was physically, and emotionally challenging and – it was true for me, at least – took a degree of courage.

Wrestling is a tough sport; I don't know if it's the toughest combat sport; mixed martial arts probably is, but MMA is professional. Amateur wrestling – called sport wrestling - has opened a professional league this year to give the chance to make some money to our elete and international wrestlers, who wrestle all year.

I was never afraid of getting hurt physically, as I would have been in MMA, which didn't exist then. What I dreaded was being hurt emotionally, being humiliated.

Speaking of courage, at fifteen it took courage for me just to have my shirt off – around girls especially, but even around guys. I was a bit of a pudge as a fifteen-year-old high school sophomore at five-ten and 165. I was positive, to my shame, that I was bustier than half the sophomore girls.

After not too many days wrestle-offs came around. A dual meet, which is to say a match between two teams as opposed to a tournament where more teams compete, was coming up. Wrestle-offs determine ranking in the weight classes. The winners of wrestle-offs became the number-one wrestlers in their weight classes and were varsity; the number-two guys (and girls now!) were junior varsity or B Squad; if there were enough wrestlers to make a third team, we were C Squad. We number-three guys wrestled if the other school had enough guys for two-and-a-half teams.

We had five guys at Sixty (wrestling people omit the one-hundred when talking weight). Two of those guys, Ron Dixon and Forest Wilbanks had played football at 170+. They would drop to Sixty by the afternoon of the first meet. ''and later to fifty-four. Dixon – who would become state champ in our senior year – had beaten Will (the Pill), and Will had beaten Ter the Bear. After that I beat our other two guys at Sixty.

Dixon and Wilbanks were way stronger than I, as were the two guys I'd beaten. I won on technique, a natural quickness, good balance and endurance (call it cardio).

Our third men didn't wear the green and gold singlets (the one-piece nylon wrestling outfit of mid-thigh-length shorts and sleeveless top) that the varsity wore. We wore green cotton gym shorts and a gold sleeveless cotton top. I was aware that my uniform was inferior to the varsity's. Still, though, it felt good to be wearing the colors.

All four sections of wooden bleachers remained full of kids and a few parents after the varsity and junior varsity matches when I ran out of our locker-room corridor with the rest of our C team onto the green forty-foot-square mat with the thirty-foot gold circle in the center and the four-foot gold circle in the center of it. We ran around the bigger gold circle, then dropped into our warm-up exercises.

When we were done with our warmups we walked to the chairs lined up a few feet behind the outer edge of the giant green mat and sat there throughout the match. There were thirteen wrestlers: 103, 112, 120, 126, 132, 138, 145, 154, 160, 170, 182, 195 and Unlimited on varsity and junior varsity. Just a few of us C-Squaders.

After weeks of practice and running more than a few miles every night, I'd dropped from Sixty to Fifty-four. Before I ran I did pushups, sits and squat-thrusts to exhaustion.

All my life as an athlete – which has been all my life until 2009 when docs at the Mayo

Clinic discovered a vascular condition in me they said would kill me before too long – I had always figured it a law of Nature that if a guy worked out until he couldn't work anymore he'd eventually be able to do it all easier and faster. I told the docs I was surprised that after a life of triathlons, marathons and hundred-mile bike rides I got something slow fat guys got. They said it was probably congenital.

I did well my first wrestling season. I can't remember how many matches I wrestled as our number-three at Fifty-four, I don't think it was more than four. I do remember, though, that I won them all. A modest number of strengths, to be sure, but quickness and good balance, along with good cardio served me pretty well on the mat.

I got a lot of takedowns. I never got pinned in a match with another school, although I certainly got beat around and munched up and pinned daily in practice by Dixon and Willbanks.

My second season went well, too. I trained like a fiend summer and fall, and when practice started after Thanksgiving, I was ready to go.

As John Irving, one of America's great novelists – and a former top-flight wrestler - says in The Hotel New Hampshire, "You've got to get obsessed and stay obsessed." I got obsessed and I stayed obsessed for years. I'm still obsessed: I'm still lifting; we have a senior center in our town with the best weight room I've ever seen, and I've seen a lot of weight rooms on three continents.

My marathon time was 2:30. I don't remember my triathlon times; they certainly weren't good; I'm a lousy swimmer.

I skipped rope before I went out and ran my miles; I still could not beat Ron or Will the

Pill. So I was only third man? So what? Just being a wrestler, even at that low level, gave me a measure of pride.

And catch this: even now, after all these years, when the marathons, triathlons and hundred-mile bike rides are behind me forever, I'm still proud of having been one.

Wrestling's a tough sport. It's a challenge a lot of guys won't take; not a lot of guys are in the condition it takes, and not a lot of guys are willing to do what it takes to get into that condition. I hear you: "Davis, not a whole lot of guys are that dumb!" Maybe you're thinking further – and okay, I don't guess I blame you – maybe you're thinking, "Pull yourself together, Davis. A high school wrestling match only goes six minutes. How tough can it be?"

Right, only six minutes. But you're using all the emotional focus, strength and endurance you've got for those six minutes. And you're out there by yourself, no teammates to distract attention from you.

I can't say for sure, but my feeling is that I never wrestled a guy I was stronger than. "Strength wasn't one of my strengths" is how I'll say it. Thinking about it from all this distance makes me remember that among my few strengths aggression and endurance were foremost. I was always working to score points, and I never got tired. I was always pushing, working for the pin. That makes me sound like I should have been a better wrestler. Still, for all the pushing I did, I only pinned one guy in three years.

I thought of myself as a wrestler after those two seasons. I didn't kid myself about my worth to our team, though; C Squad points didn't count as team points in a meet. Only once, in a tournament my junior year, did I earn points for the team.

It was a long bus ride from Spokane to Moses Lake in the middle of Washington State. Many busses were parked near the gym door.

When I got into my shorts and top and walked out of the locker room, Coach Via put his arm around my shoulder, pointed me to the far corner of the gym and said, "Fifty-fours down there. Go get 'em, Davis." I thought he'd go with me, but he walked away to where the varsity guys sat in a line of chairs alongside one of the four big mats that filled the gym.

Wrestlers and coaches stood around a table where two coaches sat; one read my

name and another kid's name from a sheet of paper; a ref – dressed in white pants and a white T-shirt, with a whistle around his neck – walked to the center of the closest big mat. The kid I was going to wrestle walked behind him. I looked at the kid and thought there had to be a mistake about this being the mat for Fifty-fours.

The kid was huge; he was taller than I and way more muscular. I haven't told you what

I looked like – except for the boobs. Here's the image in three words: Winnie the Pooh. There he was looking like a wrestler, and there I was in my blond Ivy League haircut and relative flaccidity. I didn't develop muscle tone until my thirties. My complexion was as pale as my Gramma's bread dough; I was tougher than that, but what I looked like was a self-effacing, medium-size plush toy.

I never found out what the kid weighed. I was more confused than scared. It may have been an advantage for me to have looked like the dear old Pooh Bear. I wouldn't doubt that every guy I wrestled took one look at me and figured he had the match won. I don't know what this big kid was thinking. He looked like he was ready to peel me and eat me.

At the simultaneous chirp of the whistle and upsweep of the ref's hand to begin the match, I danced away as I always did; not many kids locked up (moved close and grabbed the opponent behind the neck and worked to control his wrist to get him off-balance and take him down) all those years ago.

As I've said, the thing that scared me wasn't getting hurt physically. It was being humiliated. In the match with this big kid, as in all others, I fought the fear with aggression.

I would dance away at the whistle and the instant my opponent stepped after me and his other leg followed, I shot for a double-leg takedown. Wrestling people just say double or single,

I was on my knees with my hands behind and just above his knees, and I was ready to stand and lift him and take him to his back. I doubt I could have lifted him, but somehow he did wind up on his back; maybe I knocked him off-balance. So this big strong kid winds up on his back with Ter the Bear from Spokane on his chest.

In a blink I reached my left arm around his neck as far as my armpit and my right so deep in his crotch that my hand came up square in the lower-middle of his back. That's called deep in the crotch. I stretched my legs as far backward as they'd stretch and raised up on my toes to center all my weight on his chest; I pulled upward with my left arm as hard as I could on his neck and lifted as hard as I could with my right on his mid-back.

This pressure sent his shoulder blades to the mat. It must have felt really lousy for him to get pinned by some guy who wasn't even varsity. To the positive side of it for him, though, he probably never found that out.

I had no idea where he ranked on his team. Yes, it did feel good to have pinned a kid who was bigger and certainly stronger. I do have to admit, though, that it would have felt better if someone from my team had seen it, or even known about it.

Truth be told, I wished – and even today still wish - that my dad had seen it. I wish he'd seen me wrestle just one time. Yup, you're right. As I bet you can imagine, that one's another story.

I felt good about it all the way back to Spokane in the dark of the bus and until I fell asleep at home in my basement bedroom. I remember I didn't run that night. It tells you something about the obsessed-wrestler mindset that the thing I remember clearest about the highest moment in my wrestling life is that I failed to run.

Among the things wrestling was to me, it was a way to earn self-esteem. Practice was tough, and I worked hard at it. I also trained on my own. I took pride in that. The harder I worked, the better I felt about myself. When a guy – or girl – works at that extreme level, they feel it. The sense of pride cannot be self-delusion.

I won all my matches senior year, too. But, again, all I had was three or four. It felt good to win, but it wasn't only the winning that put meat on my confidence bones. What felt good was that I was wrestling. I was a wrestler, no need to include the rank.

Every single day wrestling gave me a reason to respect myself. A guy or girl cannot

work that hard and not learn from it that he's – and she's – worthy of at least a little respect from the world, and - maybe what's more important - from the self.

No, I couldn't beat Dixon or Wilbanks senior year either. But the other guys at Fifty-four couldn't beat me, so I wrestled the C Squad matches for another season.

Even now, even now everyday as I sit down to work on Son of Swain, the sequel to that little book I published all those years ago, I bring with me the profound lessons I learned as a wrestler: never give up, keep stroking and the far shore will appear, never miss practice. Do your pushups and your chest, shoulders, back, upper back, arms and abs grow. It's a Law of Nature.

I've wished for years I'd had the chance to wrestle Kegley, my old teacher. I'd have put a serious hurt on the man. It might be possible to look at my experience with Kegley as positive; it turned out to be motivational in the longer run. He did a number on me when I was at a disadvantage in maturity, and he created an atmosphere where I felt like nothing. But if I hadn't felt like nothing in those years headed up to adulthood, I might not have tried so hard thereafter to do things that moved me to feel like something.

ABOUT THE AUTHORS

Dan Blanchard: Bestselling and Award-Winning, Author, Speaker, and Educator. TV Host. Two-time Junior Olympian Wrestler and two-time Junior Olympian Wrestling Coach who grew up as a student-athlete. However, Dan admits that as a youth he was more of an athlete than a student. Dan has now successfully completed fourteen years of college and has earned seven degrees. He teaches Special Education and Social Studies in Connecticut's largest inner-city high school where he was chosen by the AFT-CT as the face and voice of educational reform and is now on the speaking circuit for them. Dan was with the team that put forth Connecticut's new Social Studies Frameworks and is also a member of the Special Education Advisory Board to the Connecticut State Department of Education. In addition, Dan is a Teacher Consultant for the University of Connecticut's Writing Project. Finally, Dan is a double veteran of the Army and the Air Force. Find out more about Dan and his other books: www.DanBlanchard.net.

Bryan Preece: He can't really remember a time when he wasn't involved in the sport of wrestling. His father Dennis, a Hall of Fame wrestling coach from the State of Utah, introduced Brian to the sport at a young age in the early 1970's. As a competitor, Brian won a state freestyle championship and was a 2-time region (league) champion, as well as a 2-time state placer in high school. He wrestled one year at Brigham Young University before embarking in a teaching and coaching career that spanned over 30 years. As a coach, he was recognized as the 2006 Utah Coach of the Year by the National Wrestling Coaches Association. Besides coaching, Brian also was an official, event organizer, and an early benefactor to the Utah Valley University wrestling program. But he is perhaps best known in Utah wrestling circles for the media coverage and historical perspective he has brought to the sport for parts of five decades. By joining forces with author Daniel Blanchard, the two hope to bring a fresh perspective of the father-son dynamic that is truly unique to the sport of wrestling. Brian currently resides in Provo, Utah, and with his wife Heidi, are the proud parents of two adult children (Lizzy age 20 and Zach age 18)

SOME PICTURES

Coach Brian Preece with some of his champions

CHAMPIONSHIP UTE WRESTLERS, Larry Moon, Scott Rupe, Ron Perry, Eugene Woody, Rick Massey and Jim Trick admire state championship trophy. Coach Dennis Preece, rear left, has an enviable coaching record of championships.

Brian Preece UTE championship wrestlers

Chris Miller, Brian Preece, and Darren Hirsche

Brian's brother, Scott, jumps into his Dad's arms after winning State.

Brian Preece wrestling for Unitah High School

Coach Brian Preece and his wife

Brian's Dad, legendary Coach Dennis Preece

Scott Schulte and Dan Gable

Dakota getting ready to wrestle

Dakota's double leg takedown

Dakota wins his match

Dakota and his Dad Dan Blanchard

Made in the USA
San Bernardino, CA
24 July 2020